PROTECTYOURPRIVACY

PROTECT YOUR PRIVACY

How to Protect Your Identity

as well as

Your Financial, Personal, and Computer Records

in an Age of Constant Surveillance

DUNCAN LONG

 The Lyons Press
Guilford, Connecticut
An imprint of The Globe Pequot Press

To buy books in quantity for corporate use
or incentives, call **(800) 962–0973,**
or e-mail **premiums@GlobePequot.com.**

The Lyons Press is an imprint of The Globe Pequot Press

10 9 8 7 6 5 4 3 2 1

Printed in the United States of America

Designed by Mimi LaPoint

ISBN 13: 978-1-59921-020-9
ISBN 10: 1-59921-020-7

Library of Congress Cataloging-in-Publication Data is available on file.

CONTENTS

INTRODUCTION

" After September 11, I was convinced that the United States had to do whatever necessary to secure the homeland and prevent a similar terrorist attack from happening again. I was zealous in my support of President Bush's War on Terror. I was convinced it was the battle of my generation. . . . The spying powers of the national security state bothered me little. Those concerned about privacy were uninformed people who just didn't understand that in war the government must have the power to obtain necessary information to prevent future attacks. **"**

— BEN CARMACK, STUDENT[1] —

It has been said that people living in glass houses should be careful where they undress.

Today such admonishments lack humor given that we all live in glass houses, thanks to gadgets that seem straight from a sci-fi movie. These tools can allow snoops (a group including everyone from nosy neighbors to government zealots) to see what you type on your computer, hear your every word, and even peer through walls using secret cameras to spy on you. Today's technology has put each of us into a glass house, and most of us are unaware of the dangers posed by living in such an abode.

[1] Ben Carmack, "Confessions of an Ex-Con," Opinion, *The Evening News / The Tribune*, June 27, 2006.

Most of this book will deal with ways that allow you to make your glass home less transparent, if not opaque. But before moving to the how-to, it's important to understand not only *why* these invasions of your privacy are occurring, but also what dangers they pose and what directions these incursions might take in the future.

Very private information about a person can be assembled with little expenditure of time and at almost no cost. This truth was brought home to me as I was writing this book. I received an e-mail from a gentleman who was wondering if I knew the whereabouts of another writer who had written for the same publisher that carried some of my books.

The author in question had kept a low profile, writing under a pen name. His books, while outlandishly entertaining, told of a variety of illegal activities from poaching game, to dynamiting fishponds, to building hand grenades, as well as a myriad of other illicit activities. The author of these books might have been in hot water had BATF (Bureau of Alcohol, Tobacco, and Firearms), state fish and game personnel, or other government agencies ever discovered who he really was.

His safety net had been that only his publisher and perhaps some close friends or a spouse knew who he really was, allowing him to remain anonymous for several decades.

But now the e-mail I'd received stirred my curiosity and goaded me: "You're writing a book about privacy—why not see how much you can really find out about this author?"

So I "googled" the author's pen name. Near the top of the list of Web pages returned was a story containing his pen name, published in *Salon*, an online news magazine. The article included a short interview with the controversial author, giving not only his pen name, but also a key bit of information: the town and state he lived in.

Another Google search, this time with both his pen name and his hometown and state, yielded a casual statement in a newsgroup

exchange (and I must note that the names are changed here to protect the innocent and guilty alike): "John Doe, spokesperson for
the group, is an author. He has several books out under his own
name, and dozens of books out under his pen name."

Armed with what appeared to be his real name, I searched
using that name and the pseudonym linked to the town and state
I had learned about in the previous search. This led to a listed
phone number for the author and also yielded links to a series of
articles published in the local paper by this person.

Even though some of the actual pages had been removed from
the newspapers' Web sites, I could still read the letters because of
Google's cache feature, which had preserved the communiqués for
anyone to find. Little by little, I discovered that the author had the
same viewpoints and such expressed by the guy writing under the
pen name. Reading more articles revealed that he was part of a
loose coalition of like-minded folks with a Web site.

I was now certain I had the correct (and real) name of the author.

I soon discovered his e-mail address, compliments of a site
that listed the various officers of an organization he was a member of. His name and e-mail made it possible to search Google
PhoneBook to gain his street address and verify his home phone
number. (At this point I might have used Google Maps, Yahoo
Maps, or MapQuest to obtain a route directly to his front doorstep. Had he lived in a more populated area, I could have also obtained a detailed aerial view of his neighborhood with definition
sharp enough to see how many cars were parked in front of his
home on the day the satellite or high-flying aircraft had passed
over.)

The county tax records from his area had not yet been entered into Zillow.com's database. Otherwise I might have learned
how much he'd paid for his home and when it was purchased.

I continued my search, and Google led me to other material
he'd written for various newspapers, and also a hunting book written under his own name. I also found a neighboring town listed as

his place of residence, suggesting he might have moved from one locale to the other in recent years.

Find.Intelius.com led me to his likely family members in the area, including his wife. Searching for her name with the city/state address then yielded her place of work and various organizations she is/was a member of.

I checked MySpace.com but found little info there because the site is generally employed by teenagers and twenty-somethings; this writer as well as his wife and children were all older than that demographic. (Had the author been younger, this site might have provided a wealth of additional information, from his views on current events and his favorite activities to photos of him and his family.)

Were I really intent on finding dirt on the formerly anonymous author, I could have drawn from operations that make money selling information to marketers, private investigators, and money lenders, as well as state and federal government agencies.

For example, I might have contacted a site like PublicRecords-Search.com and, for less than $50, could have drawn data from state and court records to see what brushes with the law the author might have had in the past, as well as what property, land, or vehicles he might own. For $35, Court-Record.org would have sifted through thousands of court documents to see if he'd ever run into any legal problems in his neck of the woods.

If I had obtained a cell phone number belonging to the author and were willing to cough up $110, LocateCell.com would have given me the cell phone records of those whom the author had called over the last month. For a little more, the names and addresses linked to the numbers he'd called could also be purchased.

Were I a serious snoop working for a government agency, knowing the author's e-mail address would have allowed me to contact his ISP (Internet Service Provider), and I might have pressured workers there into letting me see his recent e-mails, what Internet sites he had recently visited, and so forth, without any need for a court order, since too many ISPs cave in rather than chance getting on the bad side of law enforcement—especially in a time when Internet businesses are doing their best to avoid the appearance of helping terrorists, child pornographers, or scam artists. Thus, without a court order, I could probably see his private exchanges and examine what sites he frequented. And if he used a VoIP phone system (Voice-Over-Internet Protocol), perhaps I could listen to his calls, as well.

If I were working for the FBI, Homeland Security, or a similar agency with a lot of clout, then it wouldn't be too hard to check all sorts of data about this individual, from his credit records to his bank accounts and credit card statements. I could see who was paying him and what groups he might be contributing to. Such records would also reveal:

- His overall health (by what medications he was taking and how often he was being billed by medical institutions).

- If he were still involved in antigovernment groups (through donations to groups or payment from controversial publishers); and from there I might discover that he was using a new pen name, creating another search that would uncover even more information.

- What church he might attend (through records of donations he might make).

- If he had large amounts of money coming from sources that might be illegal (or which might be construed as potentially illegal), so that I could obtain a court order to search his home and check his computer's hard drive for possible incriminating information, etc.

- Who his employers and fellow workers might be (who then could be interviewed for more information); or, if I wanted to engage in some dirty tricks, I might cause his peers to think he might be the target of an investigation.

In sifting through his records, I might turn up information that I could employ to convince a judge that the author might present some sort of danger to society. Since he has written (under a pen name) about explosives and building illegal weapons in the past, that alone would probably suggest the need for scrutiny in these days of worry about terrorism, enabling me to get a court order to tap his phone line and listen in on his cell phone calls.

There are other avenues I might pursue were I a government snoop, as will be noted later in this book. But the point is that today, anyone can have their privacy stripped away in just moments, whether by a curious stranger on the Internet or a government agent. Equally troubling is the lack of awareness most people have of just how profound a loss can occur. As was noted in the U.S. Senate decades ago:[2]

> Tremendous scientific and technological developments that have taken place in the last century have made possible today the widespread use and abuse of electronic surveillance techniques. As a result of these developments, privacy of communication is seriously jeopardized . . .

> No longer is it possible, in short, for each man to retreat into his home and be left alone. Every spoken word relating to each man's personal, marital, religious, political, or commercial concerns can be intercepted by an unseen auditor and turned against the speaker to the auditor's advantage.

It's Easy to Break the Law

Today being charged with wrongdoing is not as difficult as it once was, given the many laws and regulations that have been spun from federal and state legislators during the various "wars" against crime, drugs, and terrorism. The once-innocent actions of the past can now place a person on a terrorist watch list or put the buyer under suspicion of being a drug abuser or money launderer. Formerly "presumed-innocent" purchases can attract attention

---

[2] Senate Report 1097, 90th Cong., 2d Session, 1968.

and are often carefully scrutinized for illegal activities by government agencies (as many a young person wanting chemicals for home experiments or building model-rocket motors may have discovered when he was investigated for possible bomb-making activities).[3]

Worse, some harmless acts can be twisted to become illegal actions. For example, many state laws designed to combat domestic methamphetamine labs can also be applied to household objects owned by most people, potentially transforming them into criminals, according to how law-enforcement personnel choose to interpret the law. Thus, a child's chemistry set or a coffeemaker can become illegal according to the whims of a policeman. As Shawn Carlson, a 1999 MacArthur fellow and founder of the Society for Amateur Scientists noted about the antidrug laws in Texas:[4]

> The Mr. Coffee machine that every Texas legislator has near his desk has three violations of the law built into it: a filter funnel, a Pyrex beaker, and a heating element. The laws against meth should be the deterrent to making it—not criminalizing activities that train young people to appreciate science.

You may get a feel for the potential danger when you consider how many methamphetamine-manufacturing chemicals you may have in your home. The list presented at the U.S. Office of National Drug Control Centers consists of common household items such as:[5]

> . . . over-the-counter cold medicines and diet pills, lithium camera batteries, matches, tincture of iodine, hydrogen peroxide, lighter fluid, gasoline, kerosene, paint thinner, rubbing alcohol, and mineral spirits. Corrosive products, such as muriatic acid, sulfuric (battery) acid, and sodium hydroxide from lye-based drain cleaners.

---

[3] Steve Silberman, "Don't Try This at Home," *Wired Magazine*, June 2006.

[4] *Ibid.*

[5] "Fighting Methamphetamine in the Heartland," Office of National Drug Control Center, www.whitehousedrugpolicy.gov/news/testimony04/020604/meth.html, February 6, 2004.

Obviously law enforcement must keep illegal drug manufacturers in check. Yet when honest people might be guilty of having illegal drug-manufacturing equipment or chemicals in their homes or businesses, simply because they own a coffeemaker or some lighter fluid, it isn't too hard to see how someone digging into your background and checking lists of what you've recently purchased might be empowered to then go after your scalp were they so inclined.

Ours is becoming a society where one man's harmless household chemicals become an illegal drug-manufacturing substance, with the decision as to who is the honest citizen and who is the criminal being left to the discretion of the police and U.S. courts.

Collecting Data

Even as more and more formerly harmless activities and purchases are capable of transforming citizens into suspects, technology is also permitting more of us to be intensely inspected for such possible infractions. As security expert Bruce Schneier noted about the situation we are seeing today with government surveillance,[6]

> It's not "follow that car," it's "follow every car." The National Security Agency can eavesdrop on every phone call, looking for patterns of communication or keywords that might indicate a conversation between terrorists. Many airports collect the license plates of every car in their parking lots, and can use that database to locate suspicious or abandoned cars. Several cities have stationary or car-mounted license-plate scanners that keep records of every car that passes, and save that data for later analysis.

Most American government agencies are prohibited from collecting data on U.S. citizens who are not suspected of doing anything illegal. But there's one big loophole. The various laws keeping government out of the spy business still permit private businesses to collect all types of information on customers, those

---

[6] Bruce Schneier, "Your Vanishing Privacy," *Star Tribune* (Minneapolis), March 5, 2006.

asking for a loan, and so forth. This data is then made available for sale to almost anyone wanting to pony up a few bucks to buy it.

Some of those buyers are local, state, and federal government agencies. Thus, various government and law-enforcement agencies that are prevented from directly collecting data about citizens can still easily and legally purchase the information from the private sector. There are a number of large information brokers selling this data, including ChoicePoint, LexisNexis, and Acxiom. Each offers a computerized file that starts with a person's address and phone number, moves through to their Social Security number and banking records, and then offers details about any brushes with the law, divorces, property owned, places of employment, and so forth.[7]

Some of these companies aren't selective in handing out information or concerned about what might be done with the data. After all, the less caution they exercise, the more money they make — and sometimes they'll even forfeit the freedom of individuals to take in a few more bucks. For example, major e-mail providers based in the U.S. have been quick to hand over data to the Chinese government, even though doing so has resulted in the jailing of those who were guilty merely of questioning whether or not they wished to have a communist government. Yahoo, for example, turned over a *draft* e-mail to Chinese authorities who then jailed the would-be sender under subversion charges. When taken to task for helping an oppressive government jail political prisoners, a spokesman for Yahoo bravely announced,[8]

> We condemn punishment of any activity internationally recognized as free expression, whether that activity takes place in China or anywhere else in the world.

Apparently Yahoo's condemnation ends when it comes time to pocket a little cash by cooperating with a government intent on squashing free expression.

---

[7] "Consumer Reports Finds Personal Privacy Concerns in Planned Uses of Radio Frequency Identification Tags (RFIDs)," *Government Technology*, http://www.govtech.net/magazine/story.print.php?id=99443, May 8, 2006.

[8] "Group: Yahoo Helped China, Again," Associated Press, April 19, 2006.

The major search engines also seem to have little trouble censoring their searches in countries like China, hiding keywords and articles that might be embarrassing to the regime. Worse, when asked by the Chinese government to do so, Google (the company whose motto is "Don't Be Evil") apparently turned over logs that linked computer users to their searches.[9]

Sometimes the government doesn't even have to pay for the data, as was the case in 2006 when U.S. attorney general Alberto Gonzales requested millions of search records from the major search-engine corporations. At that time only Google protested and appealed the subpoena in court in an effort to prevent the action. All the other companies involved complied without even a public protest or whimper, perhaps in part because the data was said to be part of an effort to revive a 1998 law designed to protect children from online pornography.[10] Microsoft, Yahoo, and AOL simply turned the records over to the government, and the whole event likely would never have come to light had Google not protested the request.

The government maintained that these millions of records were only going to be sifted through to craft better legislation, and that the names of those conducting searches wouldn't be with the records. However, this may have been less than true. While specific names were not in the records, it is very likely that the unique IP (Internet Provider) number that most Internet service providers give to their customers was linked to each search. If so, it would be simple for law-enforcement agents to link a user to a search—a fact that was not generally revealed in various statements from the government (as well as the press and the search companies) when addressing this issue.

When extreme amounts of data can be quickly assembled on any given individual, the possibilities of abuse grow as well. One recent case demonstrated how dangerous even the most innocent of data collecting can become when twisted toward selfish

---

[9] John Shinal, "Internet Privacy in China and the U.S.," *MarketWatch*, January 21, 2006.

[10] John Shinal, *Ibid.*

ends. According to the FBI, a Washington, D.C., police officer was attempting to extort $10,000 from a married man who had visited a gay bar. The officer had apparently employed a law-enforcement computer system to identify automobile license plates of cars that had been recorded as being outside the bar, and then linked the plates to the names and addresses of the vehicles. He then cross-referenced to see if the men were married, and if they were, he attempted to extort money from them. According to the FBI, the officer threatened to send photos showing the men at the bar to wives and employers if the victims didn't cough up silence money.[11]

Hanging Offenses

In the seventeenth century, French minister Cardinal Richelieu is said to have boasted, "Give me six lines written by the most honorable of men, and I will find an excuse in them to hang him." The idea here is that if a citizen can be exposed to enough governmental scrutiny, for a long enough period, it is probable that infractions of laws or regulations will be exposed. (Perhaps not enough for a good hanging today, but certainly enough to be hung out to dry by the press, with legal fines thrown in for good measure.)

When presented with the maze of laws and regulations created through decades of the "War on Crime," the "War on Drugs," and the more recent "War on Terrorism," there is a wealth of infractions for a neo-Richelieu to draw from. These "wars" are more akin to publicity stunts (albeit publicity stunts with serious goals). Yet they are powerful, and those who question the wisdom of waging such wars and passing legislative fixes to bring these wars to victory are often greeted with the same reaction one might receive when suggesting that Pol Pot's communism wasn't such a bad thing after all.

Worse, those supporting this or that "war on" treat their cause as if it were a formally declared war, with war powers in place and our way of life in peril if draconian measures fail to be taken. Yet

---

[11] Avis Thomas-Lester and Toni Locy, "Chief's Friend Accused of Extortion," *The Washington Post*, November 26, 1997; Page A01.

in each of these "wars," there has been no formal declaration. The press and politicians may profess war, but it is only rhetoric for the TV camera. While the government's actions in waging these pseudo-wars may even take on the magnitude of a real conflict, legally, they are counterfeit pronouncements that stifle debate and blur the true meaning of war and its legal ramifications.

This tactic obscures the truth with admirable manipulation. Its origins should give one pause, as the architect of the "War on" method of energizing the public was none other than Hermann Göring, the man in charge of the Nazi propaganda machine during World War II. He noted,[12]

> Voice or no voice, the people can always be brought to the bidding of the leaders. That is easy. All you have to do is tell them they are being attacked, and denounce the peacemakers for lack of patriotism and exposing the country to danger. It works the same in any country.

Now this is not to say that the U.S. government and Nazi Germany are all that similar. They are not. Yet the fact that the U.S. government has latched onto the same method of manipulating the public should make us step back and consider what is being created, and whether we might be laying the groundwork to facilitate a dangerous, heavy-handed government in the near future.

Before leaving the chilling parallel between Nazi Germany and present-day U.S. policy, it should also be noted that the Nazi Party didn't win the elections and then pass a variety of draconian laws to limit basic freedoms. Rather, Hitler and his band of thugs won the elections and took advantage of laws passed by the previous administrations, who were intent on fighting crime and communism in order to make German citizens safer. The laws were thought safe because those passing them hadn't planned to exploit them; their failure to realize how dangerous their laws might become in the hands of the unscrupulous served to expedite Hitler's consolidation of powers.

---

[12] Gustave Gilbert, *Nuremberg Diary*, Farrar, Straus & Co., 1947.

This begs the question of whether many of our laws, designed to combat drug smugglers, terrorists, or child pornographers, might just as easily become the tools of a future president willing to push the limits of the law in order to bring about a tyrannical state. Certainly U.S. governments of the past have demonstrated how fine a line exists between protecting the government and pursing personal agendas. For example:

- John Adams created the Alien and Sedition Acts.

- Lincoln suspended habeas corpus during the Civil War.

- Franklin Roosevelt placed Americans of Japanese descent into concentration camps.

- Presidents Johnson and Nixon employed the U.S. military and the FBI to spy on war protesters and civil-rights activists.

- George W. Bush thought it prudent for the National Security Agency (NSA) to collect phone-record data on thousands of citizens.

Historians may argue that each of these acts was sensible for the time and crisis faced. Perhaps most were. Yet taken in their total, they demonstrate how easily rationalizations can be made for the curtailment of privacy—or even freedom—for U.S. citizens when a president, for whatever reason, feels he is justified in his actions. Such justifications can even be made if the real purpose seems more to protect the presidency than the nation, as Johnson and Nixon demonstrated in their spying on U.S. citizens.

Deadly Actions

When governments continue to reduce the rights and privacy of citizens in order to combat this or that perceived threat, the results are often disastrous.

Consider that the great killers of human beings in recent decades have not been terrorists, or even wars between nations, but rather governments that conduct genocide against citizens. A quick look at the great slaughters of the twentieth century bears this out (with similar actions continuing as this is written):

- Ottoman Empire, Turkey, 1915–1917, 1.5 million Armenians
- Soviet Union, 1929–1953, 20 million
- Nazi Germany and Occupied Europe, 1933–1945, 13 million
- China, 1949–1976, 49 million
- Guatemala, 1960–1981, 100,000
- Biafra, 1967–1970, 1 million
- Uganda, 1971–1979, 300,000
- Cambodia, 1975–1979, 1 million
- Angola, 1975–2002, 400,000
- Suharto (East Timor), 1976–1998, 600,000
- Afghanistan (Russian-occupied), 1979–1982, 900,000
- Afghanistan (Taliban, 1986–2001), 400,000
- Iran and Kurdistan (Saddam Hussein), 1980–1990, 600,000
- Rwanda, 1994, 800,000

While some of these slaughters were between warring factions within a nation, and others created by governments set up during occupation, they all have one thing in common that makes possible the rapid and extensive slaughters of populations: government records or ID cards identifying citizens by their ethnicity or their political and/or religious beliefs.

In such societies, loss of privacy can translate into loss of life. The collection of data about a population always presents the potential danger of massive genocide should the government be transformed from one of benevolence into one that is pathological, a change that can happen very rapidly as demonstrated within some of the nations in the list above. Anyone who knows history should be concerned with privacy issues.

That being the case, our nation's current "trust us, we're good guys" solution to protecting rights and privacy is dangerous. It is a path that ultimately might lead to disaster should a single untrustworthy person come to power. It is precisely for this reason that our Founding Fathers designed our government with a system of checks and balances so it could avoid various abuses extending from the highest levels of government to the state and local ranks of office. Yet today we see this system becoming eroded, leaving an opening for abuse of power.

For example, when questioned by a senator about how information was being collected on U.S. citizens during terrorist investigations, U.S. attorney general Alberto Gonzales replied:[13]

> I can't talk about specifics about it, but information is collected, information is retained and information is disseminated in a way to protect the privacy interests of all Americans. . . . We understand that we have an obligation to try to minimize intrusion into the privacy interests of Americans, and we endeavor to do that.

The question to be asked, then, is how safe are we when citizens must simply trust government agencies to collect data behind the scenes with little or no oversight other than the promise that they will "try to minimize intrusion into the privacy" of citizens?

The Bottom Line

So here's the bottom line: *You and every other person living today are facing an army of government snoops, corporate data miners, identity thieves, and private investigators, all intent on collecting as much information as they can about you.* And once they obtain this information, they can employ it to harm you in one way or another, from making you easier to target when it comes to tax audits or marketing campaigns, to stealing your money, to figuring

---

[13] "U.S. Senate Judiciary Committee Holds a Hearing on Wartime Executive Power and the National Security Agency's Surveillance Authority," Transcript, *The Washington Post*, February 6, 2006.

out who should be on a madman's hit list or rounded up in a government pogrom.

Those collecting data about you and your family generally aren't doing it as a favor to you. They may promise to make your time at the checkout counter shorter, or offer discounts or other conveniences. But in the end, the trade-offs may be more expensive than the few advantages they provide.

Now let's take a look at how you can start protecting yourself, regain your privacy, and avoid being snagged by those who would disregard your rights.

CHAPTER 1 AT HOME IN YOUR CASTLE

" No one shall be subjected to arbitrary or unlawful interference with his privacy, family, home, or correspondence, nor to unlawful attacks on his honor and reputation. Everyone has the right to the protection of the law against such interference or attacks. "

— ARTICLE 17, UNITED NATIONS INTERNATIONAL COVENANT
ON CIVIL AND POLITICAL RIGHTS,
RATIFIED BY THE GENERAL ASSEMBLY (AND THE U.S.) IN 1948.

People innately desire privacy. We have moments when we wish to have our own thoughts, things we prefer to do without an audience. We like to put our feet up and let our hair down. We don't desire these times of privacy because we are engaging in illicit activities, but rather due to a need for spiritual renewal, introspection, and even modesty.

Those who rob us of our privacy steal something very profound and very human from us.

For many of us, our last chance for privacy lies in our house or apartment, where we hope to escape the prying eyes—both electronic and biological—that are increasingly lining our streets and businesses. Our homes are the traditional castles where we wish to remain in charge, and where we enjoy quiet times, when we can do as we please without fear of unreasonable disapproval.

SOLUTIONS

YOUR FIRST LINE OF DEFENSE

In the past, we often created a refuge with privacy fencing, high walls, or screens of vegetation. Today, to some extent, that can still be done. However, care must be taken because the screening that might hide you from your neighbor's observation can also hide a thief intent on breaking into your home—or even hide a snoop in the dead of night who has a camera zeroed in on your bedroom window.

AVOID CREATING HIDING PLACES

For this reason, one of the first lines of defense that you should consider laying down like a moat around your home is not a screen of fencing or hedges, but rather open space that makes it impossible for a person to hide without being easily observed by you or your neighbors.

This is not to say you must clear the brush until your yard looks like a barren football field. Rather, shrubs should be trimmed with an eye toward making it impossible for someone to stand behind or hide under them without being seen. You should also avoid using any large boulders in landscaping, since these also lend themselves to concealment.

You can quickly assess what is needed by touring your property as if you are a child engaged in a game of hide-and-seek. Scrutinize each potential hiding place, and then consider what might be done to make that spot inaccessible to anyone who might hide there to avoid observation from a passing car or from someone inside the house. Do this during the day, and then take another tour of the grounds at night.

When replacing landscaping bushes and hedges, you can improve your security by purchasing plants that sport thorns. These create a prickly surprise for any would-be intruder foolish enough to try to use them for cover. Ideal plants for this purpose are hawthorns, *Berberis darwinii, Berberis thunbergii*, and the Robin Hood rose, all of which boast large thorns. There are other plants that may also be available in some climates; a quick call to a local nursery will generally yield suggestions for plants that will thrive in your area.

If you need fencing for pets or small children, consider chain-link or woven-wire fencing. These don't screen your yard from view and thus make it hard for a criminal or snoop to hide in your yard while he works, since he will be fearful of neighbors or others spotting him.

LET THERE BE LIGHT

To paraphrase the Gospel of John just a bit, criminals "love darkness rather than light, because their deeds are evil." Often crime can be thwarted by simply putting up floodlights, and this is true with those snoops who might spy on you at night or exploit the cover of darkness to break into your home.

Outdoor lighting with built-in motion-detection activators are as close as your local hardware store. These are designed for outdoor use and can be adjusted to place a bright spotlight on anyone within the detection range (generally from 20 to 80 feet).

Ideally, the lights will be mounted so they cover all sides of your abode, and installed 10 to 15 feet above the ground so a criminal can't easily unscrew a bulb or otherwise disable them.

YOUR SECOND LINE OF DEFENSE

When you have the perimeter around your home lit and free of hiding places, your next task is to find likely entry points that a criminal might exploit and transform them into less-accommodating entrances. Most criminals will try to enter by back doors or windows at the side of a home if the front is well lit. Ironically, the majority of people spend most of their money on heavy doors and locks that go in front of their homes. Don't make the same mistake.

Consider replacing the glass on ground-floor and basement windows with shatterproof plastic, or glass with embedded wire. If it fits into the style of your home, think about adding decorative iron bars over windows to add another level of security. Bars over windows are not 100 percent burglarproof (they can generally be cut with a large bolt cutter), but they do slow seasoned burglars and greatly discourage the run-of-the-mill juvenile delinquent. Ensure that bars are mounted with one-way screws so they can't be easily removed. Just as important, don't block any potential fire exits with bars.

Ground-floor windows need to have locks, or, barring that, be modified so they can't be opened from outside. You can make such a modification

SOLUTIONS

by drilling a small hole through the sections where the upper and lower window frames of windows overlap, and then place a nail in the hole to "lock" it shut. Make the hole slightly larger than the diameter of the nail so the nail can be easily removed if you need to do so. (Angle the hole downward when you drill it so the nail can't fall out once in place.)

It's also possible to add a second set of nail holes to secure the window in a partially open position, allowing ventilation while still keeping the window opening small enough that no one can enter. The only thing to be careful of with this technique is to avoid leaving the window open wide enough so that a criminal can reach in and remove the nail to open the window.

Storm windows can also help to secure a window if you paint over the lower screws holding the frame in place, making them difficult to remove. Or you can mount the frames with one-way screws (making the frame easy to install but very difficult for a would-be intruder to remove for entry). To make maintenance easier, consider using screws with unusual heads that require a special driver.

Some homes may have special features that could be exploited for entrance into your home. Skylights, windows by trees that could be scaled, window air conditioners that could be extracted to provide entrance, and so forth all merit special attention.

ALL ABOUT LOCKS

The old saying that "locks keep honest people out of your home" has an element of truth to it. A determined intruder can get past almost any lock, given time and the proper tools. However, many would-be intruders will be discouraged and try elsewhere if presented with enough of a challenge.

Of course, the best locks in the world won't help you if someone else has the key to them. And someone may have a master key that will open a variety of the same type of locks. Such keys get little publicity, but are often provided by manufacturers to locksmiths, or (possibly) government agencies. Anyone having one of these keys can quickly enter a premise just as easily as the person who owns the personal key to the lock. For this reason it is a mistake to assume that your lock is totally secure. This also makes some off-brand locks more secure than their more-expensive counterparts, which are more apt to have a master key available.

An interesting expedient that can be employed to defeat master keys is to insert a key partway into a lock and then break it off. The portion of the key in hand then shoves the broken section into the lock. This permits the stub of a key to still work the lock while preventing another key from being inserted into the opening to activate the lock, even if it is an exact duplicate of the original, or a master key. The only problem with this is that afterward, only one key will work in the lock (although, in theory, if the original broken key were used as a guide, it might be possible to grind the end off a duplicate to create a second "broken" key that would also work the lock).

When you move into a home, it's wise to have the locks re-keyed; this is also a good idea if a family member loses a key. And never place your name and address on a key chain, since anyone finding it will then know where to return it—or what house they can enter to steal goods from. Re-keying costs very little; paying a locksmith to do this is money well spent. (Replacing a lock with a keyless touch pad system may be even wiser since there are no keys to lose.)

With brute-force entry through a door, even cheap locks will generally hold up, while the frame and door are usually the weak points that give way. A hard kick will defeat many doors, with a pry bar or other leverage system doing the trick if a kick fails. For this reason you can increase your security by purchasing a metal-clad or solid hardwood door, hung in a metal or hardwood frame.

The door should fit closely in its frame and swing smoothly on strong hinges. Ideally a door will open inward to make defeating the hinges difficult to accomplish from the outside. If you have an exterior door that opens outward, be sure the hinge pins can't be removed from the outside, as this can be a quick way to defeat a lock—a burglar simply pops out the pins and slides the door from its frame.

If you have a door with the hinge pins on the outside, then you can secure them by having them welded in place; by having a bracket made that covers the top of the pin; or by adding screws or bolts on the edge of the hinge-side of the door that recess into the frame, securing the door in place even when the pins are pulled out.

There are four basic types of door locks. The simplest and least-secure is the *entry lockset*, which uses a short, spring-loaded latch that

At right: Ideally an exterior door will open inward, leaving its hinges on the inside where they are nearly impossible to attack.

Below: The entry lockset employs a short, spring-loaded latch. It doesn't offer a lot of protection, but can be useful in conjunction with a deadbolt lock.

Below right: The cylinder deadbolt lock has a key on its exterior. On the side inside the home, it can have a lever, knob, or second keyhole. A longer bolt offers greater protection with this type of lock.

is part of the doorknob assembly. The entry lockset should never be used on a door that opens outward, as the lock can generally be defeated in just seconds with a credit card or a pair of pocketknives that can lever the bolt itself, bypassing the key mechanism altogether.

An *entrance handle set* employs a lever and auxiliary key-operated cylinder to create a deadbolt lock that is more secure than the entry lockset. These are generally harder to defeat, except with a brute-force entry.

The *surface-mounted deadbolt lock* can be employed to augment other locks or even placed in a series on a door. This makes it possible to quickly upgrade the security of a door and its locking system. However, this assembly is useful only for securing the door once you're inside, since it doesn't have an external key system.

The *cylinder deadbolt lock* is similar to the surface-mounted deadbolt, but has a key on its exterior so it can supplement protection whether the owner is in the house or away. This system has an exterior keyhole, while the interior side of the lock has a lever, knob, or second keyhole, this latter arrangement dictated when there's a window in or near the door that might be broken so a burglar could reach the lock through the smashed pane. With both types of deadbolts, the longer the "throw" of the bolt, the harder it will be to defeat it with a brute attack.

DEALING WITH SNEAK-AND-PEEK SNOOPS

Most street criminals will break into homes with brute force. However, if someone is interested in gaining access to documents or computers in your home or business, they will generally try to do so surreptitiously with a sneak-and-peek entry that gives no sign it has occurred. They'll employ a master key, lock picks, or a pick gun that permits them to open the door, leaving no sign an entry has taken place.

To be alerted if this happens, you should devise a system that will show if a door has been entered, even if the lock shows no sign of forced entry. The old trick of putting a small paper match in the doorframe might work. (The match falls out when the door is opened, and while anyone unfamiliar with this trick won't notice, the person who placed the match in the frame will easily notice it is no longer in place.) However, this trick is not likely to work with a pro, since he'll carefully examine the frame for just such an object.

A little creative thought should enable you to place something insignificant just inside the door which will provide such a tip-off. Remember that all you need to do is create a situation where something changes; while the intruder may realize something has been used in this manner, he still won't be able to replace it properly if it moves before he can detect it. Something just inside the door that might be displaced or tracked across the floor will serve well, letting him know that *you* will know he has entered. (Of course, in some situations you may prefer to avoid letting the intruder know that you know he's broken in, in which case you'll need to adopt just the opposite tactic.)

WHILE YOU'RE AT IT

Since you're working hard to increase the protection factor of your locks and doors, putting forth just a little more effort can also give you added protection from brute-force attacks.

The area that normally fails when doors are subjected to a kick isn't the lock itself, but rather the strike plate. The plate often rips loose from the doorjamb, allowing the door to open. You can minimize this risk by replacing the short screws that generally come with locksets with longer, three-inch screws purchased from a hardware store.

Longer screws securing a lock plate help protect against brute-force attacks. This frame actually cracked when kicked by a would-be intruder, but the door remained secure, thanks to long screws.

An even greater level of protection can be achieved if you also replace the striker plate with a beefier plate that's less apt to bend when subjected to force. A heavy plate can generally be found at a locksmith's shop, or even at a large hardware store that sells locksets. In a pinch, you could mount a second plate on top of another to increase the level of protection.

Most locksmiths have quality locksets, installed and re-keyed; you can have one key for all the locks on your house. Spending a little extra for a lock that is hardened against drilling and other attacks can also increase your level of safety.

When locks are being installed, placing them as high as is practical can increase their resistance to a kicking attack, since most people can't kick higher than four feet. A lock placed at chest level will be much more secure than is a lock at waist level.

Chain locks are almost worthless, as they are flimsy and easily defeated with a bolt cutter or a swift kick. A better alternative to a chain lock is the "Door Club" (available at most locksmith shops), which is secured in holes drilled into the floor when it is in place. These units generally have two positions: one to keep the door fully closed, and a second that permits the door to be partly opened to receive a package or speak to someone at the door.

Never make the mistake of fortifying your front door while retaining cheap locks on back or side doors. Remember that most criminals or snoops prefer to enter by these less-visible entrances.

HIDING YOUR VALUABLES
IN PLAIN SIGHT

There are two ways to protect sensitive papers, computer disks, and so forth. One is to secure them in a home safe or the like. The other is to hide them where they are difficult to find.

Locking things in a home safe is a good bet for protecting secrets when you're worried about snoops with limited resources or capabilities. A safe will stymie an ex-spouse or nosy neighbor. Even a private eye may be stopped by a good safe with a secure combination.

On the other hand, if you're worried about a corporate spy or a government agency discovering your secrets, then a safe is less secure. These snoops will have the resources to drill or otherwise defeat the security a safe might afford.

A bank safe-deposit box is ideal for avoiding non-government snoops. To add a layer of security, have your safe-deposit box in a different bank from the one in which you have accounts; this makes it hard for a snoop to know where the safe-deposit box might be—or if it even exists. (Never deduct your safe-deposit box charges on your tax forms, even if it is a business expense. Otherwise you may attract unwanted attention since the IRS sometimes obtains a search warrant to inspect such boxes to be sure they don't contain money gained through black-market endeavors and on which taxes have not been paid.)

When it comes to your computerized storage data on hard drives or data disks, the best solution is heavy-duty encryption, which will stop all but the most determined and extended cracking efforts (more on this in chapter 6). Provided you're not the head of a terrorist network or a spy caught in the White House, chances are that valuable computer resources won't be wasted in cracking the password to your encrypted documents.

Printed documents, photos, computer disks, and so forth must be physically hidden. If you don't want to use a bank safe-deposit box, think hard about a good hiding place. This is tougher than it may seem, since all human beings tend to hide things in the same places—which most government agents, spies, and even burglars are well aware of. It is not without reason that these folks first look under mattresses, in bookshelves, and in clothes drawers when searching for items of interest, or check the bedroom floors when looking for home safes. The most common hiding places are often above or below their eye level, and this is where a seasoned snoop or criminal will look first.

Whole books have been written about devising hiding places that actually work—the catch being that any snoop who reads such a book will also know where to look. So the best place is the one you come up with yourself, after long and careful thought, rejecting the first places that spring to mind.

If you need a little help to launch your thinking, then a quick Web search for "secret hiding places" might give you a good start. With a little imagination, you can come up with hiding places that will defy all but a very lucky snoop.

It's important to remember that, as with all things regarding privacy, if someone wants badly enough to find something you've hidden and he has enough time, he probably will locate it. He can either take the brutal method of beating you or someone you love until you tell him where something is, or he can tear your home apart, bit by bit, until he finds what he's looking for. Both techniques are used, and will continue to be employed in the future, simply because they work.

HOME SAFES

If you decide to use a home safe to thwart low-level snoops, be prepared to spend some serious money.

One lower-cost alternative is to purchase a gun safe, which can generally be found at a local gun shop or discount store. These safes use locks rather than a numeric pad or combination dial to help reduce costs, making them a bit more awkward to use.

You can increase the security afforded by a gun safe by firmly anchoring it to the wall and floor with the long screws provided for this purpose by the manufacturer; this helps prevent thieves from carrying the whole safe out the door and then attacking it at their leisure. Adding rolls of pennies, lead weights, or similar items to the floor of the safe makes it even harder to move.

The tighter the area you put the safe in, the harder it will be for a criminal to attack it. Putting it in a narrow closet is an excellent choice for this reason.

If you plan on storing papers in a gun safe, purchase a fireproof chest for media or paper documents and place it inside the safe. This will help preserve them should you suffer a house fire. Note that computer CDs, hard drives, and such are more sensitive to heat and therefore dictate a *media* fireproof box. Both types of fireproof boxes can be purchased at Staples or other companies that specialize in serving business customers.

Used personal safes can sometimes be purchased from a locksmith. These are generally a bargain and the locksmith can change the combination for you. You can also on occasion find a used safe for sale in classified ads or estate sales. The only caveat here is that you should always hire a locksmith to change the combination, since you have no idea who might know the combination on a used safe.

Whether a conventional safe or a gun safe, if the safe weighs less than 200 pounds, then you should frame it in with two-by-fours and Sheetrock to make it harder for thieves to cart off.

For maximum privacy, whole rooms can be placed behind vault doors with combination locks. The vault itself should have reinforced concrete walls, ceiling, and floor so that the door can't be circumvented. The cost of these doors is $2,500 and up.

A wide variety of safes and combination vault doors are available from:

- Homeland Security & Safe Co., 9612 Beverly Road, Pico Rivera, CA 90660, 562-699-8554 or 800-543-1277, Homelandsafes1 @aol.com, www.homelandsafes.com

- Pentagon Safes, 6311 Paramount Boulevard, Long Beach, CA 90805, 800-266-7150, www.pentagonsafes.com
- Fort Knox, 1051 North Industrial Park Road, Orem, UT 84057, 800-821-5216, info@ftknox.com, www.ftknox.com
- Smith Security Safes, Inc., P.O. Box 185, Tontogany, OH 43565, 800-521-0335, safeman@smithsecuritysafes.com, www.smith securitysafes.com
- Brown Safe Manufacturing, 285 Venture Street, San Marcos, CA 92078, 760-233-2293, Fax: 760-233-2297, sales@brownsafe.com, www.brownsafe.com

HOME ALARM SYSTEMS

In the not-too-distant past, home alarm systems were notorious for sounding false alarms. Today most systems have two groups of sensors that double-check each other and thus avoid false alarms.

If you're trying to avoid low-level snoops, then hiring an alarm company to install your system is the quickest and easiest route to take. A quick check of the yellow pages in a local phone book will yield businesses that can handle this, including representatives for Brink's Home Security and ADT. If you are concerned about government snoops, then you may wish to install your own system; otherwise, the government may require the installer to help defeat your alarm system—leaving you with only a false sense of security for your efforts.

A number of companies now offer do-it-yourself home alarm kits—and many of these are relatively simple to install, since they are wireless systems that don't require a lot of drilling and stringing of cables to set up. Among companies offering such equipment:

- Norco Alarms/Home Security Store, Inc., 1660 Chicago Ave., Suite N1, Riverside, CA 92507, 951-782-8494, Fax: 951-782-8499, customerservice@homesecuritystore.com, www.homesecurity store.com
- Intella-Home, Inc., P.O. Box 780392, Sebastian, FL 32978, 772-589-0970, frank@intellahome.com, www.intellahome.com

- Alarm.com, 1861 International Drive, McLean, VA 22102, 877-389-4033, info@alarm.com, www.alarm.com

Whatever system you settle on, it should have a battery backup (so the system can't be defeated by turning off the electricity), and if it has a "phone-in" feature, it should call over a cellular backup so it can't be defeated if the phone lines are cut. A basic system should include:

- A main control panel connecting various components together.

- Keypads to arm/disarm the system and set various features; one keypad should be placed near the entrance you normally use to enter the house and another near your bedroom.

- Siren or speaker system to create an alarm when an intruder is detected.

- A panic switch; a handheld unit can also serve to obtain medical help, making them ideal for the elderly or invalids.

- Infrared, microwave, or photoelectric motion detectors; more secure detectors use several types of sensors to reduce false alarms.

- Magnetic contact alarms on doors and windows.

- Glass-break detectors are small microphones keyed to the sound of glass breaking. These are located on ground-floor windows or doors that are likely to be attacked to gain entrance.

- Pressure mats can be placed at key entrances to sound an alert when someone steps on them.

- Conducting tape can be employed on windows or other surfaces that might be broken to gain entrance into an area.

- TV cameras may be used to watch the yard or other areas that might be used by intruders approaching the home. These may be augmented with motion detectors.

- Smoke detectors can also be wired into the basic alarm system. Ideally, a much different alarm will sound when the smoke detector is activated, so the home can be quickly evacuated.

A full system is going to cost between $1,000 and $2,000, with a monthly fee if a business monitors the alarms for you. Some home insurance

SOLUTIONS

companies will offer a discount if you have a home alarm system, which may offset some of the expense.

WHEN YOU'RE AWAY

The ideal time to break in, as far as snoops or criminals are concerned, is when the homeowner is away. For this reason, you're less apt to suffer a break-in if you refrain from telling service personnel, hairdressers, newspaper boys (and so on) that you're going to be gone on a vacation. Ideally, you wouldn't even let people know when you go to and from work, although this is generally harder to do. The fewer people who know about your comings and goings, the less apt you are to suffer a break-in.

Avoid subscribing to newspapers, lawn-care services, or other deliveries that might provide a tip-off if you're gone, either by the piles of newspapers on the front stoop or the necessity to tell personnel that you won't be home on such-and-such a date.

Also avoid telling people about valuables in your home. Thieves often pay for tips about what homes have coin collections, firearms, or cash in them. Letting people know that you have such items can make your home a target for criminals. Never place valuable paintings or collections near the front door where anyone who might come to your door can see them.

You can often fool would-be snoops and criminals into thinking you're at home when you are not. You can do this by leaving lights on (perhaps with a few lamps on timers to make it appear someone has gone from one room to another), as well as running the TV or radio—talk shows being ideal for creating the illusion that people may actually be in the room.

One old ploy of discovering if someone is out of the house is to dial the victim's number from a pay phone or stolen cell phone, and then listen to see if anyone answers, or whether the homeowner's phone continues to ring on and on. If he can still hear the phone ringing when he's ready to break in, he can be pretty sure no one's home.

You can prevent this ploy from working with call answering, setting the phone to pick up after just one or two rings. This makes it hard to determine whether someone is out of the house or simply using the phone messaging system to screen callers. Having an unlisted number is even better—though this will not work with government snoops who can locate this number when common criminals cannot.

Going on a vacation?

Don't make a big production of it. Leave quietly so anyone watching the house is apt to miss your leaving, which won't be the case if friends and neighbors are gathered on the lawn, waving tearful good-byes. Put suitcases and such in the car while it's in the garage, and then leave with little fanfare. If you have a recreational vehicle, trailer, or boat, then park it where it can't be seen from the street so its absence won't attract attention.

Rent a box at the post office or a UPS store, and then use the box address on tickets, motel/hotel registrations, and such. That way someone passing tips along to criminals (as can happen at some resorts) won't have your home address to give to a burglar.

Also avoid newspaper announcements of when you're having a funeral, wedding, or such, since criminals often take advantage of these events to quickly enter and steal from your home. If you must list an exact time and date, then hire a house sitter to stay at your home while you're gone. Generally it is best to make newspaper announcements *after* the fact rather than before.

PAPER TRAILS

Too many folks employ a home safe to protect private or sensitive papers (along with documents showing ownership of property, passports, Social Security cards, etc.). Such safes are great for some things, but not for things you wish to keep private, since these safes can easily be opened by a criminal, a private investigator who doesn't mind bending laws, or an overzealous government agent. If you have something you really need to keep private, it's best to have a lawyer hold onto these papers. Put them into a large envelope and hand them over to him, to place in his safe for a small fee.

In theory you might also place that envelope, labeled PRIVILEGED CLIENT/LAWYER MATERIALS, in a safe place in your home, to safeguard it from snoops—provided they obey the letter of the law. Too often this is not the case, and the purloined documents show up in court, leading to a dubious game of "he said/they said." And unfortunately, most jurors are inclined to

SOLUTIONS

take a police officer's word as truth over a defendant's—especially if that defendant is charged with a crime.

Throwing unwanted private papers into the trash might seem safe to you, but it's not. U.S. courts have ruled time and again that once something is in the trash, anyone can legally have free access to it. If you've thrown something away, the assumption is that you don't mind someone else owning it. That means there are endless possibilities for mayhem:

- A criminal Dumpster diver can obtain your credit card numbers from old bills.

- A private investigator or spouse can dig out love letters or such to blackmail you.

- A news reporter can look for a potentially salacious story in your Dumpster.

- Anyone working for a government agency can go through your trash on a fishing expedition to see if you might be breaking any laws.

So basically, tossing a document into the trash is akin to posting it on a public bulletin board somewhere. If you don't want the world to see a document, then you need to shred or burn it.

Documents run through a cross-cut shredder become impossible jigsaw puzzles, making them useless to would-be snoops.

There's a Catch-22 to this, however: If you're under investigation, then destroying documents is likely to be a crime in and of itself—provided you're aware of the fact that you're under scrutiny. As long as you are not under investigation and have not been informed that you are, then being prudent in destroying paper documents with dubious content is generally a good idea. A document that doesn't exist is not apt to be damaging. Of course, you should also remember that if a document doesn't exist, it can't be used to defend you in court, so don't overdo things when getting rid of documents. The basic idea is to never store anything that might be misinterpreted or otherwise used against you.

When in doubt, shred.

Hi-Tech Snoops

Home privacy is under assault from snoops with some very sophisticated equipment. While private detectives or even nosy neighbors may have access to some of this equipment, much of the more-intrusive devices are in the hands of various government agencies. While some of this stuff sounds more like science fiction than reality, it is in use now.

Millivision Viewer

Possibly the most obtrusive of these is the Millivision viewer. Rather than using visible light or infrared heat, these instruments detect invisible millimeter waves that penetrate clothing and other light materials. The picture presented when this scope is turned toward a fully clothed human being is basically the person without clothing, with hard objects like a pistol or a packet of explosives

Millivision viewers can penetrate clothing and even light walls, giving a snoop what amounts to "X-ray vision" — and an easy way to invade your privacy.

showing, no longer hidden by garments. Although they get little coverage, such devices are currently used in airports to check suspicious characters for drugs or illegal weapons.

Does this constitute an illegal search? Unfortunately, the question has been pretty much ignored by both politicians and the press. One person who has serious doubts is James Dempsey of the Center for Democracy and Technology:[29]

> When does a technology-based search constitute a search for constitutional purposes? How do you evaluate the level of intrusiveness? ...The use of this device is not overt and there is no warning of it. Already, there are two strikes against it. ... There are many things to consider, such as how intrusive is this search? Is it like taking a person's clothes off? Can the police see a person's body, or do they only get an image of the weapon? Those are factual questions that make a difference in how it is accessed from a privacy standpoint.

Modern surveillance cameras can spy through a variety of openings including grills and other architectural features most of us take for granted.

In addition to seeing through clothing, this device also appears to be capable of penetrating through most wood-frame walls, giving law-enforcement agents the ability to see into hotel rooms from outside the door, or to watch citizens inside their own homes. The possibilities for abuse with such a device are not hard to imagine.

The device will not penetrate dense materials, however. This means that a home with a brick facade, for example, will stop the waves that the Millivision viewer might otherwise see. This is something to keep in mind when you get ready to buy a home or rent an apartment. Careful selection of a building with a stone, concrete, or brick structure could greatly increase the potential for stopping such intrusions.

---

[29] Kelly Hearn, "Weapon-Scanner Raises Constitutional Concern," United Press International, May 30, 2001.

Today Millivision viewers carry a $60,000 price tag, making their widespread use unlikely. However, should the price drop, or should you find yourself singled out for investigation, a van sitting outside your home might be spying on you even as you go about your business behind closed doors.

What's Bugging You?

Bugs are basically a small microphone (or perhaps even a microphone and video camera) hidden in a room that a snoop wants to monitor. Cars or other vehicles, restaurant tables, or public areas can all be bugged. For this reason it's wise to avoid conducting sensitive conversations in the same place, day after day, as this makes it easy to bug that spot and capture what is being said.

Today's bugs can be very small—little bigger than a wristwatch battery. And with direction and noise-canceling properties, the microphones on bugs are capable of picking out a whispered conversation in the middle of a noisy area. Because bugs are relatively inexpensive, snoops often employ several bugs, both so conversations can be more easily monitored as well as to give a margin of safety. If one is found, the person looking for bugs may think they've found *the* bug and quit searching, leaving one or more other bugs in place.

Obviously computers or other electronic gadgets can be bugged (as noted in chapter 5), so that the information being created or viewed on them may be transferred to a snoop via radio waves or other collection methods.

Directional microphones, an old technology that is still viable, can record conversations conducted outside, or even through an open window. Directional microphones operate out to a distance of several hundred yards (although considerably less in noisy environments). These microphones are hard to hide, as they often require a dish or tube to collect distant sounds. However, they can sometimes be camouflaged to appear to be something else, such as a TV dish antenna, or concealed among junk or appliances.

It's also possible to bug an area over short distances by using a special laser listening device. These send out a tight beam of laser light that bounces off a window or an object inside a room. Because the beam of light is altered ever so slightly as the object reflecting it vibrates, it is possible for sensitive equipment to translate this vibration into the sound within a room, duplicating the conversation going on there.

Placing a white-noise generator on the windowpane can defeat laser bugs monitoring a window's surface; sometimes simply gluing a small transistor radio speaker to a glass pane and playing music can also be employed for this purpose. These cause the glass to resonate so the relatively weaker vibrations of voices in the room are masked. However, a skilled laser-bug operator can bypass a window and focus the invisible laser beam on an object inside the room, such as a mirror, metal door, or filing cabinet, and then capture the conversation from that object.

Obviously the safest spot to hold conversations that can't be picked out by a laser bug is in an inside room.

Drones

If you live in LA or another large urban area, it is very possible that the TV camera on a police drone aircraft has given you the once-over today.[30]

These Remotely Piloted Vehicles (RPVs), and the similar Unpiloted Aerial Vehicles (UAVs), vary in size from being as small as a model aircraft on up to Volkswagen-sized vehicles with wings. The "pilot" remains on the ground and flies the aircraft by remote control. In the past, the U.S. military has used these for surveying battlefields, and the CIA famously used a drone in 2003 to fire a missile into a car containing six al-Qaeda members.

The big advantage of these vehicles is that they are much cheaper and easier to maintain than are conventional, piloted air-

[30] Xeni Jardin, "Launching 'Big Brother' Flying Drones Over LA," National Public Radio, April 6, 2006.

Military UAVs (Un-piloted Aerial Vehicles) vary in size from Volkswagen-sized vehicles like this Global Hawk, to the size of model aircraft. Smaller UAVs are slowly working their way from the battlefield into the hands of police departments in the US.

craft. And because of the small size of many of them, they are also harder to detect, making them more or less invisible to those on the ground.

Efforts appear to be under way to create robotic UAVs that would fly predetermined routes of their own, perhaps alerting a human being if something of interest has been spotted. There has also been work toward a small, helicopter-style RPV which might slowly travel down hallways, hovering and peering through windows from outside a building, and so forth, giving a police officer or government official a mobile camera capable of very intrusive spying.

Most areas are not yet seeing a lot of RPV or UAV activity. But given the low price tag of some of these units, it seems likely these will eventually be employed by avariety of snoops to gain information, like a robotic Wee Willy Winky who peers through the windows and keyholes to check for wayward children.

The future looks Orwellian when one considers the possibility of every police department in the country having a small fleet of UAVs available to patrol their cities.

Eye in the Sky
One doesn't have to spend much time looking at a site like Google Maps to realize that satellites—perhaps augmented by high-flying aircraft—can give an eagle's-eye view of what is going on in your backyard.

Due to the advantage spy satellites offer military users, the U.S. government has steadily expanded its collection over the last two decades, with a twenty-year price tag estimated at around $25 billion. These are now believed capable of being trained on a target in a matter of hours, anywhere on the planet, and can track anything larger than a baseball.[31]

In theory, government satellites are being used to check for terrorism and crime rather than to spy on citizens. However, this is a very thin line, and there is no oversight system to be sure that this line is not crossed. Thus, while most of the time these satellites are undoubtedly employed to check on overseas military sites, possible violators of treaties, and so forth, it isn't unreasonable to think that U.S. satellites might on occasion be employed for domestic spying. As security expert Steven Aftergood of the Federation of American Scientists put it:[32]

> What it all boils down to is "Trust us. Our intentions are good . . ." If they deviated from their own rules, how would it be discovered? I am not satisfied that they have an answer to that question.

And satellite expert Harold Hugh suggests the U.S. government may be doing some serious spying from the sky:[33]

> When George Orwell wrote the novel, *1984*, he envisioned a TV camera in every room, spying on the occupants. Whether we like it or not, that time is here. Although we don't have cameras in every room, there are eyes in space that help our government enforce laws and can even tell if we water our lawns too much. . . .
>
> A few agencies that use Keyhole intelligence [the highest-resolution images produced by U.S. spy satellites] are the FBI, the Drug Enforcement Agency, Customs, and the EPA.

According to Hugh, even less-detailed satellite images can be exploited to reveal what condition plants are in, or even what type

---

[31] Joseph Fitchett, "Spying From Space: U.S. to Sharpen the Focus," *International Herald Tribune*, April 10, 2001.

[32] Katherine Pfleger Shrader, "Satellites over U.S.: Public Protection or Illegal Spying?" Associated Press, March 11, 2005.

[33] Harold Hugh, *Satellite Surveillance*, Loompanics, Port Townsend, WA, 1991, p. 89.

of plant is most abundant in a given area. This information has been used to do anything from catching homeowners who are watering their lawns at night (despite water rationing), to spotting farmers raising crops they agreed not to grow, or discovering drug dealers growing illegal "cash crops." County appraisers have employed government satellite photos to find out which homeowners have made improvements on their houses without reporting the changes, and DEA agents have used heat-signature photos to find underground gardens growing small crops of marijuana.[34]

It should also be noted that some satellites can "see" through the clouds by using radar or detecting wavelengths of light outside the range of human eyes. While there is not a lot you can do to protect yourself from aircraft or satellite surveillance, it is important to be aware of it.

Keeping criminals and snoops out of your home is not an easy matter. However, with a little thought, you can greatly reduce their opportunities to invade the privacy of your home.

If, despite your best efforts, there are signs that someone has managed to breech your castle walls to access your computer, steal documents, or such, then follow the directions in other sections of this book to deal with the problem and minimize your losses, both monetary and in terms of loss of privacy. When possible, always try to stop snoops at the door. If you fail to do this, don't give up. Instead, do your best to make their efforts unproductive.

---

[34] *Ibid*, 90–96.

CHAPTER 2 FACE-TO-FACE PRIVACY

" The right of the people to be secure in their persons, houses, papers, and effects, against unreasonable searches and seizures, shall not be violated, and no warrants shall issue, but upon probable cause, supported by oath or affirmation, and particularly describing the place to be searched, and the persons or things to be seized. "

— FOURTH AMENDMENT TO THE CONSTITUTION —

It is an odd truth that while new ways to invade your privacy keep coming online, the older methods remain as well. Gossips continue to be just as dangerous today as they were a hundred years ago. Whether a private investigator or the FBI, when someone wants to know more about you, they'll interview your neighbors, friends, relatives, and fellow workers.

Skilled snoops can be quite effective, so that unwitting friends who do their best to protect you will be tricked into divulging information they normally would not. A private detective can pose as an opinion-poll worker or salesperson. The FBI may claim to be investigating one thing and then very gradually work questions about you into their line of inquiry. And if a snoop should run into a real gossip, there's no telling what may go into the files about you—true or not.

As with protecting your property from break-ins, you should also give some thought as to how to counter snoops. Many police departments as well as government agencies in our post-9/11 world encourage delivery and sales personnel, city inspectors, or other workers who have access to people's homes and yards to report anything suspicious that they happen to see while working. While this does on rare occasions help capture bad guys, too often in their zeal to help law enforcement, these informants do a lot of damage. And the result can be legal expenses and, in the worst case, arrest or confiscation of your property or assets should it be discovered an obscure law has been broken.

The results can be horrific when things start to go wrong. For example, given that marijuana grows wild in almost every part of the U.S., it isn't hard to imagine a homeowner being unaware of a large clump of this illegal weed growing in an alleyway, or a shut-in who seldom ventures into the backyard being oblivious to the fact that this plant has taken over their garden. Now suppose a meter reader notices that someone is apparently growing marijuana, and promptly reports it to the police. The next step might be a SWAT team of DEA agents bursting through the front door and trashing the home, looking for contraband.

Obviously, the key to avoiding such a happenstance would be to never allow "weeds" to grow in your yard. However, chances are good that sooner or later, if they look long enough, a building inspector might find that your house is in violation of this or that code, your children may dig up the yard and leave behind decaying mud castles that look suspiciously like shallow graves (to the eye of the meter reader), or your dog may have a tag that has expired.

Some of these potential headaches are small. Others, large and dangerous. None are easily avoided given that you're likely to be totally ignorant of the problem right until someone in authority is knocking on the door.

KEEPING SNOOPS AT BAY

Given that the world will remain just as safe if no one were to discover these infractions, real or imagined, the best route toward avoiding such run-ins with the powers that be is to prevent potential informants from entering your yard any more than is necessary. You can do this by trying to purchase a home with meters on the front or side rather than the rear; and if you build a home, get the meters placed on the side rather than the back, even if it means running a longer line and incurring a little extra expense. These dollars will purchase a lot of privacy over the years you live there.

Also, avoid allowing neighbors easy access to your backyard. Many neighbors will feel they should have free run of your property if you allow them to do so, and they will often gossip about anything that (to them) seems odd. Keep them out of your yard and you'll prevent this source of erroneous information about you. While privacy fencing around your backyard is the first solution that comes to mind (as noted earlier in this book), that's not the safest route to take, since it can offer hiding places for burglars.

GOOD FENCES MAKE GOOD NEIGHBORS

Fence your yard in, ideally when you first move in, using chain or woven-wire fencing. If you have a dog or other pet (or want to simply tell the neighbors that your children have been asking for one), this will often be all the excuse you need to have a new fence. Saying something like, "I figured I should spend the extra cash and fence in the yard, since it always irritated me when the neighbor's dog at our old house came into the yard and made a mess. I want to be a good neighbor, so I decided a good fence would help."

Fencing can also be used if you want to keep meter readers out of the yard. Simply post a DANGEROUS DOG sign on the gate and then lock it. Next, call the power company and tell them that you have a dog that's not too friendly, and you don't want any of their workers to get hurt. Generally, they'll let you read your own meter (perhaps sending a guy out to check your readings from time to time—so don't be tempted to cheat). All you have to do is fill out a card once a month and mail it in. In exchange, you have one less potential snoop running through your yard each month.

SOLUTIONS

Of course, you don't want to come off as antisocial. If you do, you'll attract more attention than you might have avoided by doing nothing. Instead, always be a good citizen and good neighbor, and always have a good reason for things that you do to maintain your privacy.

DON'T CHUM THE WATERS

When the anti-privacy sharks are circling your boat, the last thing you should do is throw raw meat into the churning water. Yet that's just about what some people do. They attract unwarranted attention from government agencies, making it more likely that someone will check on them (and perhaps stumble onto this or that minor infraction of the rules).

For example, some lines of work attract a lot of attention due to government regulations. If you choose to become a firearms dealer, own an Internet service provider, or manage a pharmacy, then you can expect to be scrutinized very carefully from time to time. Basically any job that requires government certification or inspections is going to cut into your personal privacy. The more inspectors and agents involved, the more likely they are to discover this or that violation of regulations few have heard of.

Likewise, any time you purchase a product that needs special licensing, has serial numbers on it, or is in any way regulated by a government agency, you're apt to be placed on a variety of special lists that may eventually attract unwanted attention to you. Also be very cautious when buying used goods that might be stolen; pawn shops, flea markets, and garage sales all offer excellent bargains, but always avoid any place where stolen goods might be unloaded. Obviously, you should never purchase anything from a guy operating his business from the trunk of his car.

Maintaining a low profile will often keep you from meriting the notice of government agencies and thereby increase your privacy.

HOW TO RESPOND WHEN
CONFRONTED BY LAW ENFORCEMENT

One of the things lawyers always advise their clients to do is to "say nothing." That's because too often, when people are confronted by the police or others in authority, they start jabbering away and, as the government official questions them, eventually let slip that they've done this or that which is illegal. Thus, people who might have avoided it, receive fines, fees, or even jail time.

The American Civil Liberties Union (ACLU) offers advice about the actions to take when confronted or arrested by a law-enforcement officer:[35]

- Be polite and respectful. Never bad-mouth a police officer.
- Stay calm and in control of your words, body language, and emotions.
- Never get into an argument with the police.
- Remember, anything you say or do can be used against you.
- Keep your hands where the police can see them.
- Never run.
- Never touch any police officer.
- Never resist arrest, even if you believe you are innocent.
- Never complain on the scene or tell the police they're wrong or that you're going to file a complaint.
- Never make any statements regarding the incident. Ask for a lawyer immediately upon your arrest.
- Remember officers' badge and patrol car numbers.
- Write down everything you remember ASAP.
- Try to find witnesses, getting their names and phone numbers.
- If you are injured, take photographs of the injuries as soon as possible, but make sure you seek medical attention first.
- If you feel your rights have been violated, file a written complaint with the police department's internal affairs division or the civilian complaint board.

The legal system basically allows police officers to make verbal agreements that they don't have to keep. An officer may tell you that what you say will be "strictly in confidence," but that won't be true. Nor do you have any legal obligation to answer a police officer's questions, even if he has a warrant or is arresting you. It is always wise to divulge as little as possible.

---

[35] American Civil Liberties Union, *"Bustcard": Pocket Guidelines on Encounters with the Police*, www.aclu.org.

While you don't have to answer questions when you're driving a car and stopped by a policeman, you do have to produce a driver's license and registration. At the time this is being published, you still have the right to refuse to identify yourself to a police officer if you're on the street. Nor are you obligated to produce ID—provided you don't mind being taken in for questioning if you refuse to cooperate. However, it seems likely that this situation will come to an end in the near future should a national ID card or similar system be instituted with the claim that it will combat terrorism, illegal immigration, or some such problem.

If you have the misfortune to find yourself in a police station for one reason or another, remember that today's stations are wired with cameras and microphones. While it may appear that you're sitting in a private room with no one around, in fact, most rooms (as well as waiting areas) will be bugged, and anything you do or say is considered fair game for introduction as evidence should it come to that.

Even when your lawyer is present with you in a law-enforcement agency, you can't be sure that what you say isn't being monitored; you might express your concerns and then try to talk freely when you're out on bail and in your lawyer's office. While one might think that the lawyer-client privilege would prevent such invasions of privacy, it appears this practice may be widespread, and extend right up to the Justice Department, given that a former attorney general and the head of the FBI have been charged with being aware of such practices in the *Turkmen v. Ashcroft* and *Elmaghraby v. Ashcroft* cases.[36] These cases may get to the bottom of how often such monitoring is allowed, if not encouraged, in law enforcement, and perhaps may stifle such invasions of privacy to some extent.

In the meantime, one can't be too careful. Always assume that any public place, including a police station, will have cameras and microphones recording everything you do and say.

SEARCH WARRANTS

While a few "no-knock" search warrants are issued, thereby allowing front doors to be kicked in and officers to swarm in with guns drawn like in the movies, most search warrants aren't so dramatic (or traumatic).

---

[36] Nina Bernstein, "Magistrate Rules that Government Must Reveal Monitoring," *The New York Times*, May 31, 2006.

Sometimes the police may come to your door merely to "ask a few questions." This presents a dilemma, since legally, you would be wise to treat law-enforcement agents like vampires (which, according to ancient legend, are unable to enter a house unless invited to do so by the owner). When a law enforcement officer asks to enter your home without a search warrant, you are under no legal obligation to invite him inside. (Officers can enter if they suspect a crime is in progress in the home.)

But once the owner invites him in, the officer can legally look wherever he pleases, perhaps discovering this or that infraction in the process, or finding something that will allow him to go to a court and obtain a search warrant. This doesn't happen often, since the public would soon stop allowing the police to enter any premise without a warrant, so there's a social contract that dictates the police be courteous when simply questioning neighbors and witnesses in their homes. Yet it is a point that should be kept in mind.

On the other hand, when an officer appears at the front stoop and asks if he might come in and "look around," then you'd probably be wise to politely decline his request, since he's obviously on a fishing expedition. Be polite but firm.

If you refuse to let an officer in, he may ask what you have to hide, or threaten to come back with a search warrant. He may add a threat that if he is forced to do so, he will turn your house upside down or otherwise trash your property. So you will have to weigh your need for privacy against possible ramifications if you attempt to protect it in this way.

Chances are good that if an officer has no idea what you're hiding—if anything—he'll figure getting a search warrant is more trouble than it's worth. Furthermore, he may have no way to obtain a warrant since he'll have no idea what to ask the court to allow him to search for. Since he can't be specific, he will lack the "probable cause" needed to obtain a warrant.

Obviously, keeping a low profile is a good way to avoid giving an officer probable cause to obtain a search warrant. If you avoid even joking about owning something illegal, stay away from illegal drugs, and so forth, then you'll have a whole lot less to attract unwanted attention that might lead to a search warrant being issued.

SOLUTIONS

If your home has been broken into, you also need to be wary, because should the criminal who broke in get caught, he may plea-bargain to have the charges against him reduced in exchange for producing evidence against other people. One trick burglars sometimes employ when captured is to claim they've seen drugs, child porn, or other contraband in a house they've recently broken into. They offer the information and address of the house in exchange for a lighter sentence.

If you have something illegal in your home which a burglar might have seen, then you should get rid of it immediately if you've been the victim of a break-in. Otherwise, officers with a search warrant listing the dubious item may one day appear at your door. The safest route is to shred to burn anything questionable. However, if the item can't be easily destroyed (as might be the case with, say, Grandpa's war trophy firearm of dubious legality), then the safest way to rid yourself of it is to hire a lawyer who you can then give the item to with the understanding they can trash it, or hand it over to the police without revealing where it came from.

Should the police show up with a search warrant, first ask to see the warrant. On occasion, officers will claim to have a warrant when they have none. If a document is produced, examine it to be sure the name and address are correct, that it appears legitimate, and it lists what is being searched for. If you see any errors, then the warrant is not valid and the police have no right to enter your home or business.

Whether the warrant is valid or not, you should always make it clear that you are not voluntarily agreeing to the search and that you are allowing it only because they have a warrant. This sets the stage in a positive way for you should anything illegal be found that was not included on the search warrant, and if the law is strictly followed, these items that were not listed on the warrant cannot be admitted as evidence in court at a later time.

Please note that if you do fail to protest the search, or if you invite police into your home when they lack a valid warrant, in most states you will open yourself to being charged for possession of anything they may discover that is illegal, and this evidence will also be admissible in court.

While you'll likely not have a tape recorder or video camera available, if you do (or have one in a cell phone or other gadget that's handy), make a recording of any exchange with the police. This also creates an "intimidation factor," since the police have learned the hard way that having a camera rolling can lead to problems if they don't mind their p's and q's. Also add your own verbal commentary, including officers' IDs, badge numbers, etc. Officers may protest that you have no right to tape them; in fact, you do if you're on your own property, so don't be swayed by any such argument unless it starts to turn ugly, in which case it is better to surrender and take legal action at a later date.

So, if an officer's search warrant appears valid, note that you are not submitting voluntarily to the search and then stand aside and follow the officer's instructions, remembering that resistance can be interpreted as resisting an officer in the pursuit of his duties, an offense you *can* be arrested for.

If you feel your legal rights have been violated, you should bide your time until the incident is over, and *then* contact a lawyer. Never make threats or suggest you're going to take legal action when facing any government worker.

A lawyer can help you weigh the costs, and will tell you when legal action would be tilting at windmills. Remember that legal action will cause you to gain a high profile and could result in even more government scrutiny. It is not something you should do lightly.

No matter how innocent you may be, it's possible that someone carefully scrutinizing what you own and what you do in your home could turn up some infraction. For this reason it is always good to maximize your privacy and avoid any undue notice from the authorities.

AVOIDING GOVERNMENT LISTS

Some groups attract attention from law-enforcement agencies. Avoiding membership in such groups can lower the chances you'll become a target of government scrutiny, thereby preserving your privacy. The groups getting extra attention from law enforcement varies from one year (or crisis) to the next, but generally will include:

- Religious extremists, from those preparing for the end of the world to those who support violent protests or terrorism.

- Racist groups like the KKK, Black Panthers, and so forth.

- Cults and militias.
- Groups that are concerned about various conspiracies and shadow governments.

You should obviously avoid memberships in extremist groups to prevent placing yourself in the crosshairs of rival groups, as well as the hidden microphones and cameras of law enforcement. But sometimes a church or other group will gradually shift its position, little by little joining the ranks of the extreme. For this reason it is never wise to become complacent and go along with the group. Stop to ask yourself how what is being preached from the pulpit or spoken from the platform might seem if played on the evening news, or repeated verbatim in a courtroom.

Be ready to leave a group when it seems to be headed toward extremism, and avoid joining any that exhibit even a hint of such tendencies. Staying away from such groups can keep you out of a variety of problems.

We live in an age when one can have "cyber associates" as well as those in the real world. Thus, it's important to be very careful with systems that create "buddy lists" or similar listings on a site. These lists are increasingly employed by law-enforcement personnel to link people to criminals.[37]

Such police work sometimes yields fantastic results in capturing criminals, but as with most of the other hi-tech advances noted in this book, this has a dangerous flip side should you discover that one of the apparently innocent people on your buddy list, whom you know only through the Internet, is actually a criminal. If a police investigation takes an unfortunate turn, this could put you on a list of suspects simply because of an innocent association you might have with a criminal.

In such a case you probably would not be convicted, but you might see serious legal costs and perhaps even have your reputation damaged should the case be an emotionally charged investigation into terrorism, child pornography, or similar hot-button issues.

BODY LANGUAGE

While most of us are aware of verbal and written communications between people, few of us stop to realize that nearly 60 percent (at least

---

[37] "Police Use MySpace to ID Suspects," Associated Press, March 25, 2006.

according to those who study such things) of human communication takes place at a nonverbal level. In the most crude of these, the message may be given with an obscene gesture. However, much of this nonverbal communication takes place at a level that many of us are blissfully unaware of, through what has come to be known as *body language*.

The key point here is that many law-enforcement personnel, politicians, and even private detectives train themselves to learn how to read body language. Sometimes they become very skilled at this; other times they know just enough to get *you* into trouble if you're innocent but feeling nervous (as most people are around authority figures).

Those who can read these nonverbal cues have a tremendous advantage, since most people, being unaware of body language, make little or no effort to hide these giveaways to what is happening in their minds.

Oddly enough, those studying body language believe many people read the nonverbal signals given by those around them at a subconscious level, the cues intruding into their consciousness as feelings of like, dislike, fear, and so forth, or as "intuition"—perhaps explaining why some people's premonitions or intuitive feelings about others can prove to be amazingly on the mark.

More recently, high-speed film and video have revealed a special type of body language, called *micro-expressions*. These are facial expressions that last only a few moments before a person suppresses them. The person's true feelings—whether fear or other emotions—appear involuntarily and can't be stopped before giving the person away.[38]

Assuming that micro-expressions work as advertised, a detective wanting to learn what a suspect is really feeling can do so by watching the suspect's face while announcing that a crime is being investigated. If the micro-expression is one of puzzlement or surprise, then the detective assumes the suspect is most likely ignorant of the crime and therefore innocent. If the micro-expression is inappropriate, such as a grin that suggests the suspect thinks he's going to beat the system, then the officer might assume he truly is a "person of interest."

Whether micro-expressions reveal someone's thoughts or are simply a modern form of tea-leaf reading is immaterial. The key thing is that this

---

[38] "Lying Is Exposed by Micro-Expressions We Can't Control," New Release, State University of New York at Buffalo, May 31, 2006.

system is being used and taught to many in the law-enforcement community, and is therefore something you should be aware of—because to some extent, you can counter it.

For example, if the police were questioning you and a smile flickered across your face, the officer may try to hone in on that with a question like, "Did that amuse you?"

Since it isn't clear whether or not micro-expressions work, lying might quickly dig a pit for you. (Just ask Martha Stewart, who went to jail for lying to authorities rather than for the crimes being investigated.) So if you find yourself in such a situation, your best bet is simply to tell the truth (perhaps the crime reminded you of a funny story, for example), brush the question off with an "I'm not sure," or clam up and say you want to consult a lawyer. Obviously, the danger for you in most circumstances will be that you may be misread, or that officers without much experience in this area may read too much into micro-expressions.

BE CAREFUL WHAT YOUR BODY SAYS

Many police departments teach their officers that a suspect who is lying or trying to hide information from you will often very subtly cover their mouth, or make similar motions, such as tugging at their nose, scratching their lips, or leaning on a hand. In the end, they are unconsciously trying to hide a lie.

Obviously then, these are things you should avoid doing when speaking to police officers. Don't make the mistake of sitting on your hands— something more than one criminal who was aware of body language has likely tried. Instead, try to gesture and act as normally as possible, keeping your hands away from your face when you speak.

Officers are also taught that people who fail to make eye contact may be lying, and that glancing down and to the left suggests lying, while looking upward and to the right suggests you're trying to recall a fact.

Some other things most officers are taught to look for in body language include:

- People being open and telling the truth tend to assume an "open body" pose, with hands unclenched and relaxed. Women may cross their legs, but men will sit with their legs uncrossed.

- Suspects who lean back or "scrunch" in a chair have disdain for authority.

- People who drum their fingers, crack their knuckles, fidget, or fiddle with their hair are nervous and may be trying to hide something.

- Suspects who "hug themselves" by clutching their chest with both arms feel inadequate.

- Anyone placing their hands on their hips may be combative.

USING BODY LANGUAGE TO YOUR ADVANTAGE

In terms of preserving privacy by not attracting attention, body language can be important. Officers on the street will stop people if they have reasonable cause to suspect wrongdoing. And one such reasonable cause is the often-elusive "acting suspicious," almost always an interpretation of body language.

It's not hard to imagine how this works if you put yourself into the cop's shoes. Imagine you're an officer, standing and watching a crowd, and there's one guy constantly looking away from you, crouching a little, and perhaps unconsciously patting his jacket just over his hip. As a law-enforcement officer, you know that people carrying a concealed weapon often pat it to be sure it isn't coming loose. They get into the habit of doing this, so they are apt to do it when they see a cop and feel stressed.

You get ready for a fast draw, make your way over to the guy, and ask him how things are going. Maybe you search him if his response is too quick and nervous. Chances are you'll find that he's been patting a gun, or drugs, so perhaps you'll even make an arrest.

Or the bad guy may know the drill, and thus look at you, smile a lot, but remain a bit stiff and wooden. You may follow the guy to see if he breaks, or—again—may stop him for "a little chat." And perhaps you will even arrest the criminal if he is suspected of breaking the law in some way.

So, how does this help you?

Here's the key thing to remember: Much of our body language is projected subconsciously. That's what makes possible the skilled performances of Method actors. These performers have discovered that rather than try to keep track of the proper accent, gestures, and so forth, it's easier to just "become" the character. The Method actor puts himself into the character's shoes, trying to think as the character would. The result is that the actor subconsciously adopts the body language of the character and delivers a very realistic performance.

You can do the same thing in real life. If you don't want to attract the attention of police, just imagine yourself as the model citizen (as you most likely are), going about your tasks. Perhaps you'll flick a grin at the officer, but you won't overdo things. You won't appear nervous or attract undue attention. The first few moments after you adopt this strategy, you'll feel like a child who's pretending to be something he's not. But as you continue to stay in this mindset, the Method acting will convince you, as well as those around you (including the police officer), that you are indeed a model citizen, which is just what you are. This behavior will merit less attention, and thereby will help you retain more of your privacy.

CHAPTER 3 IDENTITY THEFT

"Identity theft is the fastest-growing area of crime. It's badly named—your identity is the one thing that cannot be stolen—and is better thought of as fraud by impersonation. A criminal collects enough personal information about you to be able to impersonate you to banks, credit card companies, brokerage houses, etc. Posing as you, he steals your money, or takes a destructive joyride on your good credit."

— BRUCE SCHNEIER, COMPUTER EXPERT[39] —

The process of impersonating someone to raid their accounts and exploit their good credit rating is known as *identity theft*. In 2006, the Federal Trade Commission (FTC) ranked identity theft as one of most-reported frauds for the previous five years, with reported losses approaching almost $300 million in 2005.[40]

When a criminal gains access to your personal credit card numbers, driver's license, and other data, he can impersonate you with little trouble. In the process, he can steal funds from bank accounts or drain Social Security accounts, create new charge accounts (and loot them), and perhaps even buy cars or other expensive items in your name.

---

[39] Bruce Schneier, "Who Owns Your Computer?" *Crypto-Gram*, May 15, 2006.

[40] Jack M. Germain, "How to Stop Internet Identity Theft," *Newsfactor Magazine*, April 25, 2006.

Victims of identity theft often are forced to work for months (if not years) to repair the damages done to their credit rating and regain some of the money they may have lost from bank accounts. And before the damage can be undone, the victim may lose job opportunities and be turned down for loans.

Once a criminal has borrowed your identity, there's no end of mischief that he can do. He can create new phone and bank accounts that will run up charges for you, and even write bad checks under your name. If he's really slick, he may obtain a driver's license in your name, and then get a loan for a new car. Or he might get a job under your name and then file fraudulent tax returns so the IRS and your state government send him refunds that he doesn't deserve.

He may even get you arrested when the frauds being committed in your name are discovered, and the police come to your doorstep to arrest you for crimes you did not commit.

Identity theft has been made easier than it should be because both the federal government and large corporations, in their efforts to quickly collect data on citizens and clients, have been sloppy in protecting that information.

Your Personal Data at Risk

One good example of this is the use of Social Security numbers as identification on a variety of forms, including medical records and IRS forms. Other times it is used like a password, in the case of bank accounts and other systems where an employee tries to identify a caller by asking for their Social Security number. The result is that if a criminal obtains any document with a Social Security number, they can quickly use it to gain credit information through a number of ploys, such as pretending to have lost their bank account number.

(Ironically, use of the number for any identification purposes other than to make Social Security claims may be illegal. While new Social Security cards are no longer issued with the notice, older cards included the phrase: "Not to be used for purposes of identification." This was originally printed on the cards because legislators opposed to the idea of issuing them stated that the numbers might be used to track citizens rather than simply to determine who was eligible for retirement. The worst fears of those who opposed Social Security cards were well founded.)

Often government entities make obtaining a Social Security number amazingly easy for criminals, in part because a variety of forms that may not *require* Social Security numbers still provide space for them. Consumers regularly fill in their numbers because they assume it is required. Should a criminal gain access to this data, the Social Security number and the person it is linked to are there for the taking, requiring only a moment to jot down the information.

Sometimes it goes way beyond the loss of just a number or two in the back room of a business. Recently, thousands of names, addresses, Social Security numbers, and other key data have been lost in one fell swoop. Here are some notable examples:

- State employees in Ohio released the Social Security numbers of possibly millions of registered voters on CD-ROMs distributed to some twenty political campaign operations in 2006. Ironically, the campaign operations hadn't requested the personal data.[41]

- Citigroup lost a computer tape containing the Social Security numbers, names, account history, and loan information on 3.9 million consumers in 2005.[42]

- In 1999, the Securities and Exchange Commission (SEC) posted documents online that included a number of corporate executives' Social Security numbers, including that of Microsoft's Bill Gates. The numbers and names quickly circulated over the Internet even as the SEC claimed they couldn't be taken off-line because it lacked the legal authority to remove them, even though the agency had posted the information in the first place.[43]

---

[41] "Ohio Recalls Voter Registration CDs; Social Security Numbers Included," *Computerworld*, April 28, 2006.

[42] "Info On 3.9M Citigroup Customers Lost," CNN/Money, June 6, 2005.

[43] "SEC Database Exposes Social Security Numbers," *Computerworld*, March 29, 1999.

- An Ernst & Young employee lost a laptop containing the personal data of Hotels.com customers in 2006. It is believed the data included the names, addresses, and credit card numbers of 243,000 people.[44] Worse, customers weren't alerted of the loss for three months.

- In 2005, Bank of America lost data tapes containing federal workers' customer and account information. Although a bank spokesperson said that "a small number of computer data tapes were lost during shipment to a backup data center," in fact, the tapes held data on over 1.2 million people, including one U.S. senator.[45]

- Credit card processor CardSystems had 40 million client records stolen by hackers in 2005. Included were the customer-information files for Visa, MasterCard, and American Express cardholders.[46]

- In 2005, ChoicePoint sold personal information on at least 145,000 Americans, and not to just any old buyer, but to a criminal ring engaged in identity theft. The data most likely included names, addresses, Social Security numbers, spouses' names, phone numbers, and employers.[47]

- In 2006, 17 million customers of the online payment service iBill had personal data released onto the Internet, where it may have been captured and sold to spammers and criminals.[48]

The list of such major breaches goes on and on, with hundreds of major losses of personal data occurring over the last decade. Due to the embarrassment to the companies and agencies losing

---

[44] Candace Lombardi, "Car Theft Exposes Hotels.com Data," CNET/news.com, June 2, 2006.

[45] Paul Shread, "Bank's Tape Loss Puts Spotlight on Backup Practices," www.internetnews.com/storage/article.php/3486036, February 28, 2005.

[46] Tom Sanders, "CardSystems Faces Closure After Record Hack," *VNU Business Publications*, July 26, 2005.

[47] "Choicepoint," Electronic Privacy Information Center, www.epic.org/privacy/choicepoint/, March 14, 2006.

[48] Quinn Norton, "Porn Billing Leak Exposes Buyers," *Wired News*, March 8, 2006.

this data to hackers, and the anger by consumers whose data is stolen, there has been a tendency not to make these losses public.

Because of the damage caused by identity theft, twenty-some states have dictated disclosure laws that force companies losing data to alert all individuals involved.

Data

As this is written, the federal government is working to enact a "consumer protection" law known as the Data Accountability and Trust Act (DATA). This law will supersede state laws in regard to disclosure of loss of data to consumers. DATA sounds like good news, especially if you live in a state without disclosure laws. But it may not be. That's because the federal law would override state laws, and the pressure is on to water down DATA rather than to extend the protection enjoyed in some states to all fifty states.

Obviously corporations are not keen on having to notify customers of company mistakes, so it's no surprise that they might wish to reduce such consumer protections.

The real surprise is that some in the federal government are also lobbying for watering down the law. That's because some agencies have made end runs around laws that prevent them from directly spying on U.S. citizens and collecting data about them. As surveillance expert and signal- and image-processing researcher Andrew Kalukin noted:[49]

> Information about individuals is sold and traded routinely for marketing, charity solicitations, and political polling. . . . The breakdown of privacy in the trade of personal information already makes it possible for government agencies such as the FBI to bypass the government ban against information collection for people who are not suspects of investigation by simply accessing personal information that is already commercially available.

Little wonder, then, when the legislation came before Congress, that government agencies and corporate lobbyists were busy

---

[49] Andrew Kalukin, "Privacy? Automating Camera Surveillance," *Z Magazine*, Vol. 18, No. 1, January 2005.

undermining it, even as federal politicians were describing it as a way to protect the public from identify theft. Here's how computer expert and columnist Bruce Schneier described the situation as DATA reared its ugly head in Congress:[50]

> Lobbyists attacked the legislation. . . . they went after the definition of personal information. Only the exposure of very specific information requires disclosure. For example, the theft of a database that contained people's first initial, middle name, last name, Social Security number, bank account number, address, phone number, date of birth, mother's maiden name, and password would not have to be disclosed, because "personal information" is defined as "an individual's first and last name in combination with . . ." certain other personal data.

> Second, lobbyists went after the definition of "breach of security." The latest version of the bill reads: "The term 'breach of security' means the unauthorized acquisition of data in electronic form containing personal information that establishes a reasonable basis to conclude that there is a significant risk of identity theft to the individuals to whom the personal information relates."

So it appears the law is being carefully crafted to allow a little creative nitpicking, thereby allowing companies to avoid informing consumers when personal data has been lost. For example, records with unlimited personal data can be lost without any need to report the loss, as long as that person's *first* name wasn't included. (Want to bet on how data records will be recorded in the future?)

Such data remains dangerous, since once a criminal has your address or phone number, he can quickly recover your name through a variety of search engines and reverse directories.

Yet if a company should have included first names on the data tapes that were stolen, there is still hope for management. The company can simply claim that there's a "reasonable basis" to

---

[50] Bruce Schneier, "The Anti-ID-Theft Bill that Isn't," *Wired News*, April 20, 2006.

think there's little "significant risk" of data theft. Since *significant risk* means pretty much whatever the company decides it should mean, there's plenty of wiggle room here. And thus you can be sure most statements announcing the loss of files to the press include some weasel words to the effect that there's no "reasonable basis to think there is a significant risk," etc.

(While I hope that somehow the consumer might still win out with the DATA laws that have been undergoing debate without passage for some time now, I am not optimistic.)

Corporate Lack of Privacy

One might assume that information about your private affairs is, well, private. But that isn't the case when you give information to almost any business, from your bank to the local discount stores. U.S. banks and financial services have spent possibly billions of dollars over the last seven years, creating data warehouses of customers that can be "mined" for information that is sold to other businesses—or to the U.S. government.[51]

Internet sites and retail stores—or just about anywhere else you use a credit card or establish your identify—are all quietly and busily collecting and selling information about you. As security expert Dave Methvin recently wrote,[52]

> If you really want to worry about who's tracking you, think about your credit card, your wholesale club membership, or your frequent-buyer card for the local grocery store. All of these companies know where you live, what you buy—down to the UPC code—and how often you buy it. They have big computers and don't need no steenkin' Internet connection to find out that you guzzle a couple of six-packs a week and wear Depends.

Federal laws give you some protection over your personal data, as do many states—provided you exercise those rights. Sadly,

---

[51] Rebecca Lynch, "Internet Marketers Are Getting Hammered for Trying to Build Consumer Profiles," CIO.com, October 1, 2000, page 200.

[52] Dave Methvin, "Clandestine Web Spies," Winmag.com, May 26, 2000.

many laws have been written to give companies the advantage in selling your data, even though the laws purport to protect citizens.

The catch to the laws is that the "default setting" is for information to be shared; unless you opt out of the sharing, the company assumes it is what you want. (Yes, this is the Alice-in-Wonderland view of things.) In other words, if the company can bury the fact that it's selling information about you somewhere in its "privacy policy" statement, then most of those who see the barrage of text will simply skip reading it. *Ka-ching*. The company gains another way to make money by selling personal information to anyone who wishes to buy it.

A careful reading of these privacy policy statements generally reveals that anything but privacy is being extended to clients. For example, banks will claim to collect only minimal data on clients. Yet the doublespeak in the following privacy statement paints a very different picture:[53]

> To provide services and to help meet your needs, we collect information about you from various sources. We get information from your requests for our products or services. One example is income on loan applications. We get information about your transactions with us and with others. For example, we have your account balance information. We get information, such as your credit history, from credit bureaus.

Since these documents have a wealth of other information on them, a bank in fact collects your address, your Social Security number, bank account numbers (possibly including passwords), your loan history, your spouse's name, and so forth. In other words, they collect all sorts of stuff about you.

Whom do they share it with?

A casual reading might lead you to think it stays in-house. But that's not the case. First of all, they share the information with their "family" — in other words, any business that might be owned by the same parent corporation or that is somehow connected to

---

[53] "Privacy Policy," www.chase.com/pages/chase/cc/privacysecurity/policy/policy2, JPMorgan Chase & Co., May 2006.

the company.[54] Given that today's major corporations own a variety of companies, that alone could be troubling.

But it doesn't end there. Reading on will reveal that in fact, almost *any* business that wants access to the data can buy it. Here's a typical phrase whose counterpart can be found in the privacy policy statement of many businesses:[55]

> We may share information about you with companies outside of our family as permitted by law, including retailers, auto dealers, auto makers, direct marketers, membership clubs and publishers.

In other words, your key information may be bought by a shady car dealer operating a lot in a crime-prone area of town, or by a telemarketer wanting to call you at the dinner hour. There's no hint of what safeguards, if any, the data might have when it's in the hands of buyers. The only promise the statement makes is that other groups will have access to the information.

Nor is the data sold for just one-time use. The data is shipped to other companies that can then combine it with other records, mine it for information, or otherwise process it. Which is why privacy policy statements will include a clause like[56]

> We require companies working for us to protect information. They agree to use it only to provide the services we ask them to perform for us.

So your data is protected by entrusting it to someone who "agrees" to only use it as asked by the seller.

Little wonder the data on millions of Americans has been stolen or lost over the last few years, a fact that argues that the safeguards are inadequate.

The cynical might even suggest that one might do as well turning your private information over to the Three Stooges for safekeeping.

---

[54] *Ibid.*

[55] *Ibid.*

[56] *Ibid.*

SOLUTIONS

OPTING OUT

Changing the privacy-sharing status of an account is wise and generally doesn't take much effort. However, it also is not as complete as one might hope. As mentioned, companies collecting data on you will often reserve the right to share the information within their "family" of companies. And if you've "authorized" them to share information by signing previous documents or entering into agreements previously with them or a sister company, they reserve the right to keep that previous agreement in force—without bothering to tell you.

Nevertheless, contacting them and telling them to share as little of your data as is possible is still a worthwhile effort. Most bank cards will have a number you can call listed on the actual card. Calling this number and asking a few questions will eventually lead you to the right department.

A faster route is to go to the Web site of the business and search for its privacy statement, and use the toll-free number or online form to reduce the amount of information about you the company can share.

Don't get sidetracked by the promises or wording that at first makes it appear your private information is safe. It is not, as history has demonstrated time and again. Remember: Companies regularly lose track of their data, sell it to criminals, or have it stolen. Having your information removed from even a portion of the various lists and computer tapes being sold might help you avoid becoming the victim of identity theft or other mishaps that can occur with the leakage of data.

Government's Losses

When it comes to protecting citizens' data in bureaucratic hands, the American government doesn't always do the best of jobs, either. In 2006, a worker for the U.S. Department of Veterans Affairs (VA) took home a laptop that had personal data, including names, Social Security numbers, and birth dates of 26.5 million veterans and VA employees. Thieves broke into the home and stole the computer.[57] Later it was learned that 1.1 million active-duty military personnel, 430,000 National Guard members, and 645,000

---

[57] "Vets' Personal Data Stolen," Associated Press, May 22, 2006.

Reserve members were likely included in the files, raising national security concerns.[58]

After learning the data had been stolen, the VA sat on the problem for thirteen days before informing the FBI or the public, thereby giving the thieves an almost two-week head start to avoid getting caught.[59] Worse, the event didn't result from an isolated breach of security. Rather, it was common for the employee to take a laptop loaded with private records home—a practice that had been going on for three years.[60] The only surprise is that the fiasco didn't occur sooner.

This raises the question of just how carefully various U.S. government agencies protect the data they collect on U.S. citizens. This particular incident suggests that, at least in some agencies, the protection is even less than measures extended by the corporations collecting data on citizens.

As Senator Susan Collins noted after hearing of the theft:[61]

> [It's] simply appalling. . . . The lingering result will be increased doubts among the American people about the federal government's commitment to protecting their personal information.

This same fear that the U.S. government was failing to safeguard the data it was collecting caused the highest court in the European Union (EU) to block an agreement to give the U.S. government information about transatlantic air passengers. The court ruled that the U.S. government failed to protect the data it was requesting, including the names, addresses, telephone numbers, and forms of payment used by passengers.[62]

---

[58] Ann Scott Tyson and Christopher Lee, "Data Theft Affected Most in Military," *The Washington Post*, June 7, 2006.

[59] Bob Brewin, "Senate Hearing: VA Data Theft Should be Wake-Up call," *Federal Computer Week*, May 26, 2006.

[60] Hope Yen, "VA Data Analyst Took Files Home for Years," Associated Press, May 25, 2006.

[61] Johanna Neuman, "Vets Chief Ripped over Data Theft," *Los Angeles Times*, May 25, 2006.

[62] "EU Blocks U.S. Access to Flight Data," *Guardian Unlimited*, May 30, 2006.

Likewise, in 2006 Canada lawmakers also expressed the fear that data placed on travel cards might be detrimental to the privacy of cardholders who visited the U.S.[63]

How Businesses Collect Data

In addition to information collected about each of us from government forms and business applications, many companies are busy creating detailed lists of what customers buy.

Loyalty Cards

One way of doing this is to offer discount or "loyalty cards" to customers. When the customer produces the card, it is scanned and, in return, he gets a modest savings on whatever he is purchasing. What many people don't realize is that the card also identifies them so that a record of what they have bought can be recorded in a file that includes their names and addresses.

This data can be exploited in a variety of ways. At the checkout counter it can help print a coupon (offering a discount for a product that is sold by a competitor of the business that produced the items you actually bought—with the competitor paying the store to give a coupon to you).

The loyalty card system also creates a profile that can later be sold to other companies. If your family regularly buys diapers, your name, address, and buying record might be sold to a direct marketer of baby products; the company can then send junk mail targeted to your home address, knowing that you are a possible customer for their products.

It seems likely that many credit card companies are also assembling lists of the stores their customers frequent. These lists don't contain the specific items purchased (as do the store lists), but they still contain a lot of data. And it is also possible that when a credit card is used, the merchant taking the card might strip the billing data from it and then key that information to the in-house list of products purchased at that time on

---

[63] Jim Bronskill, "Canadian Privacy Concerns Could Scuttle Joint Land-Border Card Proposal," Canadian Press, Canada.com, June 2, 2006.

the card. (It is possible this could even be done when payment is made with a check, especially in businesses that now copy the code from checks and send that data to banks for electronic withdrawals.)

In the end, all sorts of lists are collected about your buying habits when you use a credit or a loyalty card, and possibly even when you use a personal check.

As columnist Allen Pusey noted:[64]

> New technologies have created a massive market for what was once regarded as intimate knowledge of individuals. Marketing programs and devices—ranging from grocery discount cards to Internet identifiers on your computer— allow passive disclosure of consumer transactions. And for the right price, that information is available to the government or anyone else. Law-enforcement agencies, tax collectors, utility firms, collection companies, and others purchase data from companies such as ChoicePoint and BTI to create profiles for everything from screening job applicants to solving crimes.

The obvious catch to this is that as the data from various stores is purchased and compiled on an individual, not only is a very complete picture of the individual created, but the information also may or may not be exploited in ways that will be to his advantage.

For example, an insurance company might create a list of those taking medications, and then compare it to those wanting to buy health or life insurance. Or it might check to see what someone has been buying at various stores: Those with poor diets (as demonstrated by all the soda pop and frozen pizzas they've been buying) might be singled out for physical exams, while those buying running shoes might get to forgo the exam when offered a policy.

Likewise, the police might comb lists for those buying crowbars like the one found at a crime scene, or people buying products

---

[64] Allen Pusey, "Experts Wary of Personal Data Use," *Dallas Morning News*, May 28, 2006.

that might be components for various illegal drugs or bomb making. They could then get warrants from judges and conduct raids — the only downside being that the chemical used to build one man's bomb is another man's lawn fertilizer, and the druggies' "speed" formula uses the same chemical that helps keep your neighbor's antique car engine from icing up in the winter. The system works great for catching criminals, as long as you don't mind inconveniencing innocent people along the line.

As for criminals, those working in a business with access to these lists might search them for goods recently purchased that would be ideal for theft. A worker with computer access at such a business could conceivably generate a list of addresses of people who recently purchased big-screen TVs or other items, giving burglars a shopping list of homes worth breaking into.

WHAT YOU CAN DO ABOUT IT

Fortunately there are things you can do to minimize your risk of having the police bulldoze your front door to confiscate your fuel-line chemicals, or companies penalizing you for one reason or another. Simply use the discount cards when you want the picture being painted of you to be complimentary. For example, if you're buying health equipment, use the discount card and pay with a credit card.

Buying a knee brace because your legs are shot (and possibly in need of knee surgery in the future)? Or purchase lots of aspirin because of migraine headaches? You should pay with cash and avoid discount cards so the data isn't linked to you.

Purchasing a new TV set or laptop computer? Then you might want to pay cash so you won't attract the attention of thieves.

The rule of thumb is to pay cash when you don't want anyone to use the knowledge of your purchase to your disadvantage, and use other methods of payment when you won't be hurt — or might even be helped — by having the information about your purchase added to your profile.

SOLUTIONS

Social Engineering—Hackers at Work

Before going any further, I should note that by and large, hackers are not the bad guys so often portrayed by the mainstream media. Hackers were originally computer and technology workers who, when confronted with an unknown program or piece of equipment, simply messed around with the software or device until they figured out how to control it. Often in the process they came up with unorthodox procedures, and occasionally found routines and capabilities that those originating the program or hardware hadn't realized it possessed. As the wild card in an organization, a hacker can often see or discover things in engineering design that would otherwise go unnoticed.

Most hackers are naturally curious, and sometimes a bit cavalier about following the rules. They sometimes evade security systems and locks not so much to gain access to what has been protected as to see whether or not they can do so (and often this curiosity gets otherwise honest hackers into trouble).

That said, there are some in the hacking community, just as with government and business circles, who are criminals at heart. These are the dangerous hackers, and the ones most often pictured by our culture when the term is used. These are also the ones that pose the most danger to you when it comes to identity theft, either directly or through the schemes they devise that are employed by less-talented criminals.

While most of us picture hackers as tapping into secure systems through brute attacks on computers via phone lines, the Internet, or with laptop-looking devices that pump info into a card reader, in the real world the hacker's most useful tool for cracking into a system is often a telephone and a technique known as *social engineering*. Social engineering is just a modern version of the "confidence man" of days past—only instead of stealing the money from your wallet, he gains access to your computer files.

The basic technique of social engineering is simply to make a person believe that you are someone who should have access to a particular system, but for some reason, you don't have the key information (password, phone number, etc.) to gain access to a bank account or computer system—or whatever a malicious hacker's target may be. Key tools for social engineering tactics are an individual's fear of offending one's fellow workers; a tendency to conform to one's peers; and a fear of admitting ignorance.

Thus Sam, the hacker, if he's done his homework, will know a victim's Social Security number and, that being the case, he can attempt to gain access to his victim's bank account directly online, trying a few possible passwords. When those fail, he can pick up the phone, claim to be the customer of the account he's trying to access, and tell them his password doesn't seem to be working.

At that point the bank clerk will most likely ask for the account holder's Social Security number—which Sam has—and give him a new password, or reset his account with the last four digits of the Social Security as the password. Sam hangs up with access to the account.

Or if Sam doesn't want to call the bank, but has a check from his victim, he may call the owner of the account and say, "Hi, this is Sam at the Always Safe Bank and Trust. We believe someone may have tried to illegally access your account. To let you know that I'm actually from the bank, let me give you your Social Security number and bank account number." After Sam's done this, most people will assume he really is calling from the bank.

Now the trick: "I'm going to assign you a new password so your account will remain secure. Do you have your old password? I'll need that to access your account." At that point, if the victim gives out the old password, Sam has already gained access to the account. However, he'll continue talking as if that information was unimportant, instead putting all the emphasis on the new (and actually bogus) password that Sam will give his victim. Sam then hangs up and immediately starts looting the account. When Sam's victim tries to access the account, he can't, because the new password is bogus—and Sam has emptied the account.

There are all sorts of variations on such scams. Some can even be automated, such as Web sites that claim to be your bank, but are not. For example, Sam might obtain a bank's client list but lack the necessary passwords. In such a case he might mount a brute attack on the bank's system, with a program that enters possible account numbers at random. (Fortunately, most online accounts today are set up to prevent this.) Or Sam might employ some of the "phishing" scams detailed in the next section or simply buy data from stolen computer records.

Pretexting, Phishing, and Pharming

While some hackers may employ only technology to do their dirty work, most often at least part of the job is done with social engineering. When a criminal uses the phone (as in the example above) to carry out his scam, it is also known as *pretexting*. If the social engineering scam is done via e-mail or over the Web, it is known as *phishing*. And if it involves using a phony email to cause a browser to appear it is taking the user to a bank or other site, when it's actually going to a fake site set up by a criminal, the scam is known as *pharming*.

The bottom line is that each of these schemes is designed to ask for your bank account number and password, your credit card number, or other information that can then be used for various identity-theft schemes.

To carry out a phishing scheme, Sam might first visit the bank's Web page and then copy that site, putting his duplicate at a different location on the Internet that he has taken over from someone else without their knowledge. Or he may put the page on a free site, burying it below the home page so the site operator won't easily notice his criminal activities. He then sets up the dummy page so it will record the account number and password when someone attempts to enter the information, thinking it is a legitimate bank page.

Sam will then send out spam e-mails to bank clients, or maybe just execute a mass e-mailing to a range of e-mail addresses that might contain some of the bank's customers. The e-mail will look official, probably using the bank's logo that he has stolen from its Web site. The message will inform the victim that he should check his bank account immediately because it appears someone might have withdrawn several hundred dollars without permission (or some such thing). The actual Web address of the bank will then appear in the e-mail.

Here's an actual example of a rather sloppy spam that came into my in-box while I was working on this book:

> Dear valued WellsFargo [sic] member:
>
> Due to concerns, for safety of Your account [sic] has been randomly flagged in our system as a part of our routine security measures. This is a must to ensure that only you have access and use of your wellsfargo [sic] account and to ensure a safe Banking [sic] experience. We require all flagged accounts to verify their information on file with us. To verify your Information [sic] at this time, please visit our secure server webform by clicking the hyperlink below.
>
> To update your WellsFargo [sic] records, click on the following link:
> http://www.wellsfargo.com/signon?LOB=CONS&screenid= Update_Ac ct
>
> Thank You.
> Accounts Management
>
> As outlined in our User Agreement, WellsFargo [sic] will periodically send you information about site changes and enhancements.

A quick inspection of this e-mail immediately suggests something is wrong. The most glaring indicators are the capitalization mistakes throughout; "Wells Fargo" should be two words, with each capitalized. That a company would make four mistakes with its own name is doubtful, and shows just how pathetic some hacker efforts at tricking people often are. However, the real trick to this is that while the first link appears to take the reader to a Wells Fargo site, in fact it does not.

That's because this e-mail scam, like most of this type, presents a visible Web address, with the invisible HTML code used for the actual link taking the victim to a sub-page at: www.theatre-oftheoppressed.org, where apparently criminals are hoping to "free the oppressed" by lining their own pockets.

Regrettably, most people using e-mail are accustomed to clicking on a link and having their browser open on that link, rather than some other one, so with scam e-mails like this one, victims don't often notice when their browser opens on a bogus site. Thus when a victim lands on the page that is set up to appear official, he won't realize it is really a counterfeit page.

Once the victim arrives at the bogus site, he attempts to access his account by entering his account number and his password. In the process of attempting to log in, the victim will have fed his password and account number directly to a criminal's computer.

The criminal then takes this information and immediately enters the bank's real site, accesses the victim's account, and transfers money into another account at a different bank. He later withdraws the money in cash from the second account, which he then most likely discards, never contacting that bank again so it becomes a dead end when the authorities finally check it.

Big Business and Hacking

While criminal hackers generally work for themselves, or in conjunction with a small gang of criminals, it is likely that some are on the payroll of companies intent on gaining information on their competitors. Just how much business spying goes on is anyone's guess, but industrial espionage has always been a problem, and for businesses engaging in such activities, hackers would seem a logical part of the team.

In 2006, the hint of what might be going on behind the scenes became public with a lawsuit filed in U.S. District Court for the Central District of California by Torrentspy against the Motion Picture Association of America (MPAA), claiming the latter had hired a hacker to steal e-mails and other information from Torrentspy. Complicating the picture was the fact that Torrentspy was already the target of legal action from the MPAA, which claimed the business had been helping software pirates share files over Torrentspy's P2P (Peer to Peer) system.[65]

Whether or not this case has merit remains to be seen in court. However, for years software manufacturers—as well as the music and movie industries—have been battling for the right to take draconian measures against those they believe are using software, listening to music, or watching movies without proper licensing. The targets of their wrath are file sharers and those who record material from the airwaves, movie theaters, and cable TV, continuing to thumb their noses at these commercial groups.

I should note that as a writer and illustrator, I have a vested interest in ensuring that copyright laws remain strong (as this in part helps me earn a living), so I'm not overly happy with file sharers most days, but have done my best to remain objective. This is one of those stories with no good guys, since the software, movie, and music industries have not been entirely aboveboard with the public either, with shady contracts in the music industry and "creative accounting" in the movie business being almost legendary.

In 2003, Microsoft, Intel, Advanced Micro Devices (AMD), IBM, and Hewlett-Packard (HP) formed the Trusted Computing Group (TCG), which was to create standards for a "more secure PC"—a slight twist of words, since the actual goal was to minimize the computer user's ability to use software he had failed to pay for. In order to do this, software was to "phone home" to ensure it was legally purchased, and in some proposals, the software com-

---

[65] Greg Sandoval, "MPAA Accused of Hiring a Hacker," CNET News.com, May 24, 2006.

pany could employ "remote attestation," which would cripple the software if the company marketing it believed it was improperly licensed.[66]

Because of the outcry in the privacy advocate community against Trusted Computing, the company has undergone changes. Microsoft, for example, has transformed the idea first into its Palladium program, and now into the Next-Generation Secure Computing Base (NGSCB).[67] However, the basic thrust remains the same, regardless of the title: A program will assume itself stolen until a number of hoops are jumped through on the part of the buyer to verify that the software was actually purchased and in use on only one machine.

Some of the "protection" goes well beyond simply protecting the software vendor. Under Microsoft's proposed version of NGSCB, a user running new versions of Windows would also discover that he couldn't play music or DVDs on his computer unless he has the proper hardware and can verify that the music or movie is not pirated.[68]

Arguably no one should be running stolen software, music, or movies on their computer. But for systems like the NGSCB to work, the software has to basically sift through data on your hardware and perhaps "call home" over the Internet to various companies owning licenses to both software and hardware to determine whether or not the material appears legitimate.

What happens when it determines you don't have proper authorization? At least part of your computer will be unable to continue the task you were trying to do. Unanswered is how much of your computer a program can disable, and to whom it reports if it finds software, music, or movies it believes might be stolen.

Given that mistakes and glitches regularly plague software, do we really want software police deciding whether or not we should be using our own computers? It is bad enough when a computer

---

[66] Robert Lemos, "Digital-Rights Group Knocks 'Trusted' PCs," CNET News.com, October 2, 2003.

[67] Jim Rapoza, "Don't Trust Trusted Computing," eWeek.com, November 21, 2005.

[68] *Ibid.*

freezes and has to be rebooted; what happens when it first calls the police and then freezes—even though you have all your legal ownership papers in order?

As columnist Jim Rapoza has noted:[69]

> We aren't the customers of Trusted Computing … we're the untrusted enemy who is naive enough to think that we have control over the hardware and software that we've purchased and that we have some kind of fair-use rights. When it comes to Trusted Computing, don't trust it. After all, it doesn't trust us.

Where this will all end is hard to say. But it may be that in the future, corporations will have the legal right to sift through data on your computer and determine whether or not you will be allowed to use it. (At that point, old hardware and pre-NGSCB software may become the only viable way of maintaining real privacy when running a computer.)

In the meantime, while corporations are waiting on the sidelines for legal permission to invade computers, criminals are already doing their best to defeat safeguards users have in place.

They may even be stepping in to take action without legal permission. A computer virus known as *beneficial malware*, or *vigilante ware*, attempts to right a perceived wrong—at least in the eyes of the person designing the virus. Recently one very suspicious vigilante virus surfaced which deletes the very files that those in the music and movie industries regularly claim are slowing the rate of their ever-climbing profits.

Appearing in 2006, the Troj/Erazer-A locates the download folder normally created by file-trading P2P programs and then deletes all MP3, movie, and other graphics files, as well as ZIP files in that folder. Finally, it copies itself into the file-sharing folder so it can be "shared" with others on the P2P system.[70]

Of course, the catch is that there is no determination made of whether or not the files were legally being shared, as might be the case if someone had created his own music or movies and was

---

[69] *Ibid.*

[70] John E. Dunn, "Vigilante Trojan Attacks Other Malware," *Techworld*, May 12, 2006.

attempting to get some free publicity by distributing them through P2P services. This isn't a rare occurrence, and some bands are now becoming famous this way. Additionally, the Trojan turns off antivirus software, leaving the computer open to attack from other malware.

Hopefully such vigilante programs have not been, and never will be, launched by any in the software, music, or film industries. Yet it points to a method that might be employed in the future should the laws be modified to allow owners of copyrighted material to remove material from the computers of those suspected of owning the files illegally. As such, one might argue that vigilante ware is not too far removed from Microsoft's NGSCB concept.

AUTOMATED IDENTITY THEFT

As one might expect in the computer age, automated methods of stealing a person's identity have also surfaced in recent years. These are often in the form of computer viruses attached to e-mail, often disguised as a message from a friend or a document of interest. When the user opens one of these attachments, he also launches the virus (or the attachment may actually be just a virus, in which case nothing appears to happen).

Once launched, the virus then positions itself to collect data and send it to a location where it can be collated. Passwords, Social Security numbers, or other key data you may have hidden on your computer can be copied and relayed to a criminal halfway around the world in this manner. Worse, because the virus program is self-replicating, it may spread itself to your friends and acquaintances via your e-mail address book.

A more detailed look at how to deal with and prevent computer virus infections is covered in chapter 5, but suffice to say, it's wise to avoid installing software from unusual sources, and opening e-mail attachments is never without risk, especially when the e-mail comes from a stranger

The delete key can be the most important tool for protecting your privacy.

TIP

(or even from a friend, if the message seems like an odd subject or the writing seems uncharacteristic of your colleague).

Because viruses or other damaging software may be piggybacked with free software, it is also wise to avoid downloading and installing programs that come from questionable sources online or which are not really needed. Also avoid free games, file-swapping groups, and "wares" sites, as these are all notorious sources for viruses (not to mention potential legal headaches created with pirated software that finds its way to many of these sites). Many sites claiming to offer free ring tones for cell phones or screensavers actually deliver software that installs a virus or spyware (more on this in chapter 5), so be very cautious with such offers as well.

Since spam (unsolicited e-mails that are bogus) is often designed to trick you into giving out private data or will include a virus toward that end, it is wise to do all you can to avoid it. While there are a variety of filters to help sort out spam, often people are targeted for spam because they have placed their e-mail address online in a Web guest book, at a blog site, or other places where an e-mail address may be added. Spammers often employ software "robots" that search out sites with e-mail addresses on them, and then send spam to those addresses.

If you have a Web site and need to have an e-mail address online for legitimate contacts, use a small JavaScript program to hide your e-mail from address-collecting robots, while still allowing actual human beings to send you an e-mail (a quick search on the Internet will turn up snippets of code that can be put into Web pages for this purpose).

Also avoid adding your e-mail address to "chain" e-mails advocating this or that, and do your friends a favor by forwarding messages to groups of people in your address book using the BCC (blind carbon copy) feature, which will hide everyone's e-mail address from others you send the message to.

Never "sign" an online petition that asks for your e-mail. Chances are a congressman will never see the petition; instead, everyone who foolishly

One quick way to avoid spam is to never post your e-mail address online.

TIP

signs the petition will add their e-mail to a spam list, and receive a variety of junk messages for some time to come.

Also, never buy anything advertised by unsolicited e-mail ads sent to you. Chances are these are simply scams designed to get you to give up credit details and your address. Spam should simply be deleted, no matter what it promises to do for you in the way of bargains, services, or free offers.

Occasionally you may be exposed to spam or software that combines a virus with social engineering for a double-whammy assault. A good example of this is the Troj/Arhiveus-A Trojan that encrypts a victim's "My Documents" folder in Windows, and then saves the folder as Encrypted Files.als. The virus then warns the victim that they must buy a product from an online vendor in order to get the password to open their own files—and warns that if the police are contacted, they will never get the key. Of course, since people often have family pictures and such stored in the My Documents location, they may be desperate to get them back.

An even better bit of social engineering is employed when such a virus is inserted into the computer when a victim thinks he is getting pirated hardware, the serial number to software he hasn't paid for, or access to a pornography site. In such a case the victim will be between a rock and a hard place, since if he contacts the authorities for help, he'll be admitting that he was trying to engage in a questionable (if not illegal) activity.

The solution to avoiding such problems is not to pursue illegal activities.

If you are a victim of a virus that encrypts files, generally a little searching for antivirus companies that have dealt with the problem will yield the password or work-around to unlock the files (if one is available—some "encryption" may be random strings of letters and numbers, with the original file actually deleted). Obviously it is also wise to back up data that you want to preserve and then store the CDs, hard drives, or whatever you store your backups on in a safe place (ideally a fireproof media box).

Something Borrowed, Something New

Some modern social engineering hacks are built around old scams that rely on greed and people's willingness to break the law if presented with the possibility of getting a large sum of money for their efforts.

One common example of this is the "Nigerian scam" in which an e-mail claims the writer has access to an account with hundreds of thousands (or even millions) of dollars, and that he will share a percentage of the money with someone who'll help him move it from the Nigerian to U.S. accounts.

To do that, the Nigerian (or Sudanese, or whatever nationality the hacker has settled upon) will need the account number and password to the U.S. account he'll be transferring the fortune to, or he'll need to have money wired to his account.

There are many variations on this theme, but the last chorus always involves money traveling out of the victim's account. Other variants of this idea have been appearing in online dating services where, after making an acquaintance online, a stunningly beautiful young woman will proclaim her interest in marrying a stunningly naive victim—but first she will need the money to come to the U.S. Sadly, for want of love, the victim will too often send the money, never to hear again from the phisher pretending to be his true love.

AVOIDING THE PHISHER KING

Today's criminals employ all sorts of phishing and social engineering tricks. To avoid getting caught by them, there are several important rules to follow: First, don't expect important information about your bank, the IRS, or other major corporations to come to you via e-mail, especially if it is in regard to an attempt to access your account or to take legal proceedings against you.

If you get an e-mail requesting that you confirm your Social Security and other data with the IRS, or asking whether your bank account recently did or did not have a large sum recently withdrawn from it, suspect a phishing scheme.

Ditto for a notice that someone may have "illegally accessed" your eBay, PayPal, or whatever account. You can be 99.99 percent sure these are bogus e-mails.

Likewise, people calling on behalf of this or that organization, government agency, or business shouldn't have to ask for your personal information. They should have all your data (and then some) if they really work where they claim, and they should have access to at least some of it. But do keep in mind that a criminal might have some data on you that he may then try to exploit to obtain more.

He might say something like, "To confirm that I'm working for the IRS [or bank, or whatever], I can give you your home address and Social Security number." Remember that just because someone has some data about you doesn't mean that they necessarily have all they need, or necessarily represent those who should legitimately have the private information.

The best ploy when dealing with any of these situations is to immediately get in touch with the actual agency or business, using a phone number or other contact that *you* obtain from a phone book or from the actual agency's Web site. Don't use the Web address in an e-mail or the phone number given to you by a caller—either one might be phony, and lead you right back to the scam artist. Instead, get the actual number or site and go from there.

And if the people you contact are unaware of what you're talking about, then immediately report that someone has been trying to get the data. When reporting what appears to be an attempt by a criminal to trick you, be prepared to forward the bogus e-mail, or give the phone number from which the criminal called. (Caller ID may capture a criminal's number, though it is very easy to spoof ID numbers with computers or other equipment. Currently—and oddly enough—it's perfectly legal to create bogus numbers to hide one's identity.[71])

Also be prepared to help law-enforcement authorities should it come to that. Doing so will help lend you credibility should the hacker eventually gain access to your account in some other way, and you need to repair your credit rating and so forth.

---

[71] Bruce Schneier, "Caller ID Spoofing," *Schneier on Security*; www.schneier.com/blog/archives/2006/03/caller_id_spoof.html, March 3, 2006.

Stealing Money the Old-Fashioned Way

Not all data about individuals need be collected in hi-tech ways. Some of the old ways still work well with the most common targets, including bank and credit card statements (which will generally give them all the data they need to make illegal charges to your card or create bogus checks with your account number); credit card offers (which permit opening a new account using a rented postal box for the address); new checks or credit cards that can be used directly for purchases; or medical or tax forms that have your Social Security number or other information.

Some of the techniques for obtaining these are quite simple. Criminals may:

- Steal mail from your postal box to obtain credit card and check information — if not the checks and credit cards themselves.

- Do some Dumpster diving and rummaging through trash cans to obtain old documents that yield key information about your accounts.

- Obtain information about your account numbers from business records or checks sent by you to the business where the criminal works.

- Pose as a landlord or employer to obtain your credit report, and glean data about you from it.

- Steal your credit or debit card passwords by watching you enter them into an ATM (often by standing behind you but sometimes by watching from some distance with binoculars).

- Steal your purse or wallet and obtain information about you from documents you were carrying, and/or use your credit cards and personal checks.

- Use a U.S. Postal change-of-address form to divert your mail to another location where they pose as you.

• Break into your home and steal personal information about you, along with credit cards, personal checks, etc.

Often criminals will also take actions to delay your ability to quickly discover that identity theft is ongoing. For example, a criminal who has obtained your credit card information might call the credit card issuer and ask to have the billing address changed. This allows him to run up bills on the card without your seeing them. And if you fail to notice his actions at that point, he can even file for bankruptcy—in your name—to buy himself several months of additional time while running up bills.

Better Shred than Dead

Since many identity thieves rely on finding paper documents in your trash, it is a good idea to get a shredder that is capable of making Dumpster diving or similar ploys impossible to exploit against you. A good shredder will also save you from a variety of government or private snoops as well (as outlined in chapter 1).

There are shredders and there are shredders. The cheap ones simply cut a paper into strips. These may seem safe, but in fact I have talked to investigators who have hired retired folks or people in hospitals with time on their hands to go through piles of shredded sheets to piece them together. They even have a clipboard-type tool that makes it easier to shuffle the strips around until the right one is located.

The shredder that doesn't permit this type of reassembly is the crosscut or disintegrating shredder. These shredders cut the paper into little squares or odd chunks that are not easily pieced back together.

You can add a level of security by also shredding some unimportant papers—thereby making more pieces to consider if someone might try to reassemble the documents. You never want to shred just one or two sheets in an otherwise new or empty shredder, because those might be reassembled if someone were really intent on recovering them.

When a shredder is about full, reaching in and stirring up the bits of paper is another way to disturb the order of the particles, making reassembly impossible. And when emptying the shredder, leave it about one-fourth full to keep things confusing when you shred new sheets into it.

For really sensitive documents, or for times when you don't have a shredder handy, you can burn paper and then stir the ashes. This reduces pieces to the molecule level, where it's impossible to recover data. Be sure documents are really burned. It isn't unusual to see a stack of papers that someone "burned" which is mostly intact, with only the outer pages and edges burnt, while the inner pages are still undamaged. Burning sheets one at a time is a good way to avoid this, followed by a stirring of the ashes so the documents can't be carefully removed and read—something that *is* possible, and has been done by investigators.

Because information stored on CDs or data disks can also be accessed by criminals, and since it is possible to reconstruct some of this information even when a disk is scratched or cut in half, it is wise to purchase a shredder capable of chopping disks into small pieces, along with paper documents. Such a shredder is also capable of handling old credit cards, making it an ideal way to destroy them (since even outdated credit cards contain data that might be employed by a criminal).

AVOIDING INFORMATION LEAKS

In addition to regularly using a shredder, there are other things you can do to avoid becoming a victim of these criminals. First and foremost for those who regularly use the Internet for shopping and banking, or who have e-mail accounts, be very wary of possible phishing attempts to gain access to passwords and other information about you.

When in doubt, don't do business with a company online, and remember that most serious banks and government agencies don't make contact with customers and consumers via e-mail.

Never give personal information over the phone, the mail, via e-mail, or on Internet sites unless you are very certain whom you're dealing with. You should only do this when you contact the business involved—never after someone has contacted you claiming to be representing this or that business or agency. Also, be skeptical of any calls that announce you have won a prize. Generally these will be scams to get information from you or sell you something you don't need.

Too-good-to-be-true deals generally are. Phishers often offer low-priced software or other goods that are never delivered. Instead, you give up your credit card number, name, and address, along with the specific ID on the back of your card. By the time you realize you haven't received what you ordered, you may find a plethora of charges on your credit card account.

You can also plug another potential area that identity thieves employ by opting out of credit offers sent by mail. Simply visit www.optout-prescreen.com, or call 1-888-567-8688*. (Ironically, you will be asked to provide your Social Security number when making this call, but don't be alarmed; this is a legitimate request).

Your Social Security card should be stored in a secure place, such as a bank safe-deposit box. Ditto for infrequently used passports, birth certificates, or other documents that might be useful to an identity thief.

Never give your Social Security number unless required to by law. If your state foolishly uses Social Security numbers on driver's licenses, ask to substitute a random number for it instead (which is generally an option). Do the same with your health insurance company, if possible.

Since loss of credit cards and other data can be expensive, carry only the credit cards and identification you may actually need. Leave other cards and data locked up in a home safe or a bank safe-deposit box.

---

*Found online at www.ftc.gov/bcp/conline/pubs/redit/prescreen.pdf.

Keep track of your wallet or purse at all times. When at work or at the gym, lock it in a safe place.

If possible, when ordering bank checks, pick them up from the bank rather than having them mailed to your home.

Finally, keep your home secure. Some identity thieves simply walk through an open door or crawl through an open window and proceed to take the various documents in the house or apartment and use them to set up bogus accounts and do their damage.

The simple precaution of locking your doors and windows can keep such people from victimizing you. Locks are not always a solution, but they at least make the job of identity theft more difficult. And in some cases, they may thwart altogether those who would do you harm.

WARNING SIGNS

There are some warning signs that you have been the victim of identity theft. Any time you see one or more of these, you need to take action immediately to minimize the damage you suffer. Key danger signs include:

- Failure to receive bills or other important mail. A missing bill can mean that a crook has diverted your billing to another address to hide his activities in abusing the account.
- Receiving a credit card you didn't apply for is a bad sign, since it means someone else did apply for it but failed to fish it out of your mailbox before you did, or that the bank sent it to your actual address rather than his.
- Being rejected for a loan or asked to pay a higher-than-usual rate when you should have a good credit rating.
- Receiving bills or letters from bill collectors about merchandise or services you haven't purchased.
- Getting notices about goods or services you haven't ordered.

HOW TO UNDO IDENTITY THEFT NOW!

If some of the above warning bells have sounded; you have lost your credit card, wallet, or other ID; or you have reason to believe that someone may have stolen your identity in some way, then taking immediate action can at least minimize the chances for further damage to your credit rating and a variety of legal confusion for you to sort out. In the following pages, I've detailed the steps you need to take and the options open to you when dealing with identity theft.

For most people, these steps will be practical to take in a do-it-yourself manner. This will also often save a small fortune in costs, since hiring someone to do the work, especially in the case of a lawyer, can be expensive (though you may eventually find yourself in court, at which point hiring a good lawyer is a necessity).

However, if you find this process too complicated, or if you don't have the time to follow all the steps, then you might want to contact a "credit repair" business and/or a lawyer to have them handle the task for you. It is always better to hire someone to do the work competently and thoroughly rather than to do it in a slipshod matter.

1) As soon as you notice any theft on credit cards, with banks, etc. you should file a theft report. This complaint should generally be filed with your local police. If for some reason the police are reluctant to take your report, you should ask to file a "Miscellaneous Incidents" report, or try another jurisdiction such as the state police. Or you can contact your state attorney general's office to determine what state law requires of police departments (and perhaps register a complaint if the police have failed to do their job). A police report of a crime is essential if you are to avoid having to pay for fraudulent use of your accounts by a criminal, so don't take "no" for an answer when trying to file a report.

2) You may also need to file a complaint with the Federal Trade Commission in some circumstances (the police will often advise you on this matter—more on this later in this chapter).

3) After filing your criminal report with the police, there are four key areas you should immediately act to protect:

• Your financial accounts: Credit card companies and banks you use should be immediately contacted and accounts closed. Employ new passwords on all new accounts you create (more on how to do this in a bit).

- Your Social Security number: Contact the Social Security Agency Office of the Inspector General and file a complaint. You can file online at www.socialsecurity.gov/org, or you can call 1-800-269-0271. You can also send a letter detailing your problem to: SSA Fraud Hotline, P.O. Box 17768, Baltimore, MD 21235.

- Personal ID: Contact your state driver's license bureau and get another driver's license issued, and also ask for your file to be flagged so that your name can't be employed for a new license by someone else. If you have a passport or other IDs, do the same thing for these documents.

- Your credit report and rating: Call the toll-free fraud number of one of the three consumer reporting companies: Equifax (800-525-6285), Experian (888-397-3742), or TransUnion (800-680-7289). When contacting one of these services, ask them to place an initial fraud alert on your credit reports. This will help protect you by preventing someone from creating new accounts in your name, and also may lead to their apprehension when they attempt to do so.

YOUR FRAUD ALERT

When you report the possible theft of your ID, you will find that there are two types of fraud alerts you can file. The first is an *initial alert* that will remain on your credit report for at least ninety days. This is most ideal if you are not certain that you are a victim of identity theft. It will buy you some time and safety without a lot of complications.

If you don't find that bogus charges and accounts are being created under your name, then you won't need to take further action. The initial alert is ideal if you've lost your wallet or suspect you might have fallen for some e-mail or Internet phishing scam. After you file an initial alert, you'll also get a free credit report from each of the three companies listed above; check these over to be sure there have been no bogus accounts or charges made in your name, and that your address, banking information, and so forth are all correct. (If they are not, then you should contact the credit bureaus and police immediately.)

The second type of alert you can ask for is the *extended alert*, which will remain on your credit report for seven years. This is the best choice if you know someone has stolen your identity and is creating bogus accounts and so forth under your name.

With the extended alert, you will get two free credit reports within twelve months from each of the three consumer reporting companies. You will also have your name removed from marketing lists for pre-screened credit offers for the next five years, making it harder for someone to create phony accounts under your name.

Having either alert will create a few headaches for you. For example, when you want to set up a new account with a business or bank, you will be asked to produce more identification than you might otherwise be asked for. Creating accounts or buying things online or over the phone with a credit card may be more problematic. However, this is generally a small price to pay for the added security obtained.

Be sure that if you move, change jobs, or make other major changes in your life, you report these to the credit bureau you're working through with your alert. Otherwise there may be some confusion as to whether you are really you, or someone impersonating you.

CLOSING THE OPENINGS

If you discover that someone else has illegally accessed any bank or credit account, you should immediately call and speak to an officer in the security or fraud department of the company involved. Get the account closed and a new one created. Follow with a written summary of your conversation with bank or other officials, sending the letter to that business as well.

If any company asks for additional information, give it to them promptly. Remember that the more hoops you jump through at this point, the more quickly issues will be resolved and the more likely they will be resolved in your favor. Always be polite and cooperative.

Keep copies of *everything* you write, and send only copies of supporting documents to banks or loan offices. Try to minimize your phone conversations, and instead put things in writing whenever possible, since verbal agreements are hard to prove should you be forced to go to court over disputes about what you owe to a bank or loan company. Also, save all paperwork, forms, and other documentation so they'll be available should you be taken to court for bad checks, credit charge disputes, defaulted loans, or such.

Be prepared to keep correspondence, phone logs, and documentation for several years, even after the police close your case. This is necessary because problems will often crop up later, or a criminal will be arrested who is later found to be responsible for the charges made against your name.

At that point having your records may resolve some question as to what amounts you were responsible for, and may also help nail the criminal for the crimes he committed. So always file all your paperwork for possible later reference, even if it appears everything has been resolved.

When first contacting companies via phone, don't hang up until you're certain you understand everything you've been told. If you need more help or the person you're talking to is unsure about something, politely ask to speak to a supervisor. Write down the name of everyone you speak to along with the date and time for later reference.

Also write a summation of what was discussed. These phone logs can be very helpful later on, and may also prove essential should you be forced to take legal action on disputed charges or the like.

Send all letters to companies by certified mail, return-receipt requested. This will give you a U.S. postal document showing when you sent a letter to the business, which can also be useful should you be forced to go to court. Also save all documents you receive from the businesses, as your lawyer may find this useful should you become the target of a lawsuit.

If a criminal has made charges and debits on your existing accounts, or created new accounts, request a fraud-dispute form from the bank or other company involved. You must be careful to dispute all charges that you have not made. Otherwise, the companies involved will assume that you owe the money.

You may be forced to pay disputed charges for the time being, but don't do so without filling out a fraud-dispute form, or without writing a letter to the billing department to note that the charge was not made by you, and that you are paying the amount *only* until the matter can be settled.

Also request a letter from all banks or other credit companies stating that disputed or illegally accessed accounts have been closed, and that fraudulent debts have been discharged. This letter can be important if subsequent charges are made to the account or if claims saying you have not paid your bills are later sent to your credit report company.

In settling accounts, companies may ask for a copy of a police report. You can obtain this from the police department to which you first reported that fraudulent use of your identity or accounts was occurring.

DEALING WITH THE BANK

There are a variety of laws designed to protect victims of crimes, including identity theft. In general, criminal use of checks or loans created locally will be covered by state and local laws, while theft involving electronic transfer of funds or through credit card companies that are based out of state will involve federal laws.

The federal Electronic Fund Transfer Act applies to all transactions involving an ATM, fraudulent use of a debit card, electronic debit or credit to accounts, and unauthorized electronic fund transfers. This law gives you sixty days from the date your bank account statement is sent to you to report *in writing* any amounts withdrawn fraudulently from your account.

With ATM and debit cards, the amount you are responsible for is determined by how quickly you report your loss of the card. If you report the loss or theft within two business days of your discovery that it has been stolen or misused, then the maximum amount you are responsible for is $50. If you report your loss after two days, but within sixty days, you will be responsible for up to $500 in losses. After more than sixty days, you may be responsible for the full amount before you file your report.

Currently Visa and MasterCard have limited their customers' responsibility to $50 per card, no matter when the report is made. However, this could change overnight should the companies adopt a new policy.

To notify a company of suspected loss or fraudulent use of a card, phone the company that issued the card and then follow up your call with a letter (sent by certified mail, return-receipt requested). Save a copy of the letter and the return receipt.

Generally you will be expected to pay for disputed amounts until the company can investigate, at which point they will credit your account. This must be done within forty-five days of your contacting them about the loss or fraudulent use of a card.

If you believe that checks have been stolen or duplicate copies made and used, you should immediately contact your bank and ask that a stop-payment be placed on all checks. Close the account immediately. You should also ask the bank to notify its check verification service so that retailers will no longer accept the checks from this account.

Even with checks that the bank has cleared but which you did not write, you should immediately contact the business the check was written to and issue a written letter disputing the charges against your account. This can prevent the business hiring other collection agencies to go after the money if the bank withdraws its payment on the check.

Currently no federal law limits your losses if someone uses your checks with a forged signature, but most state laws will protect you to some extent, with most states holding the bank responsible for bad checks. However, these laws may not apply if you fail to notify the bank immediately upon your discovery that fraudulent use of your account may be taking place.

If you discover that checks are being written in your name on a newly created account, contact the bank that has issued the checks and have it close the account and contact its check verification company. You should also immediately contact your credit bureau to be sure other accounts and services have not been created using your identity.

CREDIT REPORTS

If you find inaccurate information on your credit report, contact the company issuing the report and get the information changed immediately. The federal Fair Credit Reporting Act (FCRA) requires that credit report companies and the businesses giving data to them are responsible for correcting fraudulent information in your report. This means that once you contact them, they must block fraudulent information from appearing on your credit report.

To do this, you must mail them a copy of your identity theft police report and a letter telling them what information on their report is fraudulent. In the letter you should note that you did not authorize or make the transactions that have led to the fraudulent reports. With the letter you should also supply proof of your identity. (Xeroxed copies of your driver's license, Social Security card, etc., will generally work for this purpose.) Send your letter by certified mail, return-receipt requested. Save the receipt with a copy of your letter and documentation.

By law, after receiving your notice of fraudulent use of your identity, the consumer reporting company has four business days to block the fraudulent information. It must also alert the businesses submitting information in dispute that it has blocked the data being submitted.

You should also contact the companies involved in reporting information to the credit report company, sending them a letter explaining that identity theft has occurred and that you did not authorize or make the charges in question. Also send this letter by certified mail, return-receipt requested, and save the receipt with a copy of your letter and any documentation in the way of account numbers, billing records, etc.

FEDERAL TRADE COMMISSION COMPLAINTS

Filing an identity theft complaint with the FTC will make it more likely that whoever stole your identity will get caught, as well as creating proof that you were anxious to get the matter cleared up—both important points to have established should you have to go to court to prove you are not responsible for the fraudulent actions of whoever stole your identity.

It is possible to file a complaint online at www.consumer.gov/idtheft, or by calling 1-877-438-4338. You can also make a complaint in writing to: Identity Theft Clearinghouse, Federal Trade Commission, 600 Pennsylvania Avenue, NW, Washington, DC 20580.

Should additional information about fraudulent use of your accounts or identity come to light after filing your initial complaint with the FTC, you can contact them again to give them the additional information. Generally, phoning will be the most satisfactory way of doing this.

If the criminal has employed the mail at some point to engage in fraud, then you may also wish to contact the U.S. Postal Inspection Service to file a report. Likewise, some out-of-state exploitation of your identity may merit contacting the FBI. Remember that while doing either of these will create more work for you, they will also increase the likelihood that the criminal will be caught, and also make you look better should you have to go to court to prove that you are not responsible for fraudulent use of your accounts.

For these reasons, the extra effort will almost always be worthwhile.

BANKRUPTCY FRAUD

If you discover that a scam artist has filed for bankruptcy using your name, write to the U.S. Trustee Program in the region where the bankruptcy was filed. You can generally find the phone number for this agency by looking under "U.S. Government Bankruptcy Administration," or by contacting your local credit union or bank and asking for the information.

When contacting your regional U.S. Trustee by letter, you will need to give a brief description of what you believe has happened, and also provide proof of your identity (again, Xeroxed copies of your driver's license, Social Security card, etc., will generally work for this purpose). The U.S. Trustee will then make a criminal referral to law-enforcement authorities.

You should also file a complaint with the U.S. attorney general's office, or the FBI in the city where the bankruptcy was filed.

Because none of these government agencies will provide you with legal advice, you should also hire an attorney to work with the bankruptcy court to convince them the filing was fraudulent.

CRIMINAL RECORDS

Often a crook who has stolen your identity will create criminal records as well. This can vary from speeding tickets to more serious breaches of the law. The best bet when facing such possibilities is to contact your state attorney general's office to see what procedures are necessary to repair your record. If charges are serious, you should immediately contact a lawyer and let him run interference for you to avoid serious troubles.

If you find yourself arrested for a crime you did not commit and suspect identity theft is behind the charge, the problem can be cleared up once you are photographed and fingerprinted, since the police may have a record of the photo and fingerprints of the person who claimed to have been you. If this is the case, you should be immediately cleared, as it will be apparent what has happened. This may not be true with less-serious crimes such as speeding, however. You may again need a lawyer to sort things out for you.

Since it is possible that there might be arrest warrants issued in states or counties other than the one you live in, upon reporting suspected identity theft, you should also ask the police to send an *impersonation report* to other law-enforcement jurisdictions. You can also take this action if you discover an outstanding warrant has been issued.

Once the impersonation report has gone out, the police should recall warrants and issue a *clearance letter*, or, if you've had the misfortune of being arrested, a *certificate of release*. It is wise to keep this document in your wallet with your driver's license in case you're wrongly arrested at a later date. It is also wise to request that the police file records of any follow-up investigations establishing your innocence; these should go to the district attorney's office and/or the court in the jurisdiction where any criminal activity took place.

Since your name is likely to have been recorded in one or more criminal databases, you should also ask the police to change the *key* or *primary* name to that of the person who stole your identity. If his name is not known, then it should be listed as "John Doe," with your name listed only as an alias.

If legal actions have been taken against the criminal while he was using your name, then you should also clear your name in court records. Most states have a formal procedure for doing this; contacting the attorney general's office in the state where the charges were filed will give you the details on how this is done.

States with no formal procedure for clearing court records require that you contact the district attorney's office in the county where the case was prosecuted and ask for the procedure that needs to be followed to clear your name from court records. Because this process can be complicated, you may be forced to hire a criminal defense attorney in order to clear your name.

DEALING WITH DEBT COLLECTORS

Although the federal Fair Debt Collection Practices Act was not designed specifically for dealing with identity theft, you can nevertheless use it to stop a debt collector from contacting you.

SOLUTIONS

You can do this by first writing a letter to the collection agency, telling them to stop their collection efforts; explaining that the amounts in question occurred due to identity theft; and include documentation and a copy of the police report you have filed in regard to identity theft. Send the letter by certified mail, return-receipt requested, and save the receipt with a copy of your letter and any documentation in the way of account numbers, billing records, etc.

Once the debt collector receives your letter, legally the company may not contact you again except to tell you there will be no further contact, and/or if it intends to take specific action to collect the debt, in which case the collection agency can renew its activities only if it sends you proof of the debt.

You may need to be a little creative if you lack documentation, as might be the case where a criminal has created a new account. Fortunately a debt collector is obligated to send proof that you owe money. So immediately contact a company claiming you owe them money and demand documentation.

When these documents arrive, often you can find a bogus signature, a wrong address, or other indication that will prove you did not make the purchase or charges that are being accrued to you. At that point, you will then have the documentation along with the police report that you need to send to the bill collector as outlined above.

Once you have notified a bill collector that you are the victim of identity theft, the company is also obligated to tell the business it is collecting for that you are the victim of identity theft.

This may stop a debt collector from dunning you, but it doesn't necessarily erase the debt itself. It's up to you to contact the business that believes you owe it money and explain why you do not believe the money is owed. Otherwise, the business may simply hire a new bill collector, report to your credit bureau that you have failed to make payment, or initiate a lawsuit to collect the money.

DEALING WITH OTHER PROBLEMS

There are a variety of other problems you may encounter if you're the victim of identity theft:

- If you believe that identity theft has led to tampering with your securities investments or brokerage accounts, report this to your broker and to the Securities and Exchange Commission's Complaint Center at www.sec.gov/complaint.shtml, or write to: SEC Office of Investor Education and Assistance, 450 Fifth Street, NW, Washington DC, 20549-0213. For answers to general questions, call 202-942-7040.

- The U.S. Postal Inspection Service (USPIS) investigates cases of identity theft that involve the mail system, whether it involves fraudulently securing new credit cards, theft of personal information from a mailbox, falsified change-of-address forms, or other schemes. Simply call your local post office, explain your problem, and ask to be connected to the USPIS.

- If your passport is lost or stolen, contact the United States Department of State (USDS) local field office (whose number should be listed in the telephone directory). With today's fears of terrorism, loss of a passport is treated very seriously.

- If a fraudulent student loan was created in your name, contact the school that offered the loan and ask that the loan be closed immediately. You should also report the fraud to the U.S. Department of Education at 1-800-MIS-USED (1-800-647-8733), or oig.hotline@ed.gov.

CHAPTER 4 PHONE PRIVACY

> *Massive surveillance is a poor substitute for real law-enforcement and intelligence work. It is an after-the-fact method of crime fighting. It is not designed to prevent crime. Massive wiretapping does not equal security. Instead, we have elected to jeopardize our national security in exchange for poor law enforcement. For example, Financial Crimes Enforcement Network [FinCEN] monitoring of all money transactions did not detect al-Qaeda, nor did it find Mohammed Atta before he boarded his last flight. It was an ATM receipt left in his rental car that led the FBI to the bin Laden bank accounts.*
>
> — BRAD JANSEN, DEPUTY DIRECTOR FOR TECHNOLOGY POLICY
> AT THE FREE CONGRESS FOUNDATION[72] —

Under the Fourth Amendment to the Constitution, government entities must first prove to a judicial officer that agents believe there is probable cause of a crime being committed. Originally this standard was applied to a person's papers, home, and other property. Later it was extended to communications a person might have over the telephone, as well as a justification to limit the obtrusive technology that law-enforcement agencies might exploit to intrude on a person's privacy, such as hidden microphones and cameras.

---

[72] Charles R. Smith, "U.S. Police and Intelligence Hit by Spy Network," NewsMax.Com, December 19, 2001.

In the mid-1970s, following the Watergate hearings, which exposed government abuse of citizens' privacy through CIA and FBI surveillance, the U.S. Senate's Select Committee to Study Governmental Operations with Respect to Intelligence Activities hearings (often called the "Church Hearings") concluded that federal agencies had regularly abused their powers in conducting surveillance on civil rights activists and antiwar protesters, even when there was no sign of these individuals actually breaking (or intending to break) any U.S. laws.

To prevent similar government abuses in the future, Congress passed FISA (the Foreign Intelligence Surveillance Act of 1978). This law was designed to prevent such abuse by laying out what government agencies could and could not do in the way of collecting data about American citizens.

FISA also established the Foreign Intelligence Surveillance Court. Under this provision of the law, this somewhat secret court is authorized by the chief justice of the United States, who designates seven federal district court judges to review applications for warrants related to national security investigations. These warrants were required before sensitive intelligence-gathering operations within the United States could be conducted.

Warrant applications were to be drafted by attorneys in the General Counsel's Office at the National Security Agency, at the request of an officer of one of the federal intelligence agencies. Each application was to be certified that surveillance targets were working for a foreign power and, if a U.S. citizen or resident alien, that they might be involved in the commission of a crime.

To help prevent abuse, FISA also established a Foreign Intelligence Surveillance Court of Review.

New Capabilities

Technology marched on, and soon the FBI and other government agencies were having trouble keeping up with the explosion of fax machines, cellular phones, and other technology coming onto the consumer scene. To keep up with the technology, the federal government greatly expanded its surveillance capabilities through the Digital Telephony Act of 1994, also known as the Communications Assistance for Law Enforcement Act (CALEA). This law gave the FBI the right to read and intercept virtually any electronic communication, regardless of what technology was used in creating the signal.[73] Under CALEA, the telecommunications industry was required to modify its equipment to make tapping phone lines an automated process. Due to the added expense of such modifications, the telecom companies all but revolted; the revolt was suppressed when the Federal Communications Commission (FCC) issued new standards for electronic equipment that basically dictated including the hardware that enabled CALEA phone taps.[74]

This legislation also mandated that cell phones made after October 2001 would have tracking capabilities to show exactly where a user was when the phone was active.[75] So today, not only can a person have his conversations listened to, but if his cell phone is in the receive mode (or in use), it is also possible to locate exactly where he is.[76]

On May 3, 2006, the FCC issued an order saying that broadband Internet access and interconnected Voice-Over-Internet Protocol (VoIP) services would be required to comply with CALEA by May 14, 2007. The agency also announced that ISPs could hire "Trusted Third Parties" for "processing requests for intercepts, conducting electronic surveillance, and delivering relevant information to LEAs [Law-Enforcement Agencies]."[77] (As this is written, the action is being appealed in court, but is expected to be upheld.)

While CALEA is seldom mentioned in the press, behind the scenes it has become one of the growth industries for government

---

[73] "Digital Wiretap Law at Key Juncture," Policy Post 4.1, *Computer Underground Digest*, Volume 11, Issue 11, February 15, 1998.

[74] Vikki Kratz, "Privacy vs. Public Protection," *Shewire*, March 21, 2000.

[75] "Digital Wiretap Law at Key Juncture," *Ibid*.

[76] "Tracked by Cell Phone," Makesecure.com, December 25, 2005.

[77] "FCC Adopts Order to Enable Law Enforcement to Access Certain Broadband and VoIP Providers," *FCC News*, May 3, 2006.

buyers, as well as for telecommunications companies upgrading equipment to facilitate easy spying on users. Here's how reporter Thomas Greene described a recent Intelligence Support Systems trade show which is held annually in Crystal City (a suburb of Washington, D.C.), where vendors displayed their CALEA-related wares for potential government buyers:[78]

> Vendors manned their booths, exhibiting the latest gadgets for mass electronic surveillance: machines capable of scouring the data streams of millions of subscribers—industrial-strength kits for packet interception and analysis, RF interception, and voice and keyword recognition. . . . In the conference rooms, salesmen pitched their solutions for "lawful interception."

> In attendance were the generally responsible representatives of North American and Western European government and law enforcement, but also numerous representatives of naked state control in the Middle East, Asia, and Africa. . . . Narus was there, maker of the kit . . . allegedly used with impunity by the National Security Agency at numerous AT&T facilities for mass, domestic Internet surveillance, and, the company boasts, used by Shanghai Telecom "to block 'unauthorized' Internet calls. . . ."

> [Other companies] offered equipment and services capable of every manner of radio frequency and packet interception, with user interfaces and database structures designed to manage and deliver not just information but "actionable data," properly organized and formatted for easy prosecutions.

Today, targeting citizens for surveillance has become a thriving business. And you are in the crosshairs.

The "F" Is for Fishing

After the 9/11 attacks, FISA safeguards were modified by the USA Patriot Act of 2001, with Section 218. These modifications included provisions for the FBI to secretly conduct physical

---

[78] Thomas Greene, "Crashing the Wiretapper's Ball," *Wired News*, June 1, 2006.

searches of businesses or homes, as well as engage in wiretaps with an eye toward obtaining evidence of crime without first showing a probable cause that any actual crime might have been committed—or even planned. The other troubling change to FISA did away with the need to notify the subjects of such investigations, unless some sign of actual criminal activity was found.

One might argue that not only did Section 218 transform FISA from a law that protected U.S. citizens from intrusive searches and wiretaps into one that did not—but the modifications also actually ignore the Fourth Amendment, since under Section 218, law-enforcement agents might secretly break into a home or business, conduct a search, tap phones, or take similar actions and never notify the target of their surveillance that such actions had been taken. As one cynic suggested, with the changes to the law, the "F" in FISA might as well stand for "Fishing."

Additionally, if a person were taken to court because of evidence found during such a search, he couldn't challenge the legality of the search or wiretaps.

As the ACLU noted following this modification of FISA:[79]

> Section 218 turns this concept upside down. It permits the FBI to conduct a secret search or to secretly record telephone conversations for the purpose of investigating crime even though the FBI does not have probable cause of crime. The section authorizes unconstitutional activity—searches and wiretaps in non-emergency circumstances—for criminal activity with no showing of probable cause of crime.

In addition to the changes wrought by Section 218, Section 216 of the USA Patriot Act also lowered the threshold of proof needed before officials could gain access to Internet communications, in part due to the failure of the language used in writing the law. The result was that nearly any Internet Service Provider (ISP)

---

[79] "How the Anti-Terrorism Bill Enables Law Enforcement to Use Intelligence Authorities to Circumvent the Privacy Protections Afforded in Criminal Cases," Position Paper, ACLU, October 23, 2001.

in the United States might be accessed with a warrant issued anywhere else in the country. As the ACLU put it:[80]

> Section 216 of the USA Patriot Act permits a federal judge or magistrate in one area to issue a pen register or trap and trace order [methods to link the sources of communications to the names and locations of the sender and receiver] that does not name the ISPs upon which it can be served, and that can be served on ISPs anywhere in the U.S. The judge issues the order and law-enforcement agents fill in the places at which the order can be served. This further marginalizes the role of the judge. Law enforcement obtains the equivalent of a blank warrant. In addition, nationwide searches of pen register and trap and trace orders effectively insulate law enforcement from challenge in court.

With some phone data now going over Internet systems, Section 216 also means that such calls aren't protected in the same ways standard phone calls are. However, this was not the only lowering of standards for some phone calls—because the USA Patriot Act also changed the law regarding roving wiretaps.

A Roving We Will Go

In the mid-1980s, as phones became more easy to install and wireless systems became widely used, the FBI requested that the wiretapping law be modified to permit the agency to follow a suspect from one phone to another without obtaining another court order for a new wiretap. Since this seemed a reasonable request to a growing problem, in 1986 Congress changed the law to allow "roving wiretaps" that would permit law-enforcement agents to tap multiple phones if agents could prove to a judge that a suspect might be changing phones to thwart surveillance. In 1998, Congress relaxed the standards for proving a suspect was trying to evade surveillance.

As generally presented to the public, the roving wiretap is pictured as following a suspect from one phone to another. But in practice, law-enforcement agencies treat it a bit differently,

---

[80] "How the Anti-Terrorism Bill Limits Judicial Oversight of Telephone and Internet Surveillance," Position Paper, ACLU, October 23, 2001.

applying it to any phone he *might* use because he is in close proximity to it. Thus, if a suspect enters the home or business of a friend or acquaintance, phones there can be tapped as well.

The USA Patriot Act of 2001 (115 Stat. 272) expanded the time periods for which the Foreign Intelligence Surveillance Court could authorize surveillance, and also increased the number of judges serving the court from seven to eleven. Section 206 of the USA Patriot Act also extended the roving wiretap authority to "intelligence" wiretaps authorized by the Foreign Intelligence Surveillance Court.

While certainly extreme measures are called for to deal with terrorism, the transference of roving capability to secretly authorized wiretaps increases the potential for the erosion of privacy. These wiretaps are authorized secretly without a showing of probable cause of crime. However, an even greater danger to privacy in Section 206 is the relaxation of the requirement that government agents first must ascertain that a target of surveillance is actually using a phone that's authorized to be tapped.

This may seem a small thing, but in fact, it opens the door to casting some very wide nets. For example, if a suspected terrorist were to enter a library and use a public computer to access the Internet, a government agency with a roving wiretap applied to that suspect could start collecting information on *all* the computers in the library, and continue to collect data even after the suspect had left the building.[81]

The contention that investigating those using computers in libraries might be commonplace is suggested by the estimated 30,000 "security letters" issued each year by the FBI to public libraries.[82] These letters require libraries to secretly turn over patrons' records without informing them that they are the subjects of investigation. While it seems likely that some of these have to do with what books a patron might be checking out, if a library

---

[81] *Ibid.*

[82] "Four Librarians Finally Break Silence in Records Case," *The New York Times*, May 31, 2006.

keys computer use to its library cards, then data about the patron's browsing habits might also be collected—and secretly turned over to the government should a security letter be issued.

TIP Be cautious in what you check out from a public library; reading books that might attract government interest in the library rather than checking them out is a much more prudent practice.

The key point with the transformations to FISA through the USA Patriot Act is that it took the lower standards that were previously applied to potential spies and others working for foreign governments and made it possible to also apply these lower standards to U.S. citizens. Thus, law-enforcement agencies now have the ability to go from investigating probable criminal activities to conducting fishing expeditions geared toward trolling for possible lawbreakers.[83]

Early in March 2006, Congress renewed the USA Patriot Act. Although members had frequently expressed worry over possible abuses of the law and publicly suggested that some sections should be removed, when the dust cleared, most of the provisions for the roving wiretap and allowing government agents to obtain warrants to search premises without informing the owner were kept in place. About the only "safeguard" for US citizens' privacy was to exempt most (but not all) libraries from having to comply with secret demands for information about patrons. At the same time, the bill had an alarming provision that prevented telecommunications businesses from telling customers that their accounts might be monitored.[84]

In the end, many concerned with privacy were worried that the new law had gone too far, undoing many of the privacy safeguards that had previously been enjoyed by Americans. As the Electronic Frontier Foundation noted,[85]

---

[83] *Ibid.*

[84] "House Approves Patriot Act Renewal," CNN.com, March 7, 2006.

[85] Declan McCullagh, "Senate OKs FBI Net Spying," *Wired*, September 14, 2001.

There is no evidence that our previous civil liberties posed a barrier to the effective tracking or prosecution of terrorists. In fact, in asking for these broad new powers, the government made no showing that the previous powers of law enforcement and intelligence agencies to spy on U.S. citizens were insufficient to allow them to investigate and prosecute acts of terrorism.

The process leading to the passage of the bill did little to ease these concerns. To the contrary, they are amplified by the inclusion of so many provisions that, instead of aimed at terrorism, are aimed at nonviolent, domestic computer crime.

Roving Wiretaps

Since CALEA requires phone companies to build mass surveillance capabilities into their networks, tapping a phone is now a very simple matter that can be done remotely without having to physically modify a user's phone or get anywhere near his property. The "roving wiretap" is likely the type most often employed. This tap works like the Six Degrees of Kevin Bacon game, starting with phone numbers that might be used by the subject of a criminal investigation, and then branching out to any phone number contacted by any of the suspect's phones.

These taps might then spread to those numbers called by the secondary phones. This can continue, with taps being legal for any phone number contacted by any of these or subsequent phones. Exactly how far this roving can legally go and how often it does so is a bit murky, but in theory, after a few days' time, a single roving wiretap might involve the tapping of hundreds (if not thousands) of different numbers across the nation, or around the world. And each phone tap would be perfectly legal under the blanket of this single, court-approved roving tap.

At one time the mountain of recordings that could result from such roving wiretaps was impossible to handle. That's changing today with inexpensive digital storage, faster computers, and voice-recognition software. This technology enables snoops to sift through thousands of messages in minutes, sorting them into suspicious and non-suspicious groups. Worse, these records can be stored for future searches involving much different crimes and even more capable equipment.

Thus, today's roving wiretap to thwart terrorists might become tomorrow's fishing expedition to ferret out tax evaders, deadbeat dads, or anything else the government declares a criminal activity.

In 1997 the FBI announced that it was working toward the capability of conducting 1,360 taps at any given time—a number that would be larger than the total the agency often claimed to be making each year. Additionally, the FBI asked for the cellular industry to build in the capacity to monitor 103,190 calls simultaneously nationwide.[86]

So in theory, at any given moment, the FBI might be employing a roving wiretap that actually encompasses hundreds, or even thousands, of phones. As Lisa S. Dean, vice president of technology policy at the Free Congress Foundation, noted about this situation:[87]

> Roving wiretaps represent a serious change in the conduct of federal law enforcement. This is a huge power grab where abuse is almost a certainty. With a roving wiretap, federal agents have the authority to tap any phone of any persons who are "proximate" to the subject of criminal investigation. It is an open invitation for the government to monitor anybody who opposes the government under the guise of fighting domestic terrorism.

This trend continued into 2000, when the FBI asked for over $75 million in budget appropriations to continue its information-technology expansion, including "Digital Storm," which permitted widespread court-sanctioned collection and electronic sorting of

---

[86] John Markoff, "Dispute Arises over Proposal for Wiretaps," *The New York Times*, February 15, 1997.

[87] Lisa S. Dean, "Totalitarian Government Has Already Begun," *Coalition for Constitutional Liberties Weekly Update*, Volume I, Number 34, October 16, 1998.

data collected from telephones and cellular phones. Along with the proposed expansion was the creation of a "foundation for an up-to-date, flexible digital collection infrastructure," fancy wording for wiretaps permitted under the Foreign Intelligence Surveillance Act. Finally, money was earmarked for an "enterprise database" that would store the data collected and share it around the world on a high-speed network similar to the Internet.[88]

Almost as troubling as the massive levels of wiretapping that may be going on is the apathy of the public. Stories of widespread tapping may garner a little hand-wringing in right-to-privacy circles, but generally there's a collective "who gives a rip." As Dr. Robert Bruen, the director of systems and operations at the White-head Institute/MIT Center for Genome Research, has noted:[89]

> The right to privacy is not mentioned explicitly in the Constitution, but it falls within the penumbra of the rights that are explicit. There has been a constant and continuing effort by various agencies of the federal government, law enforcement, and state governments to chip away at this right. These efforts have been resisted by a number of groups through legal challenges and media publicity.
>
> The battle is raging, but it does not appear that most of the citizens in America realize the extent of the consequences of this war. It is the difference between a police state such as George Orwell envisioned in his novel *1984* (perhaps as demonstrated in East Germany and the former Soviet Union, without quite the high-tech capability) and a free society as envisioned by the framers of our Constitution. The very future of our society is at stake.

Of course, part of the problem is that most Americans remain in the dark as to how much surveillance is going on with phone calls. When a federal government spokesperson claims only 1,773 wiretaps were conducted in 2005, for example, the number of actual

---

[88] Robert O'Harrow Jr., " 'Digital Storm' Brews at FBI, *The Washington Post*, April 6, 2000, p. A01.

[89] Dr. Robert Bruen, "Book Review—Privacy on the Line. The Politics of Wiretapping," *Cipher*, January 12, 1998.

phones that were monitored might be hundreds or thousands of times greater due to the way roving wiretaps work. Furthermore, such numbers don't take into account state and local police surveillance that is currently outpacing federal activity in criminal cases, nor does it include FISA surveillance (which saw over 2,000 applications for surveillance and searches in 2005).[90]

Worse for those concerned with privacy, these wiretaps are just the tip of the iceberg.

Nothing New Under the Sun

In 2006 it was discovered that the National Security Agency (NSA), operating outside FISA rules, was conducting warrantless wiretapping. According to some reports (and given the secrecy involved, there is much confusion as to how large an operation this might be), the NSA had amassed tens of millions of American phone call records from Verizon, BellSouth, and AT&T/Southwestern Bell. Very possibly, the collection formed the largest database ever assembled, and there appear to be no plans to curtail or reduce it, at least during the George W. Bush administration.[91] (While political opponents of the president charged that the collection of such data was illegal, interestingly, the government has maintained that only the account numbers and the numbers dialed were collected—data that is perfectly legal to collect without a warrant, according to an earlier Supreme Court ruling.)[92]

The software the NSA is most likely using to eavesdrop on telephone calls is created by Narus, which just happens to have a former deputy director of the NSA on its board of directors. The software is said to be capable of scanning 10 billion bits of data *per second*, and is capable of dealing with e-mail as well as phone calls.[93]

---

[90] "Headlines," *Security and Freedom*, Center for Democracy and Technology, http://www.cdt.org/security/, May 2, 2006.

[91] Ray Rivera, "Eavesdropping to Go On, Cheney Tells Midshipmen," *The Washington Post*, May 27, 2006; page A03.

[92] U.S. Supreme Court, *Smith v. Maryland*, 442 US 735, 1979.

[93] Elise Ackerman and K. Oanh Ha, "Wholesale Snooping," *Mercury News*, May 28, 2006.

Although many in the American press seem to view the NSA phone-monitoring program as something unusual, in fact, it was simply the logical outgrowth of other programs the U.S. government had been engaged in for several decades.

One of the oldest of these has been codenamed Echelon. Many of us who first heard of the program in the 1980s assumed it was more hoax than reality, the stuff that has been inspired by conspiracy theorists.

The Echelon program appears to have been created by the United States, Britain, and other allies for spying on the USSR during the Cold War. After the collapse of the Soviet empire, Echelon continued to be funded, collecting data via a group of satellites. How much data it collected is open to debate. Some conspiracists claimed it intercepted millions of phone calls per day and relayed the data to ground-based computers for storage, processing, and analysis, something that would have been an amazing feat back in the 1980s.

In 1998, the European Parliament confirmed that the program existed when it expressed concern that its citizens were having their privacy violated by the system. This concern eventually led to investigations, which, as they became public, revealed that the NSA actually was engaged in activities that involved intercepting private phone calls and other communications.[94]

Here's what the European Parliament believed the NSA was busy doing:[95]

> Within Europe, all e-mail, telephone, and fax communications are routinely intercepted by the United States National Security Agency, transferring all target information from the European mainland via the strategic hub of London, then by satellite to Fort Meade in Maryland via the crucial hub at Menwith Hill in the North York Moors of the

---

[94] Ian Black, "Britain Warns EU to Drop Spying Debate States Over Echelon," *The Guardian*, April 8, 2000.

[95] "An Appraisal of Technologies of Political Control," Scientific and Technological Options Assessment of the European Parliament, Working Document (Consultation version), PE 166 499, Luxembourg, January 6, 1998, section 4.4, "National & International Communications Interceptions Networks."

UK. The system was first uncovered in the 1970s by a group of researchers in the UK. . . .

Echelon is designed for primarily nonmilitary targets: governments, organizations, and businesses in virtually every country. The Echelon system works by indiscriminately intercepting very large quantities of communications and then siphoning out what is valuable using artificial intelligence aids like Memex to find keywords.

The European Parliament also discovered another listening program that may be a part of the Echelon program—or another previously unknown one. According to the charges leveled by investigators, this program tapped into ground lines by detecting weak electronic magnetic transmissions.[96]

It seems likely—though it is impossible to connect the dots without having access to information that is not public—that the current NSA efforts of collecting telephone call information is actually a part of the Echelon program. But whether it is or not, it is safe to say that there is a whole lot of collecting going on. More than in any time in history, and likely to continue to grow as the prices of computer storage systems drop and the speed and capabilities of computers grow.

Because a number of nations are involved in Echelon, it may be that a system has been devised to sidestep various national laws that prevent governments from spying on their own citizens (much as is done with the U.S. government purchasing datamining information from private corporations while being prevented by law from collecting data about citizens directly). The trick here could be that technically, one country—say, Australia— might handle data collected from U.S. phone calls, and then the U.S. would trade data it collected on Australians for the data collected on U.S. citizens. While this may or may not be what is happening, it isn't too hard to imagine that some such bit of tortured logic and playing with the rules might be ongoing.

---

[96] Joseph Fitchett, "Spying From Space: U.S. to Sharpen the Focus," *International Herald Tribune*, April 10, 2001.

The Taps of Lesser Snoops

Of course the government is not the only party that might be snooping on your phone calls. Sometimes it might be the person you're talking to. Only twelve states (California, Connecticut, Delaware, Florida, Illinois, Maryland, Massachusetts, Michigan, Montana, New Hampshire, Pennsylvania, and Washington) have laws that require that both parties on the phone must agree to a conversation being taped.

That means the tape may be rolling any time you call someone living outside of any of these states. Given that a phone recorder can be purchased for as little as fifty dollars, no questions asked, it is not hard or expensive to put one of these devices on a line, letting it record every time the phone is picked up. Nor is the legality completely clear when it comes to one spouse placing such a device on a home line and then "accidentally" recording the other partner's conversations.

Although many people still picture phone taps as gadgets that are dropped into phone mouthpieces or attached to lines in your home, today's tap can be much more subtle, transferred from a variety of points within a home or even outside on the line, attached to the junction box or the "punch-down box" in an apartment. These taps are also often capable of transferring phone conversations, faxes, computer modem data, or telex signals.

There are devices sold that purport to detect phone taps, but these only work (if at all) with a very few types of taps installed directly on the household wiring, and only create a false sense of security.

On occasion, taps can be easily spotted in a junction box or connected to an open phone jack. Usually taps employed by small-time snoops are connected into the wiring, often at points not easily spotted.

Phones can be modified slightly to create an "infinity bug," which basically causes the phone's mouthpiece to activate while the phone is still on its cradle, thereby allowing someone to listen to what is going on in the room, within earshot of the phone, even though it is still on the hook and never rings.

PHONE SOLUTIONS

Whether you use a landline, cell phone, or Internet phone, your conversation may be intercepted. Perhaps the only relevant question is just how many different individuals and groups may be listening or recording your every word. The best advice is to never say anything on a phone that you wouldn't yell into a megaphone while standing on a busy street. Disposable cell phones may be purchased with cash at some discount stores. These give a little privacy since they aren't tied directly to you, though conversations might still be monitored on either end of the call.

TIP Since cell phones can have their precise position located when they are on or in use, switch yours off when you wish to travel without the possibility of being tracked.

Assume your cell phone calls are being recorded, because there's nothing you can do to stop it.

When it comes to dealing with snoops in the private sector, if you believe that your phone is tapped, you can ask the phone company to inspect your line. If an illegal tap is found and it has been placed there by a non-government entity, the phone company is required to tell you. But if a tap belongs to a government agency, the company is required to lie and tell you there is no tap.

If you're dealing with government snoops, the solution is not quite so easy. Philip Zimmermann, the creator of the encryption system PGP (more about this in the next chapter), has recently poked another software stick into a hornet's nest, releasing a computer program called Zfone (with versions available for Windows, Macintosh, and Linux operating systems). The program, coupled with a suitable microphone and earphone headset, permits encrypted calls to be placed between two computers.

Two other similar programs are also available for use as secure Internet phones: Speak Freely and Invisible IRC. Of the three, it seems likely that Zfone is the least likely to have a built-in back door or to be otherwise compromised. With any of these, calls must be made from computer to computer, and both must be equipped with the same program. (The programs don't work with Skypes or Voice-Over-Internet Protocol [VoIP] systems.)

It's likely that these programs are causing a bit of consternation in government circles, since so many efforts have been made to keep all communications systems easily accessible for law-enforcement officials. Terrorists and criminals undoubtedly know this, leaving the government to spy mostly on honest people and dumb criminals and terrorists.

You should remember that while Zfone and similar programs may offer protection from snoops, it doesn't prevent them from putting a bug next to your computer and simply recording your side of the conversation, or placing a sensor in the computer's sound card to capture both sides of the dialogue. In such circumstances, systems like Zfone can be less secure than one might hope, and can also lull a person into thinking he is protected from spies when he is not.

CHAPTER 5 COMPUTER PRIVACY

" In the last few decades much of our privacy has been lost. And it's not only computers that deserve the blame. They have only been useful magnifiers of what the prying eyes of Big Brother have wanted to see all along. "

— CONGRESSMAN RON PAUL[97] —

Viruses

As most readers know, computer viruses are small, self-replicating programs that often damage computers by erasing other software or, in extreme cases, reformatting hard drives or taking other actions that can create serious problems. Like a living disease, virus programs often spread by inserting copies of themselves into e-mail or files that may be shared. What isn't often noted about computer viruses is that increasingly, they collect data from the victim's computer and employ that data in a variety of ways.

Today there are a number of types of these programs, including worms, Trojans, and malware, as well as destructive macros designed to attack Microsoft Word, PowerPoint, or other programs. Although these various programs are quite different from a technical standpoint, they are usually classified generically as "viruses," since modern antivirus programs are being designed to detect and remove all of them. This book will do likewise without going into

---

[97] Jennifer Jones, "Financial Institutions Grapple with New Privacy Regulations Info World," *Infoworld*, October 27, 2000.

great detail as to how these various threats work. Suffice to say that today's antivirus programs can deal with nearly all of these.

Often viruses will be set to take certain actions on a specific date. This can vary from displaying an odd message to actually deleting data. This delay permits the spread of the virus to other computers before users even realize that their computer is infected. Other viruses may be triggered by a specific action taken by the computer user, such as opening a specific program or trying to share a certain type of file.

Windows systems are most commonly targeted due to the popularity of the software, as well as the animosity that a successful company like Microsoft often attracts. But viruses designed to attack other systems are starting to pop up, suggesting that the day is fast approaching when all types of computers will be regular targets of virus writers.

Obviously it is essential to have an antivirus program on every computer these days. The program should constantly run in the background, where it can often intercept and shut down a virus should it somehow be launched. And the program should also be employed to regularly scan all the programs and files on the computer to be sure a virus hasn't slipped into the system at some point.

Since nearly all antivirus programs detect viruses through a list of known components in various viruses, it is also important to update the virus list of a program at least daily as well. You can have this done automatically by selecting this option on the software.

TIP Update your antivirus software daily.

There are a number of antivirus programs available today. An important consideration is that on occasion, an antivirus corporation may be tempted to give spyware (more on this in a moment) designed to collect data for corporate use a free pass rather than classify it as a virus. For this reason, it may be wise to select antivirus software from sources that are less apt to have a vested interest in helping their corporate friends or, worse yet, from those that protect spyware created by the same corporation that is offering the antivirus program to begin with (one reason that Microsoft antivirus software is suspect in some more-paranoid circles).

Additionally, governments could conceivably pressure antivirus companies to allow government spyware to remain undetected. This possibility might operate with a carrot-and-stick approach, with the threat of anti-monopoly or other legal actions on one hand, and the promise of purchases by government agencies on the other (perhaps with patriotic or crime-fighting appeals as well). Given the already-cozy relationship that exists between corporations and the U.S. government when it comes to sharing data, it isn't too far-fetched to imagine this being done.

For these reasons, going with different companies for your antivirus, firewall, and anti-adware software makes a lot of sense, especially if these are different from other software you use for browsing, word processing, and so forth, since to some extent you will be pitting the corporations against each other. By the same token, a "security suite" that handles all potential problems for you might not be the best solution. If the company has compromised with the government or corporate spyware producer, then the software might give a free pass to a program that was leaking private information about you. That this might happen is not a matter for speculation—it already has; Sony's infamous rootkit program that raised the ire of many a computer user in 2006 (more on this in the section below) is a clear example of this. Many antivirus programs still won't detect it.

So antivirus software is good, but not necessarily 100 percent capable of stopping big-time snoops should the corporation that makes the software decide to cooperate with other companies or government agencies. This caveat aside, here is a list of the top antivirus companies worth considering:

- Grisoft (offering AVG, including a freeware version; www.grisoft.com)
- Friske Software International (offering several versions of F-Prot; www.f-prot.com)
- McAfee (www.mcafee.com)
- Symantec (www.symantec.com)
- Microsoft (www.microsoft.com)

Newer antivirus programs are becoming part of suites of software designed to do more than simply stop viral activity on a computer. For example, McAfee's Falcon (being rolled out for the consumer as this is written) is slated to contain antivirus, anti-phishing, anti-spyware, and rootkit detection features, and will also automatically handle some backups and monitor network security.

Sites that can check a PC for various viruses and spyware are also available. But generally these should be viewed as an additional resource rather than a replacement for software that runs on your computer. Obviously great care should be exercised to be sure the site offering such services is trustworthy; otherwise, you might be opening your computer to attack from a site that only claims to be there to help you.

Spyware

Programs that permit spying on a remote computer have come to be known as spyware. Basically, the spyware program is installed on a target computer, often piggybacked on a program that is not spyware and offered for free. Once installed, the spyware collects data from the computer and then connects to the Internet and relays the information to a distant computer. Because the spyware generally installs itself so it will start each time the computer is booted, spyware can steal enough memory from other programs to greatly reduce the performance of the computer. And since spyware is often poorly written, it can cause a computer to freeze or crash.

As noted elsewhere in this book, the U.S. government sometimes purchases data from businesses and then transfers these records into government data banks. This gives those in charge of government policies a vested interest in keeping it easy to collect information on citizens. Thus, when something like spyware raises its ugly head, the tendency is for those charged with protecting the privacy of citizens to look the other way.

Of course, the idea that the government might support some spyware is often far from the picture presented to the public. For example, in 2004, and again a year later, several congressmen introduced the "Spyblock Act," which purported to outlaw spyware. One of the supporters of the legislation, Senator Conrad Burns, said:[98]

> Computer users should have the same amount of privacy online as they do when they close the blinds in the windows of their house. But ... computers across the country are being hijacked every day as users unknowingly download unwanted and deceitful programs that spy into their online world.

Even though the savvier computer users were howling at the hidden software that was targeting them for advertisements and pop-up boxes keyed to the sites they visited, and relaying information about their computers to businesses (and perhaps criminals) around the world, Congress never quite came to grips with how to deal with the problem. The bill went to committee and was not passed in 2004, nor in 2005, and has yet to make another appearance as this is written.

Some state legislators have attempted to curtail spyware. However, these laws are often poorly written, and state law-enforcement agencies by and large see their powers as ending at the state line — not ideal if you're trying to stop a manufacturer of spyware who has based his operations in, say, Norway.

But regardless of whether you're looking at state or federal regulations, laws—whether enacted or tabled—often leave broad loopholes for businesses that wish to use spyware. These make it

---

[98] John Borland, "Legislators Take Aim at Spyware," CNET News.com, March 3, 2004.

legal for a company to market programs capable of transmitting data from your computer, over the Internet, to whomever the program is configured to give information.

Much of this legal spyware is marketed as a way to spy on workers or children—supposedly by employers and parents, though the lack of restrictions on such software makes it probable that it can be misused to spy on spouses or corporate competitors. These give the user the ability to log keystrokes, track what Web sites have been visited, and read instant messages received on a target computer where the spyware is installed. Some programs will also record what files and documents have been opened or created, log passwords, and record e-mail messages that have been composed. Some will even take screenshots to forward to whoever is spying on the computer. In short, these programs are designed to totally invade a user's privacy.

Such spyware is marketed freely on the Internet and regularly used in businesses to monitor employees. (And, yes, the courts have ruled that this is perfectly legal.) As one site crowed about such software, "This program is great tool for supervision of home or work computers. Remote control is enabled for more than one computer."[99]

TIP If you use a computer at work, always assume that your boss may be peering over your shoulder.

Big business has its hand in the pockets of spyware development more deeply than this, however, since some corporations are making their own spyware, while others are making money from third-party spyware.

"Why Should They Care About It?"

Perhaps the most infamous use of spyware by a large corporation occurred in 2005 when Sony BMG released fifty-some CDs that

---

[99] "Legal Spyware," www.spyware.lt/legal-spyware.html, January 30, 2006.

were designed to thwart computer users intent on copying the CDs for use on other devices (such as MP3 players) or—most likely Sony's goal—for file sharing. Sony's solution was to put what amounted to a virus on each CD. When a user popped one of these CDs into his computer, he was presented with a notice that he could only make copies of the CD to use on three different devices, and would have to use a special program (supplied on the disk) to play his CD on his computer. If he agreed, the small program designed to play the CD on his computer was installed, without any fanfare.

What a user *wasn't* told was that part of the program was installed as a rootkit, placing itself in the core area of the hard drive normally reserved for the operating system. Worse, the program became invisible to the user and was next to impossible to remove because it couldn't be detected with the normal file viewers found on most computers.

This program transmitted the computer's Internet address to a Sony BMG site whenever a CD was loaded into it. If the spyware was detected and an attempt made to remove it, the CD drives on the computer would stop working, dictating a new installation of the operating system before the hardware would work properly. However, Sony had apparently done such a poor job of designing the spyware that it allowed virus designers to "hide" their software within the rootkit area as well, making computers with the spyware vulnerable to a variety of secondary attacks from malicious hackers.[100]

It is interesting to note that, even though it was obvious Sony's spyware could be exploited by other viruses and spyware, and that it was reporting private data to Sony sites, the antivirus software companies at first refused to classify it as spyware. Instead, they contacted Sony, even after being rebuffed at times, and tried to give them as much wiggle room as possible, seemingly to justify leaving it off their virus lists. It was only *after* independent bloggers in the security arena started telling the public about

---

[100] Wade Roush, "Inside the Spyware Scandal," *Technology Review*, May/June 2006.

Sony's rootkit that the antivirus companies admitted they knew about the problem.[101]

Sony then infuriated computer owners when the president of Sony BMG's Global Digital Business division, during an interview on national radio, dismissed the problem, saying, "Most people, I think, don't even know what a rootkit is, so why should they care about it?"[102]

Many computer users heard this as, "The consumer is too stupid to care, so we can do whatever we want."

Meanwhile, computer-security experts were discovering that the rootkits had been installed in a variety of computers on half a million networks, including military and government sites.[103] (Had a teenage hacker done this, he would have been dragged away in chains.)

Finally, Sony released an uninstaller that worked (the first leaving behind software that could also be exploited by a hacker).[104] But one has to wonder what the results might have been had a government agency, claiming such software was necessary to fight terrorism, released the spyware. At best, the Sony rootkit fiasco speaks of corporate arrogance that does not bode well for those who wish to maintain their privacy when using a computer.

Eventually over a dozen class-action lawsuits were brought against Sony (most of these were consolidated into one proceeding in New York). Other than having to supply replacement CDs to consumers who'd bought the originals with the rootkit software, Sony suffered little punishment. It was required that they submit any future copy-protection software to an independent review, but only until the end of 2007.[105] It seems likely that this legal slap on the wrist will do little to discourage companies from taking similar actions in the future.

---

[101] *Ibid.*

[102] Thomas Hesse, Radio Interview, National Public Radio, November 4, 2005.

[103] Quinn Norton, "Sony Numbers Add Up to Trouble," *Wired News*, November 16, 2005.

[104] Wade Roush, *Ibid.*

[105] Anne Broache, "Sony Rootkit Settlement Gets Final Nod," news.com.com, May 22, 2006.

Sony may have been one of the biggest corporations to get caught using spyware, but it certainly is not alone, nor is it the worst offender. Perhaps the record holder is SmartBot.net, which was fined $4 million by the Federal Trade Commission (FTC) in mid-2006 for exploiting weaknesses in Internet Explorer to reset the user settings on a PC, changing their search-engine default, and bombarding them with pop-up ads. Adding insult to injury, the modifications included notices telling the owner of the PC he needed to purchase Spy Wiper or Spy Deleter (for $30). Only if he went to the trouble of doing that did he discover that the programs failed to remove the virus that had been responsible for the troubles the computer was having in the first place.[106]

At that same time, the FTC also charged that the software company Odysseus Marketing hijacked computers by promising users an anonymous P2P (Peer-to-Peer) file-sharing program that was bogus. The software instead changed the default search engines to another search engine. Worse, according to FTC charges, the program captured names, addresses, e-mail addresses, phone numbers, Internet shopping history, and other data, relaying it to the company for possible criminal use.[107]

Today there's a wealth of small companies that manage to get spyware installed on computers. The amount of spyware that may be installed with a single free program can be staggering. For example, computer expert and writer Eric L. Howes found that when he installed the file-sharing program Grokster, it also added a large bundle of other programs, much of it spyware, including Claria, 411 Ferret/ActiveSearch, AdRoar, Altnet/BDE, BroadcastPC, Cydoor, Flashtrack, MyWay/Mybar, SearchLocate/Side-Bar, Topsearch, TVMedia, VX2/ABetterInternet, Browser Hijack, two different versions of TopMoxie, and some other programs that, somewhat ominously, he couldn't identify. Grokster even installs the programs if the user has second thoughts and presses "cancel" during installation. As computer expert and blogger

---

[106] Armando Duke, "FTC Fines SmartBot $4 Mil Over Spyware Use," *AXcess News*, May 5, 2006.

[107] *Ibid.*

Benjamin Edelman noted about all the spyware installed along with Grokster:[108]

> These programs, in combination, place a major burden on users' computers: Loading and running so many extra tasks leaves less memory, less bandwidth, and less CPU time for whatever users actually want to do. My lab PCs are fast and well-maintained, but installing Grokster and its bundle makes them sluggish and hard to use.

In order to get users to take a chance like this in installing software, those writing spyware offer a variety of enticements. In the case of Grokster, the enticement is the ability to share music and software—perhaps illegally—with others. With other spyware, the inducement is to offer the spyware capable of doing a variety of other tasks often handled by more expensive programs. These "free" programs exact their toll once they are installed and the user's privacy violated.

TIP Beware of free programs with hidden spyware.

As was the case with Sony's spyware, most spyware is also designed to be very hard to remove from a computer. Thus when a user removes the freeware that installed the spyware, the useful components of the program are removed—but the spying components are often left behind, continuing to transmit data via the Internet connection to who-knows-where whenever the user connects to the Net.

Some large corporations have been found to have rather close relationships to spyware companies as well. For example, Benjamin Edelman discovered in 2005 that several notorious spyware marketers have received payments from Yahoo through

---

[108] Benjamin Edelman, "Grokster and Claria Take Licenses to New Lows, and Congress Lets Thems Do It," www.benedelman.org/news/100904-1.html, October 9, 2004.

the company's pay-per-click program. Some of these ads that legit-imate companies pay for appear in the pop-up ads that spyware shows, and then these advertisers, thinking the ads are appearing on Yahoo's actually search pages, pay Yahoo, which in turn makes payments to the spyware vendor. Thus Yahoo was not only ap-parently being mislead, but also supporting the spyware compa-nies.[109]

This affiliation between a spyware company and a large corpo-ration is not unique to Yahoo. The notorious Gator spyware (often installed with file-sharing programs like Go!Zilla and Kazaa) transformed its name to Claria Corporation in 2003 (many said to get away from the antipathy many computer users felt toward Gator after having the software foul their computers). Today the company continues to create spyware, but has $58 million in sup-port from investors, including U.S. Venture Partners, Greylock, Crosslink Capital, Garage Technology Ventures, Rosewood Stone Group, The Well, Investor AB, and Technology Crossover Ventures (with the last also perhaps hedging its bets by investing in a com-pany making the spyware-removal program Webroot).[110]

Spyware and Crooks

Criminals have also started using spyware and various phishing schemes involving software over the last few years. These pro-grams are often distributed for free over the Internet, with unsus-pecting users having their computer hard drives searched for whatever the programmer has deemed a good target. Once this data is located, the program then sends the data over the Internet to a criminal's computer, to be accessed later for the data.

In 2006, Panda Software (a security firm) studied the various types of freeware/spyware floating around on the Internet. It found that an astonishing 70 percent were designed specifically for crim-inal use, with a full 40 percent being designed to steal personal

[109] Benjamin Edelman, "The Spyware/Click-Fraud Connection—and Yahoo's Role Revisited," http://www.benedelman.org/news/040406-1.html, April 4, 2006.

[110] Benjamin Edelman, "Investors Supporting Spyware," www.benedelman.org/spyware/investors/, April 7, 2006.

data and relay it to a criminal, Trojan programs designed to steal information pertaining to online services, or programs that would download secondary malicious applications and install them on the user's computer.[111]

Obviously you need to exercise caution when obtaining software from the Internet. In general, you can determine the safety of software by doing a Web search with the name of the program and the word "spyware" or "malware," checking for messages that suggest it is not on the up-and-up. Also download only from larger sites that have established a reputation for checking out their software.

TIP Never get software from P2P file trading sites—and be sure your children or others using home computers avoid these sources as well.

Some malware employs sophisticated social engineering that makes it appear that a pop-up is actually a system warning. These may warn that a computer has a virus or is otherwise compromised, and offer to install a program to take care of the problem. Of course the trick is that the computer is fine—until the program that promises to fix the nonexistent problem is installed. At that point the computer becomes infected.

While it might seem unlikely that corporations would ever have the right to delete files without asking from a user's computer, it is important to note the clout the movie and record industries already exercise over Congress (which is not surprising, given that they have the ability to sway public opinion for or against government policies, as well as having deep coffers for campaign contributions and lobbying efforts).

This was demonstrated in 2006 when the proposed modifications to the Digital Millennium Copyright Act—which would extend protection rights to various types of software, movies, and CDs—came to light. The proposed law would dictate a maxi-

---

[111] "Seventy Percent of Malicious Software Aimed at Theft: Survey," Agence France-Presse, May 4, 2006.

mum sentence of ten years for software or music piracy, giving the FBI the power to wiretap suspected pirates. This compares with getting up to five years in most parts of the nation for assaulting a police officer or seven years for engaging in a child-porn ring.[112]

Perhaps tomorrow's hardened criminals can sound off in prison: "I'm in for five years for gun running."

"I'm here for eight years for being an accessory to murder."

"I'm doing ten for downloading a movie."

It would be funny were it not so tragic. And it suggests that the day may well be coming when something akin to "vigilante viruses" may be created by record companies or movie studios and unleashed on the public, just as Sony's rootkit was not that long ago.

DEALING WITH SPYWARE

If having someone steal data about you weren't bad enough, often those collecting it via spyware could care less how secure it is. Thus, second parties can sometimes purchase the data, or even steal it from the spyware company. In 2002 an anti-spyware group was shocked to discover that one spyware manufacturer had left its Web site virtually unguarded with default passwords on its Web server. Anyone stumbling onto the site (or locating it by tracking where the spyware was sending information) gained almost instant access to the data being collected. As one of the researchers noted, "I would not trust these fools with my grocery list."[113]

Instead, they had access to trusting souls' most personal information.

Given that spyware might collect your passwords, credit card numbers, bank account info, or anything else you have on your computer, it is easy to see how dangerous such programs could be, and how they might be exploited to breach your privacy in a major way.

---

[112] Nick Farrell, "Piracy Worse than Child Pornography," *The Inquirer*, VNU Business Publications Litd., April 26, 2006.

[113] "Advertising Spyware: Blackstone Data Transponder and Its Derivatives," Counterexploitation, http://www.cexx.org/vx2.htm/, January 2002.

A number of independent programmers have created a variety of anti-spyware programs (and, interestingly, few major corporations have until very recently). Among the best of these are:

- Ad-Aware (www.lavasoftusa.com)
- Spybot Search and Destroy (www.spybot.info)
- Spy Sweeper (www.webroot.com)
- MacScan (for Apple users; macscan.securemac.com/)

(Microsoft has attempted to create an anti-spyware program called "Windows Defender," but it's currently in beta testing, and to date has not seemed to be very well implemented.)

The success of anti-spyware (like antivirus programs) depends on updates that help it discover programs that should be removed. For this reason you should always check for update lists before running it, or set the program to automatically update itself periodically.

Since some legit software can also act as spyware, it is wise to check default settings when installing software to be sure you aren't "agreeing" to also install spyware or permit the program to "call home" with data about you. While not essential, it can also be a good plan to *not* register software, since this often links your name to your IP address and other data that might be employed in ways similar to spyware.

Having a good firewall that alerts you when a program is trying to contact an outside computer is also wise (see page 119). Set the firewall so that you will be asked before a program establishes an outside contact via the Internet. As a rule of thumb, any program that doesn't need to be connected to the Internet should be blocked by the firewall from being able to connect to it. (This can also prevent a virus or other software from replacing a program and then "pretending" to be it when connecting to a remote computer. Allow only programs that must connect to the Net to do so.)

You can often vote with your pocketbook as to whether you're happy with companies that support spyware. Many consumers have started their own, private boycotts of Sony, Yahoo, and other corporations that create spyware or support shady businesses that do. Companies that treat customers as something to be exploited for cash don't deserve your business. Little by little these personal boycotts are having an effect. It may be that, in the end, people's decisions to use freeware (programs offered for free) and programs that aren't spying on them will have a more profound effect in doing away with spyware than any efforts by Congress could ever have.

Search Software

Internet search engines have transformed the Web from a hodgepodge of odd information—much like piles of books placed in a huge room without any order to them—into a place where information is easy to find, sort of like a public library with automated robots fetching anything you want to read. As such, services like Google make the Internet a useful place to learn and be entertained.

As hard drives have become larger and larger, many home and business computers are becoming like the early Internet: They contain all sorts of useful data, but finding it is the trick. Today many users quickly lose track of various documents, e-mail, and so forth that are on a computer's hard drive.

The solution to the problem is a search program that will locate the data on a hard drive by keyword, file type, date created, or other parameters. Toward this end, Google, Microsoft, and various other software manufacturers have created programs that will search a hard drive.

In order to make finding a file faster, most of these search programs index the hard drive, creating a compact record of various files so they can be located in a hurry by the software. This indexing generally goes on in the background, when the computer is not accessing the hard drives, thereby slowing the computer only slightly when the actual indexing is done, and then quickly adding new material to the index as it is created and saved to the hard drive.

But, there's a catch, and one that could have grave ramifications to a person's privacy in some circumstances. The catch is that this index basically gives someone a very good idea of what is on a hard drive—or what was on it after a key file was removed. Thus, if someone gained access to your computer after you had erased, say, porn that was attached to a spam e-mail, illegal MP3 files the neighbor's kid downloaded when he and your son were fooling around with the family computer, or if your computer contains other sensitive and perhaps perfectly legal documents you don't want made public, there would still be a record that it was once on your computer.

Anyone who gains access to that index might have a very good idea of what the files actually were, and whether or not they were legal.

Worse, some of the indexing systems place index information online, outside of the computer user's control. For example, Google's Desktop 3 search system, released early in 2006, places personal data collected when the "Search Across Computers" feature is used on Google's servers for up to thirty days.

This data supposedly is encrypted and access to it restricted.[114] But it seems likely that a court order, or perhaps just a request from an interested party, would be sufficient to gain access to the data. As Electronic Frontier Foundation staff attorney Kevin Bankston said,[115]

> If you use the Search Across Computers feature and don't configure Google Desktop very carefully—and most people won't—Google will have copies of your tax returns, love letters, business records, financial and medical files, and whatever other text-based documents the Desktop software can index. The government could then demand these personal files with only a subpoena rather than the search warrant it would need to seize the same things from your home or business, and in many cases you wouldn't even be notified in time to challenge it. Other litigants—your spouse, your business partners or rivals, whoever—could also try to cut out the middleman (you) and subpoena Google for your files.

---

[114] "Privacy Fears Hit Google Search," BBC News, February 10, 2006.

[115] "Google Copies Your Hard Drive—Government Smiles in Anticipation," www.eff.org/news/archives/2006_02.php, Electronic Frontier Foundation, February 9, 2006.

And as for the protection offered by Google's privacy policy, computer expert and columnist John Lanchester noted:[116]

> As for privacy in relation to governments, the company's existing privacy policy says that "we may share information" if "we conclude that we are required by law or have a good-faith belief that access, preservation, or disclosure of such information is reasonably necessary to protect the rights, property, or safety of Google, its users, or the public." You don't have to be Diogenes the Cynic to think that this gives Google the latitude to do pretty much whatever it wants.

KEEP YOUR SEARCH ENGINE AND KEEP YOUR PRIVACY

These search engines are very useful. However, it is better to turn off indexing features and wait for a few extra seconds when doing searches—a small price to pay for the added security. It is also wise to use these programs behind a firewall (as outlined below) so that they can't "phone home" data they may have access to on your computer. Also turn off any features that search across several computers in a network, as well as any off-site storage features.

Forego using search programs' indexing features, despite the convenience they offer.

TIP

Online Software

Presently, several companies—including Google and Microsoft—are working toward offering a variety of online software. This allows visitors to a Web page to create spreadsheets, read e-mail online, or write documents without the need to have any software other than a browser installed on their computer. The advantage for the user is that he doesn't have to buy a full-blown program (although he may

---

[116] John Lanchester, "Big Google Is Watching You," *Sunday Times*, http://www.timesonline.co.uk/article/0,,2092-2014215_2,00.html, January 29, 2006.

have to pay a monthly fee or view ads on the site), nor does he need to install the software and update it from time to time. The advantage for the company offering the software is that it provides a revenue stream through small fees or display advertising.

The catch from a privacy standpoint is that the data being assembled on a distant site is there for whoever owns the site to store, search, or otherwise access. It is not only possible that the user's data being uploaded and assembled will be explored—it is also likely, given that advertising may be cued to keywords within the user's document. It isn't hard to imagine that this data would then be employed in data-mining operations to be accessed by a variety of buyers, from small advertisers to government agencies.

> **TIP** Your privacy is more secure if you take some time to install programs on your computer rather than using the slightly more convenient online programs for such tasks.

As for those who decide to take advantage of these various online programs, their privacy may sink like a rock. After looking at a possible future in which e-mail, word processing, and other activities were all handled by online software, computer expert Will Harris wrote:[117]

> The guys at Google know everything about your search habits, and you can bet they want to link 'em up to your e-mail and calendar and whatever else you end up using online. . . . Our social networks, searching habits, visual identifiers, and personal preferences will be mercilessly sold to anyone who wants to get their hands on our particular demographic. And when your photos, your files, your e-mail, and your friends are all online . . . you'll always be able to be online. And as long as you're online, they can market to you.

And you can bet that some of that marketing will include some very personal information about you and your friends.

---

[117] Willl Harris, "Why Web 2.0 Will End Your Privacy," Bit-tech.net, June 3, 2006.

FIREWALLS

When the Internet first become widely used by the public, most people didn't know what a firewall was. Not all that long ago, I can remember contacting a friend in the computer security business who was baffled when I asked him if he knew what a firewall was. Those days are pretty much over, at least for those using the Internet and who are concerned about keeping their computers free of a variety of malicious programs and junk software. Today, even for users of Linux and Apple systems (and especially for Windows users), firewalls are an essential part of computing if the computer has access to the outside world.

A *firewall* basically keeps track of everything that comes into and leaves your computer, from a removable storage drive (CDs, DVDs, etc.) as well as via the computer's modem. Many firewalls also keep track of what program is trying to launch another program. In doing all this the firewall can keep someone from easily accessing your computer without your knowledge, and can also thwart some viruses, Trojans, or other programs that attempt to send data from your computer or launch a secondary program that might damage or compromise the system in a variety of ways.

The necessity of a firewall can be demonstrated by connecting a computer to the Internet via a cable modem without a firewall, as was done by security experts Stuart McClure and Joel Scambray. They equipped the PC with software that would detect hacker attempts to gain access to the system and discovered that over a year's time, there had been over 3,000 Trojan-related port scans of the computer.[118]

There are a variety of firewalls available. One of the old standbys is ZoneAlarm, which continues to be among the best. McAfee Personal Firewall and Kerio Personal Firewall (recently purchased by McAfee, so its future may be a bit shaky) are also excellent. Microsoft has started adding firewalls to its OS offerings as well, and these are certainly better than running the system without a firewall. But the catch with the Microsoft firewalls to date is that while they block unauthorized incoming attempts, they fail to stop outgoing messages that might be sent by a Trojan or spyware. No doubt this is useful for corporations (perhaps including

---

[118] Stuart McClure and Joel Scambray, "Here's a Little Advice to Help You Defeat the Internet's Leading Trojan Horse Viruses," *InfoWorld*, December 4, 2000.

Microsoft) wishing to gain information from your computer without your knowing about it; it is not ideal from a privacy standpoint.

Since software seems to come and go overnight these days, there may be other choices available, and/or the firewalls mentioned above may not be available next time you check. The best firewalls will block not only unauthorized attempts to access your computer via the Internet, but they'll also block unauthorized attempts from programs running on your computer to send data over the Internet without your approval. Otherwise, spyware can easily compromise your privacy without your being any the wiser.

If you have really sensitive data on a computer, keep the computer off-line. A truly secure computer has no connection to the Internet. Many people today assume that a computer must be connected to the Net, but that is not the case. Word processing and a variety of other tasks can just as easily be done without a modem running.

One alternative is to run a second computer that connects to the Internet and acts as an Internet server. You can then connect your more-sensitive-data computer into this computer server, with each computer running its own firewall. Even the most skilled hacker who can gain access to the server will have little luck reaching your main computer with such a setup. (A quick Web search will yield the how-to for configuring a server system; often an older, slower computer can be pressed into service for this purpose.)

NETWORKED SYSTEMS

Networked and wireless systems often create ways for snoops to gain access to one or more computers connected into a system.

With networks, it is important to maintain a firewall with each computer connected to the system. Ideally a firewall will also be used between the network and outside connections to the Internet via a router. Many newer routers come with a hardware firewall that gives added protection, but should never be depended on as a substitute for having a firewall on any given computer.

A little extra security can be enjoyed by having just one computer hooked into the Internet and then designating it as the ICS (Internet

Connection Sharing) host. The other computers on your network then access the Internet through the ICS host. The only drawback is that this dictates having the host computer on whenever some other computer must access the host, making this generally less satisfactory. With most routers having their own hardware firewalls, using an ICS host is not all that advantageous for most people, especially those running a small home network.

Because anyone that gains access to your network will also have access to your shared folders, printers, and other devices, it is wise to minimize sharing as much as you can. If you seldom move files between computers, then don't allow any sharing options. Putting these shared appliances or folders in one of the computers inside the system rather than on the ICS host (if you have one) can also improve your protection level, since this will put shared items behind another firewall.

Wired networks are much more secure than area wireless systems. However, wireless networks can be more convenient, since laptops, palm computers, Web phones, and so forth all become more versatile when run in a wireless environment. The key to securing each unit is to be sure that it is working behind its own firewall (the memory capacity of the device allowing), and that the wireless router has its own firewall and is set to require a password before a connection can be made to it. Connect only the devices you use at any given time. This will also make it more difficult to illegally access your network.

Many routers have a default password that is employed when connecting the system. Once your system is running, change the password. People sometimes leave the default password, and that makes breaking into their networks the proverbial lead-pipe cinch.

As wireless routers have evolved, the security capabilities have become better. Today these newer security features are nearly essential because snoops are more capable of circumventing older defenses. The original system for securing a wireless net was WEP (Wireless Encryption Protocol), now more or less obsolete if you are serious about privacy. (If you have a WEP system, then setting it for 128-bit protection will improve things somewhat.)

The MAC address filtering (also known as hardware filtering) offers more protection by interrogating devices connecting to it, demanding the unique identifier for that device (generally something like 00-07-F5-4D-C7-95). The catch to this is that it is possible for a snoop to "listen" to the traffic from your network and discover the MAC address of one of the devices approved to connect to the net. He can then spoof that code on his own device and tap into your network, and—at that point—any files you may be sharing between computers.

A wireless router's SSID (Service Set Identifier) sends out a beam for wireless devices to find. The trouble is that it also acts like a beacon to attract snoops looking for wireless systems. This means that you can increase the security of your system by disabling SSID. This is possible—though it takes effort—only with non-XP systems, however.

Since most wireless routers use DHCP (Dynamic Host Configuration Protocol) to distribute the IP addresses for the clients in the network, disabling it will increase your security as well. This can be done with most operating systems, and only requires that each computer or device connected to your network have its own address. Use the standard subnet mask (usually 255.255.255.0), and then create a logical address for the device (such as 192.168.65.x).

Some of these modifications are a little tedious. But a quick search on the Internet will yield a step-by-step how-to for your operating system. Taking the time to do this will increase the security of your network for a WEP system.

Yet, WEP can still be cracked pretty easily. WiFi Protected Access (WPA) and Virtual Private Networking (VPN) are more secure, and also easier to set up. If you have computers with sensitive information on them, you would do well to use these higher standards. Of course these will never be quite as secure as a wired system using Ethernet cards. And the best security is a computer that isn't networked and which lacks an Internet connection altogether.

If you're operating a WiFi router from your home, it is wise to take a laptop, tablet, or whatever you use to connect to it, and go outside your home and see how far away the system can be detected. Many people want the maximum range for their system, not realizing that in fact they have made it possible to easily attack it from some distance away. If you discover that you can access your wireless router from several houses away, then you need to turn the aerials down or otherwise modify it so the range is decreased. Because metal, water, and other materials degrade the signal, it is also possible to create "shields" to block signals somewhat. Thus, if you have your router at the side of your home, you can attach aluminum foil or other dense material on the wall and reduce the signal being sent toward the neighbors; an added benefit is that you may also block signals that might otherwise interfere with your system (as is the case with some cordless phones that operate on the same frequencies as WiFi systems).

Some wireless routers will have "flashable" firmware (hardware that can be updated over the Internet). The only catch to this is that it is possible to screw up a system if the download is interrupted. However, this is rare and generally worth the risk, since manufacturers periodically release critical security enhancements.

If your system has an option to monitor and log unusual events and/or show you the MAC and IP addresses on your network, watching these can sometimes alert you that someone is trying to penetrate your system. If this happens, shut down the system. This may thwart him. Scout out your area to detect the snoop trying to break into the system, since he will need to be nearby to break into a WiFi router.

It should be noted that when connecting into a WiFi "hotspot" at a coffee shop, library, city park, or other public WiFi connection point, your privacy is minimal at best. It is very easy to monitor the transmissions to and from the computer and pick out data, including passwords used to access e-mail or Web sites, as well as capture messages you may send. Your firewall will protect the data that is on a computer connected to a public WiFi connection, but the communications leaving and entering the device via WiFi are totally exposed.

To some extent you can browse freely on a public system, since the IP assigned to your computer will be more or less random and likely shared with others connecting at a later date, as well as one used previously. But this is not as private as it might seem, since "cookies" (small bits of identification code placed on a computer by a Web site via the browser software) and other identifiers might still track a user. And it is very likely that methods will eventually be found and put into place by law

SOLUTIONS

enforcement to permanently link users to their communications should public WiFi become widespread.

In fact, corporations intent on selling advertising may build this capability into systems, leaving the privacy of users open to any government agency willing to obtain a subpoena. For example, when Google and EarthLink worked toward creating a system in San Francisco, Google proposed that users be tracked so advertisers in an area could have their ads pop up on devices near them. The fear among privacy experts was that these records might then be used by those willing to buy the data, or by the police.[119]

You can also achieve a little protection by encrypting the messages you send via a public WiFi system. But given the potential loss of passwords and interception of data, public systems should be avoided when possible if you're concerned about your privacy.

If it is essential that you use a public WiFi system (or a computer at a hotel, public library, or similar location) to access e-mail while you're on vacation or on a business trip, create a "throwaway" e-mail account that you can discard after your trip is over. Creating such accounts is relatively easy, and you can even have your regular account modified to forward mail to your temporary "travel" e-mail account if you wish. This doesn't prevent interception of your password or data, but will often be enough and, if worse comes to worst, you will plug the privacy leak once you discard the travel e-mail account and return to your old one.

A less-effective alternative is to change your password after using a public computer or WiFi system to access your e-mail. However, this is not as safe, since you will have given away your e-mail address with only the password protecting it at that point. Not letting anyone even know what the account is adds another level of protection.

TIP

Avoid using a public computer at a cyber café, university, hotel, public library, or other place with computers available. Simply adding a keyboard logging program or hardware to the computer will transfer it into a system that can capture passwords and other data flowing through it—a snoop's dream come true.

---

[119] "Privacy Concerns Over Google's Wi-Fi Network in SF," cbs5.com/local/local_story_098154932.html, April 8, 2006.

MAKING MICROSOFT WINDOWS MORE SECURE

If you use something other than Windows on your computer, then just skip on down to the next section. The Windows operating system allows users to do many things, thus its popularity with independent programmers; if you want to do something with a computer, chances are someone has already made a program to do it, and possibly a freeware version, if you are a Windows user. Other operating systems may have fewer headaches or face fewer security threats, but if you like to dig into your computer, modify things, and have a huge choice of software, Windows can't be beat.

In the past, the downside to Windows was that it wasn't as stable as some other operating systems. But with the introduction of XP, that changed as well. While most Apple users are too proud to agree, today's XP is every bit as stable as Apple's offerings.

But Microsoft still has a glaring weakness: It manages to leave a variety of "ports" open in its operating system, which hackers are more than happy to exploit in order to gain entrance to your computer via the Internet. Some of these openings are necessitated by various features and services; others appear to be the vestiges of programming ideas that were discarded before coming to term.

Needless to say, closing these unused ports will make a computer much more secure from hackers and various online attacks.

One programmer who offers several worthwhile programs to close these software openings is Steve Gibson, a security expert and software designer who has undoubtedly saved more than a few computers from becoming roadkill on the Internet superhighway. Gibson's site at www.grc.com/default.htm offers these small programs for free. Among the useful offerings:

- The *DCOMbobulator* disables Microsoft's Distributed Component Object Model (DCOM) features (which are almost never used but can be exploited by a hacker).

- *Shoot The Messenger*, which shuts down Windows Messenger along with the pop-up ads and other trash that Messenger often attracts.

- *UnPnP* (Unplug n' Pray) removes Window's Universal Plug and Play service, which can be exploited to install a variety of malicious software on a computer.

- *XPdite* protects computers from an exploit (a technique program that takes advantage of vulnerability or a security hole) that can delete files when a malicious Web site is visited.

Gibson also offers a Web page designed to test a computer to see if it has any security holes in its firewall and operating system, as well as check the various ports that might be exploited in a system. Known as ShieldsUP!, this online test can be found at www.grc.com, and is great for testing a computer to be sure it is secure.

And if you discover that your computer has some "holes," take steps to plug them immediately.

It is also wise to log onto the computer as someone other than the "administrator." That's because when someone logs on as the administrator, they can install software and make major changes to the system. Having the default log-in be a user will protect the system against some attacks designed to install viruses or otherwise damage a system.

If a computer might be accessed by unauthorized people (say, in an office where the staff is gone during the noon hour, or a home that might be broken into), then using a secure password to log onto the computer is in order. This protection can be circumvented in a variety of ways, but it will slow pros and will often stop less-talented snoops.

Regularly check for security updates and install them. These can be found at Microsoft's Web site, and most are self-installing. They will patch possible security holes in the operating system, as well as various programs, thereby decreasing the possibility that damage will be done to your computer by a virus or other malware.

For getting rid of various programs that may be booting, running in the background, and generally creating problems (and perhaps even harboring spyware or such), CCleaner and JV16 Power Tools (both available on the Internet), perhaps used in conjunction with Windows' Task Manager, can often weed out unneeded memory vampires. However, this can be a time-consuming job of looking up various processes on the

Internet to see what they are, and can also lead to disaster should you inadvertently disable one of the files needed for the operating system to function.

If you are only concerned about less-powerful snoops, then Windows can be secured to offer protection. However, if you have secrets to keep from corporations or government agencies, then Windows may not be the best choice—and the fact that large businesses and government agencies around the world are switching to versions of Linux suggests the route you should consider taking. Yes, backdoors may be built into this operating system (and most likely will be dictated in the future if they are not already there). But at this stage, the Linux operating system appears much more secure and has the added advantage of being targeted less often by spyware, viruses, and other problems that can plague Windows users.

If you're interested in obtaining a freeware version of Linux, be very careful what site you download it from. Avoid questionable file-sharing sources, and also aim for a download site outside of the country you're in, thereby making it less likely that a government entity working within national boundaries will have pressured the distributor into offering a compromised version of the program.

PRIMARY TARGETS

Many schemes created by phishers and pharmers depend on getting a percentage of suckers to reply to their enticements. That means the more people they can send a virus or spam to, the more apt they are to get a few people to respond and give away valuable data. That means the hacker can increase his odds of meeting with success by targeting more-popular programs that people might be using, and it also means he isn't apt to waste his time on programs that are less popular.

That makes Windows users almost always the target of various viruses, Trojans, and worms, while Linux and Apple users get pretty much left alone ("pretty much" being the key point here). It is the same reason that Internet Explorer and Microsoft e-mail programs regularly see security holes exploited, while less-popular browsers and e-mail programs do not. It's not that Microsoft products are less secure than others (though on occasion that seems to be the case), but rather that the "targets" are more apt to be found within the greater number of users with these more-popular programs.

Obviously then, you can lower the possibility of being targeted by various scams by avoiding popular software. Rather than using MS Word, go with WordPerfect or OpenOffice.org. Rather than using MS Outlook Express for e-mail, use Eudora or Thunderbird. By choosing the less-popular software, you take yourself out of the herd being stalked by a variety of criminals.

If you discover that you really need to use a certain piece of popular software (like Word), then use an older version to avoid trouble. For example, in 2006, Word 2003 was targeted by a "Zero Day" macro virus being spread by e-mail. For those who were tricked into opening the fake Word document attached to the e-mail it installed a rootkit into the computer and apparently employed the computer to spread the macro to other computers via e-mail, as well as possibly send data to a distant computer.

While those using the latest version of Word had this problem, Word 2000 users who opened the e-mail only suffered a lockup of their version of the program. And those using an older version of Word didn't even suffer a glitch when exposed to the macro.

Older software can often be purchased for a fraction of the cost of the new software, and also is more stable because the various bug fixes have already been released for the program. Going to the manufacturer's site will yield these updates that can then be installed.

TIP Use older and/or less-popular versions of programs to become less vulnerable to viruses.

The exception to this rule may be with browsers. A new generation of browsers is being designed to collect a watch list of known phishing sites, blocking users from going to any of those sites. Additionally, most browsers now have a way of showing that a user is on a certified "secure site" where online orders can be placed, and so forth. Neither of these features is entirely foolproof, but if a little common sense is exercised along with letting the browser help protect you, the chances of becoming a victim of online snooping are greatly reduced.

It should be remembered, however, that the data collection that goes on at brick-and-mortar businesses is usually far less than what is going on when you order online. If you are buying something sensitive or which might be detrimental if the knowledge leaks to the public, then the Internet is not the place to buy. Instead, buy from a store, and pay with cash.

COMPUTER PRINTERS

Computer printers are capable of creating amazing graphics, and unlike typewriters of the past, they seemingly produce identical fonts. Given these points, one might suppose that a printout would be impossible to trace back to a user.

That is not the case.

With little fanfare, in 2004, major manufacturers of laser printers placed routines in the hardware that encode a serial number and manufacturing code into color laser printers and color copiers. Every document produced on these machines has a unique microscopic code embedded in it, showing what computer the document was produced on.[120]

Today every document produced on most quality laser printers contains a code that keys each document to that hardware. And governments around the world, including the United States, already use the code to track citizens.

Of course the stated reason for embedding this code into laser printers is to combat counterfeiting. And undoubtedly, that is one of the major tools used to thwart counterfeiters—especially when one is talking about high school and college students foolish enough to try such a stunt with a laser printer.

But the temptation to use such systems to track critics and organizations was too much to resist. Thus in 2005 it was learned that the FBI was amassing files of documents on various political organizations, with over 1,100 pages of documents from the ACLU, as well as other organizations, including Greenpeace and United for Peace and Justice.[121]

---

[120] Jason Tuohey, "Government Uses Color Laser Printer Technology to Track Documents," *PC World*, November 22, 2004.

[121] "Is Your Printer Spying On You?" www.eff.org/Privacy/printers/index.php, Electronic Frontier Foundation, December 5, 2005.

The Electronic Frontier Foundation (EFF) noted that this collection of data demonstrates how a government agency can run roughshod over citizens' privacy, even when they present no real threat to society:[122]

> No law regulates what sort of documents the Secret Service or any other domestic or foreign government agency is permitted to request for identification, not to mention how such a forensics tool could be developed and implemented in printers in the first place. With no laws on the books, there's nothing to stop the privacy violations this technology enables.

When this ability to identify a page produced by a laser printer is coupled with computerized purchase histories and company tracking numbers, it would seem possible if not practical to link a printer first to the store it was purchased from, and then to the credit card or other payment system used to buy it, and from there to the purchaser and his computer.

It appears that ink-jet printers do not yet contain a similar code, but one must wonder if such coding won't be quietly placed in these printers just as it was with laser printers years ago.

Obviously you should treat any document you print as if it has your name and address printed on it. For all practical purposes, it does.

One can only guess how countries that crack down on dissidents must use this ability to track documents, and how much damage this ID system may cause to whistleblowers and others who fail to realize that a government can link a printer to them. Certainly the day of the anonymous letter is over.

PHYSICAL SECURITY

The best firewalls, virus scanners, and a computer full of unpopular software won't give you much protection if someone gains access to your computer. Once that happens, they can add a key logger to your keyboard cable, copy files from your hardware, install a Trojan, or even yank whole hard drives or the computer itself and take it to their lair to inspect it at their leisure.

Anywhere that you have a computer with sensitive materials on it merits good physical protection. Your computer should have the same

---

[122] *Ibid.*

level of security as your credit cards, driver's license, and other important papers do—even more protection, in fact.

This is also true of any hard drives you may discard inside or outside a computer. While it is nice to donate old computers to charity and such, often people who do this simply delete the files on the hard drive and give the equipment away. If the new buyer is so inclined, he can run software designed specifically for the purpose of restoring the hard drive to its original configuration, thereby gaining access to a lot of free programs—and your data.

There are more than a few horror stories produced when hard drives are revived or a user forgets to remove data from them. Perhaps one of the worst occurred to a student attending school in England, who sold his laptop on eBay. The buyer later claimed that the student had misrepresented the laptop as being in working order when it was actually broken, and the buyer had waited two months for the laptop to be delivered. The buyer claimed his protests went unanswered and so decided to take revenge when he discovered that the hard drive still worked—and it still contained all the student's files and programs. According to the buyer, the hard drive also held pornographic images, some allegedly taken by the student. Angry, the buyer posted some of these pictures on the Internet with a notice of where they had come from; for good measure, the buyer apparently sent a notice to all those in the student's address book, announcing that the pictures had been taken by the student, and then gave the URL where they could be viewed. Additionally, what were purported to be the student's personal "Dear Diary" writings, also taken from the hard drive, were posted. Eventually over a half million people viewed the site, and many others heard about the young student from news stories about the feud. In the end, the student has been left in the position of perhaps never being able to return to a religiously conservative nation that takes a very dim view of pornography.[123]

To avoid such mishaps, it is wise to pull the hard drive from a computer and then take a sledgehammer to the drive (and yes, I have done just this to more hard drives than I care to think about). The second best step is to use a wiper program (as outlined on pages 144–46) to make the data unreadable. Although this is a long process with today's larger drives,

---

[123] "Revenge of the eBay Customer," *Daily Mail*, May 30, 2006.

it might help you avoid having your most private information posted on the Internet.

Lest anyone think that taking a sledgehammer to a hard drive is overkill, it should be noted that following the 9/11 attacks, computer hard drives were taken from the rubble of the World Trade Center and data recovered from them. One such operation was handled by Convar Systeme Deutschland, a forensics company, which used a laser tool that acquired samples from the broken bits of sixty-nine shattered hard drives to create virtual drives, which then created a copy of each of the damaged hard drives. The cost was as much as $35,000 for each hard drive.[124] That means a big-time outfit will be wanting your hide before they go to this trouble; but for a government snoop, or for valuable corporate data on a drive, that might be chump change.

Never assume that data on a discarded hard drive, CD, or other media is gone until you've thoroughly wiped or even destroyed it. Otherwise, discarding it is very much the same as making a Xerox copy of your important documents and then putting them out on the curb with a small "take one" sign so any Tom, Dick, or Crook who comes along can help himself to your private information.

Tempest in a Hotspot

When an electrical current is run through a wire, it generates a magnetic field around the wire itself. If the current is modulated, the result is a radio wave. Which is just what computers and their monitors do; they create a lot of "noise" in the radio spectrum— as anyone who's set up a radio near a home computer has probably noted. What most folks don't realize is that these short-range "radio broadcasts" created by a computer actually contain data that, with the proper equipment, can be reassembled to give a picture of the letters—or even pictures—that are appearing on the computer screen.

And that presents a way to spy on almost anyone typing at a computer.

[124] Francis Till, "Hands Off! Personal Computer Privacy," www.sitepoint.com/article/personal-computer-privacy, May 30, 2002.

The technique of harvesting information via the radio broadcast from a computer has become generally known as a TEMPEST attack. "TEMPEST" is the code name under which the U.S. government apparently conducted research into this effect. Whether the name is an acronym or simply a random code name is unknown, though the "EM" suggests electromagnetic.

Originally the TEMPEST work conducted by the U.S. government appears to have been directed toward *preventing* eavesdropping on American government computers. However, it seems likely that the program quickly branched out to cover the development of ways to eavesdrop on nongovernment computers. Thus, there is no small amount of confusion today when one talks about TEMPEST, since it can be in regard to preventing eavesdropping on a computer, as well as the best ways to spy on systems.

Of course, governments around the world are interested in doing both—as are corporations. Possibly more than a few ideas have been borrowed using TEMPEST eavesdropping techniques, which often fall into legal gray areas but which are undoubtedly worth the risk to companies wanting to get ahead in a hurry.

The public is kept in the dark about TEMPEST threats. A cynic might suggest this is at least in part because keeping citizens ignorant allows both the government and corporations to do a lot of spying on Joe Citizen without the risk of actually breaking into an office to monitor a computer that is in use by the subject of an investigation, or by someone who is creating a rival industrial process. All that is needed is a van parked on the street with the proper dish antenna pointed toward the computer in question, with a crew of technicians in the van adjusting their equipment to the right frequency, and then recording the data streaming onto the screen.

However much this seems like an invasion of privacy, legally, it probably isn't considered so. The 1986 Electronic Communications Privacy Act not only reduced the penalty for intercepting cell phone calls and other such communications from a felony to a $500 fine, but it also specifically exempted from punishment the eavesdropping on electronic transmissions between home portable telephones and base stations.[125]

It therefore seems likely that monitoring the radio broadcasts of a home computer might be viewed as being liable only for a $500 fine, at worst. Thus a government agent or industrial spy has very little to worry about if he's tapping into the radio stream created by a user's computer.

Perhaps the most bizarre project that came to light involving TEMPEST was conducted by the University of Cambridge in the late 1990s. There a group developed a special program that could be installed on computers as part of an operating system. Once in place, the software (without the knowledge of the user) would start broadcasting data that included the type of software running on the computer, along with its serial numbers. The thinking was that software companies could have fleets of vans that would go up and down streets, checking serial numbers against lists to see whether or not the home user had purchased his software or was using a bootleg copy. Companies would, the thinking went, have the ultimate tool to fight piracy.[126]

Software companies never put the technique into service, apparently because of fears that the public backlash would be counterproductive. More importantly, software developers were creating other systems that would require users to register software before it could be used, thereby creating an equally efficient anti-piracy process that would be cheaper to maintain since it could be automated. (Interestingly, the technicians in a van snooping for piracy have been employed to snare people stealing TV cable services.)[127]

There is some indication that the U.S. government may have adopted this technique of placing a software Trojan into a computer

---

[125] John Markoff, "At the New Frontier of Eavesdropping," *The New York Times*, January 19, 1997, p. 5.

[126] John Burgess, "British Technology Might Flush Out Software Pirates," *The Washington Post*, February 7, 1998; Page H01.

[127] *Ibid.*

so that a program running in the background will broadcast key data via the electromagnetic waves produced by the computer. In an NSA document that was made public, a TEAPOT program was briefly noted, with a hint that it involved a system that would pick up data covertly broadcast from a user's computer through the introduction of a software program.[128]

It seems likely that such software is in use, and one might even speculate that major U.S. software manufacturers might have incorporated such code in their programs in order to help the U.S. government, whether as a quid pro quo agreement or as a patriotic measure. Even if this were not the case, then it would be simple to create a freeware program that could contain the code; distributed on the Internet, this would also be capable of snaring many users.

If either of the possibilities has taken place, then many computers around the world are patiently waiting, ready to start broadcasting coded information about their owners when the right e-mail is delivered or certain Web sites visited, thereby activating the broadcasts. And unlike the standard TEMPEST attack, which can harvest only the data appearing on the screen, this TEAPOT attack is capable of searching for the information on a hard drive that someone is interested in finding, thereby making it considerably more dangerous in terms of leaking secrets.

The good news for those concerned about their privacy is that this system is not yet automated. The need for a human crew to mount a TEMPEST attack against computer users makes it expensive and time-consuming. Thus, it is mostly a worry of those with state secrets or new industrial processes.

Do you need to worry about this type of exposure?

Possibly not.

Yet the fact that almost nothing has been done to prevent these radio emissions is troubling. If anything, current digital monitors generate even more radio waves than their older analog

---

[128] Markus G. Kuhn, "Compromising Emanations: Eavesdropping Risks of Computer Displays," Technical Report 577, Computer Laboratory, University of Cambridge, December 2003.

counterparts. Additionally, new specifications for TrueType and other fonts used on modern computers have made it easier to mount TEMPEST attacks against them. (For the cynical, this might suggest that industry and governments are interested in making TEMPEST monitoring easier.) Where older systems permitted use of low-contrast fonts that greatly reduced electromagnetic waves generated by monitors, modern operating systems allow only the use of high-contrast fonts.

Neither the U.S. government nor the computer industry has done anything to reduce the potential emission levels of computers. As computer security expert Markus G. Kuhn has noted:[129]

> No public emission-security standards exist today. Two types of electromagnetic-emission limits for information technology have been widely accepted by the market, but neither was designed to reduce the risk of information-carrying emanations, or is even remotely suited to do so. . . .

> Shortly after 1990, many manufacturers of CRT [Cathode Ray Tube] computer monitors introduced new "low radiation" models with improved electromagnetic shielding. These products confirm to ergonomic/hygienic standards, aimed at reducing the exposure of humans to electromagnetic fields and their potential biological effects . . . This standard limits only low-frequency fields below 400 kHz, which are generated by CRT deflection coils. Compromising emanations are typically significantly weaker and occur at much higher frequencies in the HF/VHF/UHF bands (3 MHz–3 GHz). Therefore, a TCO'92 conformance test will not provide any information about the emission-security properties of a device. . . .

> The second class of publicly available electromagnetic emanation standards is aimed at minimizing interference with radio communication services. . . . [But] eavesdroppers can work with significantly lower signal levels than what might cause interference with radio and TV reception.

---

[129] *Ibid.*

Thus, most computers sold today are wide open to being compromised by a TEMPEST attack. Worse, the equipment needed to mount such an attack has grown cheaper. In fact, if a guy knows what he's doing, he could walk into a large electronics store or make a few online orders and purchase the equipment he needed to monitor someone's computer from across the street or the next apartment. And the how-to for doing it is freely available online as well.[130]

TEMPEST COUNTERMEASURES

There are countermeasures that can reduce the emissions of equipment to make it harder to pick up data from your computer. Taken together, they can reduce emissions enough to make it impractical to eavesdrop on you with a TEMPEST attack.

- Remove all unneeded wiring going into the computer, as any length of wire can act like an antenna to increase the range of the radio waves a computer produces. Disconnect modem wires, cable wiring, printer cables, etc., that aren't in use and you'll lower the electromagnetic emissions of most computers.

- Reduce the contrast of your monitor using the system software (rather than simply adjusting the monitor itself) to reduce the emissions the video cable and monitor produce.

- If your operating system permits it, create a page color that is nearly the same as the font color. This may reduce the ability of a distant monitoring system to distinguish what you're viewing on your screen.

- Use proportional fonts rather than fixed-width fonts; OCR (Optical Character Recognition) programs, as well as human operators, have more trouble reading proportional fonts.

- Exploit unusual fonts when writing sensitive information on your screen, then block the entire document and change the font to a more easily read font just before saving the file. Gothic fonts,

---

[130] *Ibid.*

SOLUTIONS

alien/sci-fi fonts, and the like (available for free on the Internet) can be quite hard to read with any deterioration in screen resolution— as occurs with TEMPEST captures. After you use such fonts for a time, you'll discover they don't slow your own reading abilities.

- Reduce the size of fonts on your screen to the smallest resolution that you can read. This will make the screen harder to intercept in a readable form.

- Place your computer as far away from potential eavesdropping points as possible. If the most likely possibility is a next-door apartment, then put your computer on the opposite side of your apartment; if a parking lot or street would be an ideal place to park a TEMPEST van, then move your computer to the opposite side of your home or office building.

- Whole computer rooms can be protected in a "Faraday Box" as covered in Chapter 8. However, this technique is not convenient for most people.

TIP

Don't install software of dubious origins or open e-mail attachments and such which might install software. Doing so might install codes that will cause your computer to broadcast key information via its radio-frequency emissions.

CHAPTER 6 THE INTERNET

" Most Americans are unaware that government Big Brother no longer has a monopoly on domestic spying. There are in fact thousands upon thousands of Big Brothers in cyberspace and on the digital airwaves. These Big Brothers are intent upon criminal gain rather than national security. These Big Brothers exist in the underground hacker community, among other places. Since the widespread adoption of e-commerce and e-finance, the burgeoning hacker community has evolved into a force to be reckoned with on the world stage. **"**

— TOM KELLERMANN[131]

CO-FOUNDER OF COMPUTER SECURITY FIRM CYBRINTH LLC —

Our society has been transformed in very profound ways by the personal computer, as well as through the connection of the PC to the Internet. Currently this tool has made it possible to communicate freely with any other person who has a PC almost anywhere in the world.

However, as noted in previous chapters, this freedom is under attack in profound ways. Some nations are worried about the ability it gives citizens to circumvent government censorship, and many corporations are concerned that they are losing potential customers through the use of freeware, sharing of various types of

---

[131] Tom Kellermann, "Privacy Lost: It's Not Just Uncle Sam Spying on You," www.cbsnews.com/stories/2006-06/07/opinion/main1690428.shtml, June 7, 2006.

files, and so forth. Thus there is currently a push from some governments as well as large corporations to take back some of the freedom and privacy the PC has brought with it.

A variety of software and hardware modifications have been proposed to help governments and corporations regain control over citizens and consumers. These range from programs designed to limit how data can be used by an individual to identification systems that make it easy to identify a computer and link it to a specific location and user. None of these modifications to the PC are helpful to the user. The changes may be couched as ways to prevent piracy, fight terrorism, or curtail child pornography, but for most users the real result will be a loss of freedom and privacy, often with little done to actually combat the problems the modifications were intended to combat.

As computer expert Bruce Schneier has noted about this battle to gain control over PCs:[132]

> If left to grow, these external control systems will fundamentally change your relationship with your computer. They will make your computer much less useful by letting corporations limit what you can do with it. They will make your computer much less reliable because you will no longer have control of what is running on your machine, what it does, and how the various software components interact. At the extreme, they will transform your computer into a glorified boob tube. . . .
>
> Just because computers were a liberating force in the past doesn't mean they will be in the future. There is enormous political and economic power behind the idea that you shouldn't truly own your computer or your software, despite having paid for it.

The Nightmare

Picture this: An airline traveler steps off the plane in a foreign nation (or perhaps upon returning to the U.S.), and an inspector takes the traveler's laptop computer to a back room. A few tense

---

[132] Bruce Schneier, "Everyone Wants to 'Own' Your PC," *Wired News*, May 4, 2006.

minutes later the inspector returns to announce that his team has discovered pornography on the hard drive. Even as the traveler is protesting that a mistake has been made, he's placed under arrest. Worst of all, when he finally gets his day in court, he discovers that there really *was* porn on his computer, and he is found guilty. With a reduced sentence, he'll still experience the loss of no little money to pay for legal fees. Worse, his good name will be tarnished for the rest of his life.

This isn't the only nightmare some ordinary citizens have experienced. More than a few have found themselves in court where prosecutors, seeing an easy way to discredit defendants, have announced to the courtroom that pornography, pirated movies, stolen software, etc., were found on the defendant's home computer. Undoubtedly such revelations produce an audible gasp in the courtroom—including from the jury box. For a prosecutor, it is downhill from there.

What about your computer?

Chances are your home or business computer would yield the same sort of incriminating evidence, even if you believe you've never visited any questionable sites and know you aren't addicted to porn or pirating movies and software. You may think you have nothing to hide, but in fact, the odds are that there are data time bombs waiting to be found on your hard drive. It's very likely your computer is a disaster waiting to strike.

Because of the intrusive nature of many government agencies both in the U.S. and abroad, and a tendency of lawsuits and prosecutors to take information out of context to bring charges against citizens, great care must be exercised in protecting yourself. You can't expect the government to offer you much help, as most courts have ruled that documents you create aren't protected under the Fifth Amendment. That means any photos, papers, computer files, or other materials can get you in trouble if they can be misinterpreted and employed to create circumstantial evidence against you.

Before looking at how to rid your computer of materials that might come back to haunt you, it is important to note that paper documents, tapes, photographs, and so forth can hang a person just as quickly. And with laws constantly in flux these days, it isn't too much of a stretch to suggest that what might have been legal yesterday could be a heinous crime tomorrow. Yesterday's innocent photos or downloaded MP3s become tomorrow's "crime of the day," with agents battering down the front door to arrest you.

Handy Wipes

Spam often contains pornography. And it isn't rare for someone to accidentally visit an X-rated Web site with a name similar to a business or government agency. What many Web surfers fail to realize about these sites and e-mails is that even if you back off the site in a hurry or delete the offensive e-mail, often your computer will keep a cache copy of the offensive document somewhere.

Various snoops in government as well as private agencies know right where to look for these, and are often more than happy to introduce them into court to make you look bad. Thus an event you had completely forgotten about, and which was innocent on your part, may be employed to make you look like someone addicted to pornography or such.

It is also possible that anyone who knows your e-mail address could set you up this way. While hopefully government agencies or your enemies won't stoop to this, it's impossible to be certain they will not. Indeed, in the past, government agencies have sent suspected pedophiles materials designed to lure them into taking action that would reveal their nature—even though some of these people only yielded to the temptation upon the receipt of this government material.[133]

Even if such tactics might be tossed out as entrapment, once the charges have been made, a person's good name is tainted.

Former UN weapons inspector and vocal antiwar advocate Scott Ritter is a good example of how such charges can destroy a

---

[133] *U.S. vs. Weber*, Fifth Circuit, No. 93-4998.

person's credibility, if not their life. Shortly after making critical comments about the U.S. government's handling of the Iraq crisis, Ritter was arrested for "engaging in a sexual discussion" and attempting to meet with "a person whom he thought was a fourteen-year-old girl." In fact, the person was an adult posing as a child, so one might argue that no crime had been committed, or even that the government was guilty of entrapment.

It's even quite possible Ritter had done none of the things he was charged with, given that the case against him was "adjourned in contemplation of dismissal" and the record sealed with Ritter set free, a seemingly very light sentence for a child molester.

The dismissal of the case, especially coupled with the lack of any punishment for the charged crime, carries the presumption of innocence. Yet because the records are sealed, it's impossible for the public to see what the charges really were—an ideal way for a government to leave a lingering doubt about whether that person was guilty. So Ritter was sidelined from political discussions for the next few years. Perhaps the most horrifying aspect to such stories is that those government agents who have basically destroyed a person may do so feeling morally justified in their actions which, they might believe, will protect society from pedophiles and/or those who endanger our nation's security and interests.

It is not easy for lawyers to mount a defense for suspected sex offenders. The secret, then, is never to get into a position where you might be smeared as someone interested in anything suggestive of illegal or deviant behavior. That means you need to be able to get rid of any materials on a computer hard drive that might brand you as such, even if they were placed there by a spammer, or an overly zealous government agent intent on bringing criminals or unpatriotic citizens to justice (or injustice, depending on your point of view).

Most people assume that once they delete a file on their computer, that data is gone forever. In fact it's not. It's still sitting on the hard drive waiting to be discovered.

TIP

Deleting a file doesn't erase it. The file is still sitting in the "free disk space" on your hard drive, unless it gets overwritten or "wiped."

The reason for this is no grand conspiracy on the part of computer programmers. Rather, it came about from the time when home computers were slow beasts and programmers wanted to speed things up. To do so, they designed operating systems that would merely discard the location of a file but not actually erase it. With small storage space, this was pretty safe, since in a short time other material was recorded over the old data, thereby making it hard if not impossible to recover.

Today, large hard drives may go months or years before recording new data over the location of old, deleted data on a hard drive. That means a file that was "deleted" can be waiting to be recovered by anyone who has the right software—and such programs are available, for free download, just a quick Web search away.

Think about that. Any document with your passwords, e-mails, letters, pictures, programs, or anything else you thought you had erased when you deleted them could very well be sitting on your hard drive, waiting for anyone to find. Worse, today's operating systems give you no clue as to where these might be hidden on your drive, so while you can't easily find them, a snoop with the right software can!

WIPING YOUR HARD DRIVE

The good news is that there are programs that can actually erase these files from your hard drive. Called *wiping*, *wiper*, or (occasionally) *shredder* programs, this software basically records data over the files that you want removed.

These tiny programs come and go since there's not a big market for them, and government agencies may also place pressure on programmers to discontinue work on such software. (One can imagine a call in the night from an agent saying, "Hey, you know child pornographers are walking because of your software?")

But the programs are is out there. A little time with a search engine will lead you to what you need. Some good programs that may still be available include:

- DPWIPER (freeware), www.dpaehl.de
- Mutilate File Wiper (shareware), www.mutilatefilewiper.com
- BCWipe (shareware), www.jetico.com
- Eraser (freeware), www.heidi.ie/eraser/

Regardless of what software you settle on, it should offer several levels of wiping. That is, it will record data over the area the file is on, one or more times. Each of these passes makes it less likely that a snoop will be able to recover the data. But each pass also takes more time. Make several passes to be sure no one can recover the information. Leave the program running overnight, as this process can take time, depending on how large your hard drive is.

Wiping can also be done to floppy disks. CDs, DVDs, or other optical media will need to actually be destroyed to get rid of the data—many paper shredders are built strong enough to do this job, and I would recommend buying one of these when you buy a shredder for paper documents. (While in theory putting a few large scratches on a CD makes it unusable to most systems, data can be recovered from these. For this reason most companies and government agencies destroy data CDs rather than simply snapping them in two, scratching them, etc. A quality shredder should be capable of handling CDs or DVDs, making it an ideal way to discard these media.)

For an added level of security, the cache area of a hard drive should always be wiped. Unfortunately, locating this is problematic with most systems. Thus it is necessary to wipe all the empty areas of the drive—something that is very time-consuming with large hard drives.

There is a good solution for making this problem manageable: Create a RAM drive and use it for caching. This virtual drive is created from extra memory on a computer, so to work efficiently, a computer needs plenty of extra RAM. These conditions met, various program data can be cached on the RAM drive, which vanishes when the computer is turned off, permanently removing everything in the cache when the RAM drive vanishes. When the computer is restarted, a new RAM drive is created to record cache material, which again vanishes when the machine is turned off. (Note that the machine must be turned completely off, rather than placed in sleep mode, standby, or other states that may preserve the RAM drive.) Once the RAM drive is created, you should then set the cache location on your browser and other programs to use the RAM drive.

A lower-tech solution is to create a small partition within a larger hard drive, make it a virtual drive, and then use that for caching. This can then be quickly wiped. And even if it is not, the constant writing going over the same area will gradually cause data to be recorded over the same spots so that it is slowly lost (though not as thoroughly as when wiped). (A quick Web search will give you the step-by-step details of how to create RAM drives or partitions with your operating system.)

If you can't create a RAM or a partition for a virtual drive, hiring someone to create it for you can be a worthwhile and simple way to protect your privacy.

CACHE FOR THE MERCHANDISE

Now what about that Web site you accidentally visited with the questionable pictures on it? Where are they stored on your computer? How do you find those files?

Most browsers store material on your hard drive automatically in specific locations. This makes the operation of the browser faster if you visit the page again. Normally that's a plus. But when you hit a site with information that might be used against you, it presents a danger. One place to start is to go to the options or preferences drop-down menu in your browser and then locate the "clear cache" or "delete temporary Internet files" command. Then you can simply clear the cache (an option with most browsers). Once this is done, you can order a wiper program to wipe all the free disk space (where the deleted files now are).

"Wiping" the free disk space on your computer should be done on a regular basis.

TIP

Wiping this area of your drive is a good idea anyway, and should be done periodically for the added security it gives you. Just remember it takes time. It isn't something you can start fifteen minutes before heading for the airport on an overseas trip.

If time is limited, you may need to find potentially damaging files quickly, rather than wiping down all the empty space on your drive. In such a case, you can employ File Explorer (or a similar program) to locate the area where your browser caches its temporary files. It will generally be a folder under the one containing the browser program. Most cache folders will be marked "temporary" or "cache," so you can easily identify them; these can be safely wiped without hurting the operation of your browser.

Ad-Aware SE (freeware at www.lavasoftusa.com/), and CCleaner (freeware at www.ccleaner.com/) both have options for clearing cache files in the Firefox and Internet Explorer browsers, as well as various "history" sections in Windows which show where you have been browsing, what files you've recently opened, recent search terms, and other possibly compromising information that you might not want to let anyone gaining access to your computer discover.

Now all this may seem like a lot of extra work.

It is.

And it might even be a bit paranoid and unnecessary most of the time.

But being aware of how to prudently wipe files is a good skill to have. It might even keep you from being unjustly persecuted in some foreign nation intent on stopping pornography or piracy. Files that you simply deleted, once wiped, won't be coming back to haunt you.

Online E-mail Services

It should be noted that online e-mail services, which have become popular and convenient, are also anything but private.

> **TIP** When you use online e-mail services like Gmail, you should treat your communications as messages posted on a public bulletin board.

For example, Google's privacy policy with its Gmail service states that deleted e-mail "may remain in our off-line backup systems." For how long? Forever, if they so wish. In other words, just because you delete it or assume your e-mail should be private, doesn't make it so. This fact came home with a vengeance in a 2006 court case, when a U.S. magistrate judge in San Francisco ruled that Google had to turn over e-mail records, including those that users under trial had deleted.[134]

Worse, free e-mail services like Gmail earn money through advertising and the ads aren't selected by random. Advertisers buy keywords (as is done with most search engines). Gmail then employs "content extraction," searching through the e-mail for the keywords sold to advertisers. Thus, if you were writing a friend about an antique clock you'd purchased, the ad displayed might be for antiques or clocks—or both. This is done for both incoming as well as outgoing mail, meaning that those who haven't signed up for the service, nor agreed to have their e-mails searched for keywords, will have their letters searched for keywords. Additionally, Gmail users have cookie info from their use of other Google searches keyed into their Gmail account, suggesting that data from searches is also logged into the account.

Such searches and e-mail keywords are thus all linked to the user, and preserved along with the original e-mails the user sends and receives. These may remain for some time, waiting to be data mined by law-enforcement agencies—and possibly by various buyers of the data, should Google change its policy of not selling the information in the near future (and there's every reason to think it will; otherwise, storing e-mails for an extended time makes no sense).

---

[134] Declan McCullagh, "Police Blotter: Judge Orders Gmail Disclosure," CNET News.com, March 17, 2006.

Should such a policy change occur, then an agency like the IRS might buy the data and search for "offshore banks," "tax evasion," or other key phrases that could lead them to people who are cheating on their taxes. Ditto for a variety of other law-enforcement and government agencies.

If you want to protect your privacy, avoid such online e-mail services. Beyond that, you need to be very careful when you reply to someone using a free service that searches through the user's e-mail for keywords.

Currently users of these systems are more or less protected by the sheer volume of e-mail going through most systems. But with data storage becoming less expensive and computers more powerful, this protection will slowly erode away.

This all means that your e-mail is less than secure even today, and unlikely to be at all secure from government agencies and, increasingly, from criminals working in businesses controlling this data. You can protect your communications from snoops who gain access to your computer, but you can't control the messages once they leave your computer. From then on, it is anyone's guess as to how private a message may really be.

Backdoors

In the 1990s I had the privilege of working on a writing project with a security expert for several months. During that time I got a good demonstration of how "secure" many programs and computerized systems really are. One day he sent me a program to test; it was slick, encrypting any files selected on the hard drive so they were impossible to read without a password.

Or so the company claimed.

My friend did a little social engineering and discovered that was not the case.

He called the company, told them he had lost his password, and asked if there was any way to get his data back. The company official gave him the password to a "backdoor" built into the program. And that backdoor not only opened my security friend's encrypted files, but mine as well—and I suspect the files encrypted by any other copy of the program, too.

Sure, a backdoor can be handy if you've foolishly forgotten your password, or if an employee leaves the company in a huff, with important documents encrypted on his hard drive. In such cases, a backdoor can be the only way to easily gain access to the data.

But as my friend, the security expert, demonstrated, often anyone who can do a bit of fast talking can also get through that backdoor, no matter how good the encryption may be at the "front door" of the program. Nor is the use of backdoors likely to decrease; in these days when governments are intent on rooting out everyone from child pornographers to terrorists, you can bet many companies put backdoors into otherwise fine encryption programs out of patriotic duty, if not simply to protect themselves from government pressure.

Backdoors make it easier for government agencies to catch bad guys, but it's not necessarily a plus for citizens. One of the basic freedoms we have enjoyed in free nations is the ability to conduct private communications with anyone we choose, whether a friend, lover, or business partner. Without that right to converse without fear of being overheard, there's no real freedom in any society. A high level of intrusion via electronic means may make a society safer, but it also transforms the individuals in an adverse way, making them anything but completely free or, as our Founding Fathers put it, "secure in their persons, houses, papers, and effects against unreasonable searches and seizures."

It seems likely that backdoors may be (if they are not already) a required feature for all computer software. Early in 2006 when it was learned the new version of Windows would have stronger encryption built into it, members of the British parliament expressed the opinion that backdoors should be built into the operating system. When the British press contacted the Home Office about this possibility, a spokesman said simply, "The Home Office has already been in touch with Microsoft concerning this matter and is working closely with them."[135]

As for Microsoft, when asked about this possibility, their spokesperson issued this cryptic statement:[136]

> We are working with law enforcement to help them understand its security features and will continue to partner with governments, law enforcement, and industry to help make the Internet a safer place to learn and communicate.

Does anyone think that Microsoft would surrender its lucrative markets in order to protect customers' privacy?

This wouldn't be the first time a government has pressured a company to place a backdoor into software. In 1995 the NSA managed to get backdoors placed into the products of the Swiss firm Crypto. This permitted U.S. agencies to easily circumvent encryption for years, as over 120 countries purchased the product (including Iran, Iraq, and Libya).[137]

It is very possible that Microsoft has yielded to this pressure in the past. When computers with encrypted files were found among Taliban hideouts in Afghanistan in January 2002, government officials were able to immediately open and read the files that had been encrypted using Microsoft programs. The official reason was that the terrorists had employed a low-level encryption setting; one must wonder if, in reality, Microsoft gave investigators the keys to open a backdoor that bypassed or easily decoded the encryption.

Little wonder then that a number of nations have now stopped using U.S.-made encryption programs, and several have stopped using Microsoft operating systems, since they might easily contain a variety of backdoors.

Of course, the use of backdoors in software is a two-way street. If our nation can exploit backdoors, then a criminal or foreign spy

---

[135] Ollie Stone-Lee, "UK Holds Microsoft Security Talks," *BBC News*, February 16, 2006.

[136] *Ibid.*

[137] Declan McCullagh, " 'Lantern' Backdoor Flap Rages," *Wired News*, November 27, 2001.

might do the same should he discover how to do so. The fact that many U.S. government agencies concerned with security avoid Windows suggests this might be the case. For example, U.S. marshals have used Sun Microsystems or Red Hat Linux for years, not only to lower costs, but also because these programs better protect the agency's data.[138]

Interestingly, Red Hat has also developed the "Security-Enhanced Linux" version for the National Security Agency.[139] The question is whether this edition is security-enhanced because of add-ons to it, or because of the subtraction of a backdoor.

Sadly, U.S. citizens may not have the same option. In 2005, the FCC, with almost no fanfare, released a three-page document that included the following notice:[140]

> To encourage broadband deployment and preserve and promote the open and interconnected nature of the public Internet, consumers are entitled to run applications and use services of their choice, subject to the needs of law enforcement.

Notice this change in viewpoint. Instead of having a right to privacy, consumers are "entitled" to run software, as long as it meets the "needs of law enforcement." In other words, government law-enforcement agencies could dictate weaker encryption, or require that backdoors be placed in software as they saw fit, strictly for the convenience of the government.

This modification to the regulations received almost no notice in the press. It did inspire computer columnist Declan McCullagh to write at his blog:[141]

> The clearest reading of the pronouncement is that some un-elected bureaucrats at the commission have decreed that

---

[138] Michael Arnone, "U.S. Marshals Switching to Red Hat Linux," *Federal Computer Week*, May 29, 2006.

[139] Brad Grimes, "Red Hat Pushes for Linux in Federal Market," *Government Computer News*, January 24, 2005.

[140] Policy Statement FCC 05-151, Federal Communications Commission, September 23, 2005.

[141] Declan McCullagh, "FBI to Get Veto Power over PC Software?" CNET News.com, September 27, 2005.

Americans don't have the right to use software such as
Skype or PGPfone if it doesn't support mandatory backdoors for wiretapping. That interpretation was confirmed by
an FCC spokesman on Monday, who asked not to be identi-
fied by name.

The bottom line here is that the privacy offered by an encryption program is often marginal. By capturing keystrokes, or by
using a backdoor built into the encryption program, it is possible
for officials to quickly read files that were thought to be safely
hidden away. For this reason the very concept of privacy and the
freedom it conveys has been greatly eroded through the actions of
the FCC and other agencies.

Yet, even if a government doesn't abuse its ability to intrude
(something recent history has consistently proved otherwise), the
backdoor might be exploited by any government that knows
about it. There's also the rogue agent, the private eye, or even a
nosy ex-spouse or neighbor who poses a variety of threats to you
when your privacy is breached. An NSA agent on the take might
sell the how-to for using a backdoor to a criminal gang or a hacker;
a Chinese agent might gain the know-how to circumvent the defenses of U.S. State Department computers running the software.

What evades safeguards for law enforcement can also defeat
it for the bad guys. Little wonder then, as noted earlier, that many
government agencies are switching to non-Windows programs.
This may also be why many foreign governments and corporations are doing the same.[142]

The loser in all this is the citizen using any program with a
backdoor built in. Make no mistake about it: When someone intercepts and reads any file or message that a person expects to be private, it is an unreasonable invasion of his privacy. In the U.S., that
invasion makes us anything but "secure in our papers and effects."

Before leaving the subject of backdoors, it should be noted
that these could be built into hardware as well as software. One
sign that this may be ongoing appeared in 2006 when the U.S.

---

[142] Brad Grimes, "Red Hat Pushes For Linux in Federal Market," *Government
Computer News*, January 24, 2005.

State Department abruptly announced that the Chinese-made Lenovo computers it had purchased would be pulled from its secure embassy network. According to U.S. congressman Frank R. Wolf, the reason had to do with the fear that the Chinese could use the computers to spy on embassy networks:[143]

> This decision [to use Chinese-made computers in secure networks] would have had dire consequences for our national security, potentially jeopardizing our investment in a secure infrastructure. It is no secret that the United States is a principal target of Chinese intelligence services.

Carnivore

In the mid-1990s, as e-mail was starting to be employed by many Americans, along with citizens in other nations as well as big business, the FBI devised a scheme for quickly inspecting massive amounts of e-mail, looking for signs that the messages might be connected to criminal activity. Code-named Carnivore, the system was designed to check on the e-mail address and subject heads of the messages, and then compare these to lists of words that might indicate criminal activity. (Though never stated, it has always been assumed that should signs of criminal activity be found, the FBI would then contact the ISPs involved in sending/receiving the e-mail and obtain records of the messages, going to court to obtain a warrant should the ISP prove uncooperative.)

The use of the program alarmed many concerned with privacy, while also providing a bit of comic relief, with first the FBI's refusal to admit the program existed, and then, when the secret was out, trying to downplay the dangers the system might present to privacy, calling the program a "diagnostic tool."[144] This was followed with then-attorney general Janet Reno announcing that she had only learned the program was operational when she heard about it in news accounts.[145]

---

[143] "U.S. Pulls Lenovo PCs from State Department," *Washington Times*, May 19, 2006.

[144] http://www.fvi.gov/hq/lab/carnivore/carnivore.htm.

The catch to Carnivore is that it may be a bit too hungry to be useful. For example, if the FBI were worried about terrorists exploding a dirty bomb in the U.S., they might search for the words "nuclear" or "dirty bomb." But often news reports, as well as various security experts, will also be "chattering" about the same thing. Thus, programming that is searching for these keywords is going to collect the names and addresses of people who are at the exact opposite end of the spectrum from terrorists.

As Chris Hoofnagle, a privacy advocate with the Electronic Privacy Information Center (EPIC) remarked about this situation,[146]

> When [the FBI] says deliver to me all the packets that mention the words "crop duster" or "anthrax," you get this situation where people who are reading innocent materials might be viewed with suspicion.

This collection of too much information may have indeed happened in April 2000, according to an FBI document obtained by EPIC through the Freedom of Information Act. An internal FBI memo seems to indicate that the FISA data captured by Carnivore basically overwhelmed investigators due to a setting that allowed the program to capture an excessive amount of data. In the process, the target of the investigation went undetected.

The subject?

"UBL," a designation the FBI used for Usama bin Laden.[147] One can only speculate, but it seems possible that had the FBI not been so ham-handed in its handling of data, the 9/11 attacks might have been thwarted.

As Carnivore was used, the FBI continued its attempts to paint the program as something very unlike what its name suggested. Perhaps the clumsiest of these attempts occurred when the Justice Department offered to allow a group of independent computer

---

[145] "FBI Says Carnivore Will not Devour Privacy," CNN.com, July 21,. 2000.

[146] "An Invasion of Privacy? Civil Liberties Groups Battle Patriot Act," TechTV, November 5, 2001.

[147] "FBI Memo on 'FISA Mistakes'," Electronic Privacy Information Center, http://www.epic.org/privacy/carnivore/fisa.html, 2006.

experts to look over the program, thereby certifying that it was harmless.

A committee was formed and their work begun. But soon there was grumbling in the ranks. As Jeffrey Schiller, a security expert and network manager at the Massachusetts Institute of Technology, who was one of those asked to evaluate Carnivore, protested,[148]

> They [the Justice Department] were not looking for an independent review. In essence, what they wanted to do was borrow the reputation of any institution doing the review.... It's not really about technology, it's about oversight. The verification needs to be more than just "we trust the FBI."

Soon experts and university computer departments asked to verify the Carnivore program were announcing they no longer were interested in taking part in the evaluation.

The FBI hired the IITRI (IIT Research Institute) to handle the evaluation (to the tune of $175,000).[149] And the IITRI offered the following in Draft Report, Sec. 5[150] of its paper, entitled "Independent Technical Review of the Carnivore System":

> Although IITRI specifically excluded questions of constitutionality and of illegal activity by the FBI from this evaluation, IITRI is concerned that the presence of Carnivore and its successors without safeguards as recommended below: (1) fuels the concerns of responsible privacy advocates and reduces the expectations of privacy by citizens at large, and (2) increases public concern about the potential unauthorized activity of law-enforcement agents.

In plain language, the FBI had asked them to evaluate whether the program might violate privacy, apparently with the

---

[148] Patrick Riley, "Scientists Refusing to Review FBI's 'Carnivore'," Associated Press, September 6, 2000.

[149] Research Institute to Review FBI's Carnivore," *Government Computer News*, October 2, 2000.

[150] "Independent Technical Review of the Carnivore System," Draft Report, ITT Research Institute, Contract No. 00-C-0328, IITRI CR-022-216, November 17, 2000.

understanding that they should ignore any and all questions of legality or constitutionality. And even then, they voiced their concerns that the program needed safeguards.

The group also hinted at some poor design features; in Section ES.5 of the draft report, the researchers wrote:[151]

> While the system was designed to, and can, perform fine-tuned searches, it is also capable of broad sweeps. Incorrectly configured, Carnivore can record any traffic it monitors.

And the program was also designed in such a way that almost anyone could use—or perhaps abuse—it. In Section 4.2.4 of the report, the group wrote:[152]

> It is not possible to determine who, among a group of agents with the password, may have set or changed filter settings. In fact, any action taken by the Carnivore system could have been directed by anyone knowing the Administrator password. It is impossible to trace the actions to specific individuals. Auditing is crucial in security. It is the means by which users are held accountable for their actions.

To the misfortune of the American public, following the attacks of September 11, 2001, the congressional fears of illegal invasion of privacy and warrantless searches were soon swept to the wayside, as politicians jumped on the bandwagon to give the FBI more—rather than less—power, and to keep Carnivore in place.

In fact, just hours after the World Trade Center attacks, the FBI had agents at major Internet services installing Carnivore programs in the servers. As reporter Declan McCullagh put it:[153]

> Just hours after three airplanes smashed into the buildings in what some U.S. legislators have dubbed a second Pearl Harbor, FBI agents began to visit Web-based e-mail firms and

---

[151] *Ibid.*

[152] *Ibid.*

[153] Declan McCullagh, "Anti-Attack Feds Push Carnivore," *Wired News,* September 12, 2001.

network providers, according to engineers at those companies who spoke on condition of anonymity.

An administrator at one major network service provider said that FBI agents showed up at his workplace on Tuesday "with a couple of Carnivores, requesting permission to place them in our core, along with offers to actually pay for circuits and costs."

The person declined to say for publication what the provider's response was, "but a lot of people" at other firms were quietly going along with the FBI's request. "I know that they are getting a lot of 'OKs' because they made it a point to mention that they would only be covering our core for a few days, while their 'main boxes were being set up at the Tier 1 carriers [the lines that carry the majority of Internet traffic]'—scary," the engineer said.

Even if the FBI is merely looking at headers of e-mails and only with specific addresses, there is no one checking to be sure that's all that's going on. In effect, the public and courts are told, "Trust us" from an agency that has in the past regularly "lost" papers and evidence and been guilty of rearrangement of evidence at crime scenes.[154]

As David Sobel, general counsel of the Electronic Privacy Information Center, has noted, there's no way to be sure that the agency or a rogue agent is not overstepping the legal bounds and collecting as much data as they please with Carnivore. He noted that there are no safeguards in place:[155]

If the FBI had a subpoena or warrant for a particular individual's bank records, we would never accept a situation where the bank sits the agent down at a computer and says "Look for whatever you want." Law enforcement has never been given unchecked access to everything and then trusted to take only what they are authorized to take, but that's what happens with Carnivore.

---

[154] Jon Sawyer, "FBI's Troubles Could Imperil Its System of E-mail Surveillance," *St. Louis Post-Dispatch*, June 2, 2001.

[155] *Ibid.*

But now even the small checks and balances offered by the need to get a judge to issue a warrant before Carnivore could be unleashed have been curtailed. Because buried in the USA Patriot Act of 2001 was the permission for FBI agents to install the program after simply obtaining an order from a U.S. or state attorney general, bypassing the need to go before a judge.[156]

Thus the bar was lowered considerably for the FBI. It had a program that could be modified—from getting simple headers from e-mail messages, to obtaining the entire e-mails—without an agent having to leave any clues that he was responsible for his actions. An attorney general (who often works hand-in-glove with FBI agents) rather than an impartial judge had the right to issue a warrant for the use of Carnivore, and Congress by its actions had turned a blind eye toward the use of the program.

Worse, Carnivore was only the FBI's first attempt to collect massive amounts of information from computers and e-mail. Once this beachhead had been established, the agency started rolling out more sophisticated software with even more capabilities. Today Carnivore has been retired with newer and more efficient systems taking its place.

Before going on, it should be noted that government agencies aren't the only ones regularly checking e-mail. A survey conducted by Proofpoint/Forrester Research in 2006 found that about a third of big corporations in the U.S. had staff regularly reading employees' e-mail, checking it for legal, financial, or regulatory risks.[157]

Cyber Knight and Magic Lantern

In response to a Freedom of Information Act request filed by EPIC in 2001, the FBI released a series of unclassified documents relating to Carnivore, including some that told of an "Enhanced Carnivore Project Plan" apparently code-named "Cyber Knight." Although little is known about this project, some believe that Cyber Knight was intended to create a database by sorting through material collected from a variety of Internet sources, in-

---

[156] Bob Sullivan, "FBI Software Cracks Encryption Wall," MSNBC, November 20, 2001.

[157] "Companies Read Employee E-mail," *Wired News*, June 3, 2006.

cluding e-mail, chat-room messages, instant messages, and possibly Internet phone calls. The software may have been employed with a program called Magic Lantern, to match encryption keys to the data collected, thereby giving agents access to encrypted data as well.[158]

Magic Lantern appears to be designed to capture keystrokes on the computer the software is installed on. A keyboard logger basically makes a record of each key depressed on a computer keyboard, thereby giving access to passwords, documents, or whatever else might be typed into the computer. This data goes to a file hidden on the computer, which can later be retrieved over the computer's modem or by physically entering the premises and copying the file from the computer. The program is believed to be especially adept at capturing encryption key passwords, according to computer security expert Bob Sullivan:[159]

> It watches for a suspect to start a popular encryption program called Pretty Good Privacy. It then logs the pass phrase used to start the program, essentially giving agents access to keys needed to decrypt files.

Before it can do any of this, such a program must be installed onto a computer. Such a task once meant that an FBI agent would have had to enter the home or business where the computer was and install the software. The more elegant solution, and one that apparently is part of the FBI's Magic Lantern program, is to create a Trojan program that will entice the person owning the computer to install it himself—or have it surreptitiously installed by a computer virus. Once secretly installed, the key logger can collect data from the target computer and place it into hidden files for later retrieval by an FBI agent.

Releasing a computer virus or Trojan "into the wilds" is normally seen as a criminal activity. But it now appears this is just

---

[158] Bob Sullivan, *Ibid*.
[159] Bob Sullivan, "FBI Software Cracks Encryption Wall," MSNBC, November 20, 2001.

what the FBI has done on at least one occasion, causing Mike Sposato to write:[160]

> Under a new initiative called Cyber Knight, the FBI has launched into the business of creating "Trojans"—a particular type of computer virus—to infect computers. Yes, that's correct; the FBI wants to infect your computer with a virus. Launch a program from an infected e-mail, and the FBI will have a record of every keystroke you make on your machine. They call it their "Magic Lantern."

Since a thriving industry has created software to thwart malware, including Trojans like that created by the FBI for Magic Lantern, the agency also had to convince these companies to ignore the FBI's Trojan.

This was undoubtedly a tough task, since some of these companies were based outside the U.S. And all faced consumer backlash should it be learned that they lowered users' defenses so spyware could be installed on a machine. Although most of the debate appears to have been carried on outside of the public arena, chief executive John W. Thompson, manager of the antivirus company Symantec, said about the proposal, "Symantec's first priority is to protect our customers from malicious and illegal attacks. We have no intention of creating or leaving a hole in our software that might compromise that security."[161]

There was another important reason for companies to be reluctant to go along with the FBI's proposal. Any security hole left in an antivirus program designed for the FBI to exploit might also be employed by hackers to circumvent the software. As Fred Cohen, digital forensics professor at the University of New Haven, noted, "If you leave the weakness for the FBI, you leave it for everybody."[162]

Additionally, if a non-U.S. company agreed to lower its program's antivirus guard for the FBI, what was to prevent it from

---

[160] Mike Sposato, "The FBI's Magic Lantern," WorldNetDaily.com, November 28, 2001.
[161] "Antivirus Firms: FBI Loophole is Out of Line," Reuters, December 11, 2001.
[162] *Ibid.*

being forced to do the same for law-enforcement agencies from Britain, France, or wherever? It was a case of the slippery slope. And with each exception added to the software for this or that government agency, another hole that might be exploited by a hacker would be added as well.

As security expert Robert Lemos advised his readers about the dangers presented by such "copware":[163]

> If domestic vendors turned a blind eye to copware, and re-fused to defend customers from law-enforcement tools that criminals will turn to their own purposes, many of us would have a duty to look elsewhere for protection.
>
> Overseas vendors stand to benefit. After all, criminalizing the use of effective tools from overseas would be no more suc-cessful at stopping the bad guys from using them than firearm laws are at preventing crooks from owning guns.

Since its brief appearance in the limelight in 2000–2001, little information about Magic Lantern has been leaked to the public. It seems certain that the system is in use, and equally likely that various antivirus manufacturers have given in to government pressure and enticements to "overlook" the program.

Before leaving this subject, it should be noted that in 2001, the "BadTrans.B" worm infected a number of computers around the world. The program created a record of keystrokes in every open window of the computer, and when connected to the Internet, sent these files to a distant computer. The owner of one of the sites receiving this data claimed the FBI had approached him and taken 5,857,277 files filled with private information stolen from people's computers by BadTrans.B.[164]

There has been some question as to what happened to the data. Did the FBI sift through it for keywords? More ominously for those inclined to conspiracies, did the FBI itself *create* Bad-

---

[163] Robert Lemos, "FBI's 'Magic Lantern' Snooping Technology Old Hat," ZD Net, November 23, 2001.

[164] Thomas C. Green, "FBI Surveillance Bonanza in BadTrans.B Worm," *The Register*, December 18, 2001.

Trans.B? It is a bit unsettling to think that the government might seize such private data with seemingly no action taken to safeguard the privacy of those whose data had been stolen.

Key Logger Hardware

Several hardware key loggers are currently being made, with the FBI as well as lesser snoops employing them from time to time. These generally consist of a small piece of hardware that can be inserted between the keyboard cord and the input jack on the back of a computer.

Since few users look at the back of their computers other than once in a great while (and even then may not notice the small change of a key logger when it is in place), these generally go undetected.

The only tough part is placing the hardware on the computer since this requires gaining physical access to it. But once in place, the device starts recording data. Later the hardware must be retrieved to access the data that has been collected—another shortcoming of the system.

During the 2001 case against Nicodemo Scarfo Jr., accused of running loan-shark and gambling operations in New Jersey, a hardware key logger was apparently employed to capture data, including the password to the encryption program Scarfo was using. Once agents gained the password, they were able to access the encrypted files and eventually bring a case against Scarfo.[165]

The Illusion of Privacy

Given both the "cracking power" of the modern computers owned by the various governments of the world, as well as the pressure to place backdoors into computer programs, it's wise to assume that anything you write or save to your hard drive might be seen by government snoops or hackers exploiting such programs. Never place anything in an e-mail or on a hard drive that might eventually get you hung out to dry. Whether it's a questionable picture or

---

[165] William Matthews, "FBI's Key Logger Under Scrutiny," *Federal Computer Week*, August 9, 2001.

a piece of software you haven't purchased the rights to, or an e-mail that makes disparaging remarks about a government official—never place anything on your hard drive that might be embarrassing if made public.

E-mail gives us the illusion of a private message. We're used to thinking of mail as private, and we also write and receive e-mail in a relatively private way. Yet this is all an illusion, because without encryption, any e-mail is like a message sent via postcard. A postcard first delivered across the street to your neighbor who a day later brings it to your home. Maybe it has been read by a snoop, and maybe not.

With e-mail, chances are no one will intercept and read it. But if you value your privacy and want to avoid identity theft and other problems (which are a consideration when you send an e-mail with financial or legal information in it), privacy with our e-mail is a necessity, not a luxury.

Unlike your physical mail, e-mail is also extremely durable. While you may delete an e-mail message from your computer (which, as noted previously, only removes the record of its position from your hard drive but leaves the information on the drive where it can be read by special software), it is also stored in the ISP archives for some time. Additionally, a copy of anything sent to or from you will be on the computer of the person you have an e-mail exchange with. And some companies also back up all e-mail sent to or from business offices.

So never, ever send an e-mail that might be misconstrued to transform you into a criminal of one sort or another, be it racist, sexist, criminal, or other crime that is often defined in large strokes. E-mails without encryption are not private. They're like telling your secrets on Main Street, by whispering them into a bullhorn.

It's possible to encrypt and protect material from anyone with less power than a government agency. This sort of protection allows you to continue to engage in private exchanges without fear of being "overheard" in one way or another.

ENCRYPTION: PUTTING YOUR E-MAIL INTO AN "ENVELOPE"

Again, the best way to avoid trouble is to never send a questionable e-mail. But sometimes you will need to send data or communicate in a way that can't be easily intercepted. It might be sending your Social Security number to an employer. Or a secret letter to a lover. Or any of several other cases when information needs to be private. In such a case you can put an "envelope" of encryption around your message to prevent snoops from easily reading it.

Even though computer-generated encryption can, in theory, be cracked by the brute-force method of crunching numbers, most encryption is now so complex that too much time is needed to break these codes to make it worth anyone's while. Such expensive work is generally reserved only for really serious cases. Unless you're a member of a terrorist cell, chances are no one will be able to justify the expense of cracking your private encryption. So, provided the system you use doesn't have a backdoor built into it, today you can employ encryption that is nearly impossible to conveniently crack.

The first such encryption software to reach the public was Pretty Good Privacy (PGP), created by a programmer named Phil Zimmermann who saw his software as a human-rights tool that would keep tyrannies from harassing citizens. Interestingly, the Clinton administration didn't see PGP as such, and tried to squash its release by classifying it as, of all things, a "munition." Ultimately the code for this encryption found its way onto the Internet in 1991, and from there was spread around the world by people who realized that their ability to carry on private exchanges far outweighed the need of any government to read such messages whenever it so chose.

The Clinton administration continued to harass Zimmermann with a three-year criminal investigation, claiming the programmer had violated the export restrictions for the "munition." Eventually the case was dropped, and Zimmermann continues to this day to refine his program. Meanwhile PGP became the most widely used e-mail encryption software in the world. (This drama remained uncovered by the mainstream press, so

SOLUTIONS

most citizens remain ignorant even today of PGP and the attempt by the U.S. government to suppress it.)

Zimmermann also has released the code for PGP, making it possible for people to examine it for possible backdoors. To date, none have been found. This and its global distribution, with all sorts of people constantly scrutinizing it, makes it the first choice for encryption software. Early versions of PGP were hard to use, but the newer ones aren't, thanks to software "front ends," small programs that handle all the commands sent to PGP, making it like a conventional piece of software.

Like most other modern encryption software, PGP uses "keys" to encrypt and decrypt messages. The *public key*, as its name suggests, can be given away without too much loss in security. Your public key can be e-mailed to friends, posted in public forums, or even used as a "digital signature" on e-mail. It is a simple string of characters that you can cut and paste into any digital document.

Anyone having your public key can then use it to lock a message into an encrypted package of data that can be sent via e-mail, stored on a drive, or burned to a CD and mailed. It can only be opened by your private key, and then, only if you give the correct password for that key. Without a private key and password, the message remains a string of seemingly random and totally meaningless characters.

There are several weak links in such systems. One is that someone might create a public key and claim it is yours. If you start getting e-mail that can't be decrypted with your password, this might be the problem. (However, sometimes encrypted e-mail will get "dinged up" along the way so it can't be decrypted—a much more common problem.) Nevertheless, it's good to be aware of this.

The second weak link is that if the private key can be found out, a number-crunching attack can be used to guess the password to that key. For this reason, you should never distribute your private key. Keep it on a secure computer if at all possible.

Finally, it is important not to get lulled into a feeling of false security. Some assume that if their encryption is safe electronically, they are safe physically as well. This is not the case. As a security friend put it, "They can put you and a loved one in a dark room and proceed to beat the living daylights out of your child or lover until you give them the password to your private key."

Brute force can be extremely effective even in a high-tech world.

One other important point to keep in mind when sending encrypted e-mails is that you must not draw attention with the subject heading. Since many systems currently sift through e-mail via the header, sender, and recipient lines, placing words that might be searched for can draw attention to the message and perhaps even be a tip-off as to what is being said, so keep subject lines vague and innocuous.

THE BEST PASSWORDS

When choosing passwords, whether for bank accounts, Web accounts, or an encryption key, avoid easily remembered words, digits in your address or Social Security number, your mother's maiden name, etc. All are easily cracked these days, or even easily guessed. Instead, passwords should be more or less random combinations of words and numbers, at least eight letters long and ideally much longer. Some banks and other institutions still employ Social Security numbers or the mother's maiden name for identification of customers. When presented with these upon the creation of an account, ask if you can use a randomly created password instead, as this will be much more secure.

You might consider using password-generation software. While the passwords created in this way aren't perfect, they are generally better than those people create on their own. A little time with a search engine will yield several. Avoid online generators, since you don't really know how secure the site might be; while unlikely, a site could be recording your unique IP number and password to link them together at a later date.

I recently had a good demonstration of why random-combination passwords are considerably more secure than actual words, while using a program designed to guess at passwords for a friend who had forgotten his. While the random-combination section of the program might have taken hours (or even days) before getting the password, using the word-cracking section of the program—which I did, since the user was certain he had used a word as a password—opened the document in under three minutes. I didn't even have time to step out for a Coke. Obviously, a single word is not a wise choice for a password these days. He had also used a short word, making the task even easier. Had he used a longer word, or even a sentence, it would have been much harder to acquire the password through a brute-force assault like this.

If you have to have both a long password (for security) and must also have it memorized (so it can be entered each time you access a system or decrypt a document), then using random combinations of numbers and letters gets iffy. A better route is to use a very long phrase, or even a sentence. It needs to be something hard to guess at, but something you can remember, along with the punctuation that goes into the sentence. Part of a poem you memorized in school, a nursery rhyme, or such can work well.

The only important point is that it should not be something you use often today, and it should be hard to associate with you for any reason. Once you've settled on it, you'll have a long password that you can easily remember and enter, but which will be hard (or nearly impossible) to crack without a huge amount of computer resources.

A British security company called Lockdown.co.uk recently ran tests to see how long it took to crack various-sized passwords with brute computer attacks. While space doesn't permit going into great detail here, suffice it to say that:[166]

- For passwords consisting only of numbers, those with six digits could be broken in less than two minutes, while a nine-digit password took a little over a day—for the less effective cracking. For those with quality computer power, all of these could be cracked in ten seconds or less!

- For passwords of all upper- or all lowercase letters (like many banks use for online systems), six-letter codes took 8.5 hours for low-level attack, while the cracking was instantaneous for sophisticated computing power. Interestingly, when the number of letters was expanded to just twelve characters, even the best system for cracking would take up to 3.5 years to guess the correct password, and for twenty letters, even the best would take 631 *billion* years to crack with today's technology.

---

[166] "Password Recovery Speeds," http://www.lockdown.co.uk/?pg=combi&s=articles, April 4, 2006.

- For upper- and lowercase letters and numbers along with other characters (the ones over the number keys), an eight-character password took up to 83.5 days for even the best systems to crack.

The key point to remember in this is that if you make your password twenty characters long, you have a good chance of making it impossible to hack the password with today's technology (which is, of course, subject to change as computers continue to advance, or should a new algorithm be discovered for cracking passwords). However, if you use a password of less than six characters, it can be defeated in less than a day by those with access to the right know-how and equipment.

HOW TO GET YOUR IDEAL ENCRYPTION SOFTWARE

Probably the best bet for encryption today is still Pretty Good Privacy (PGP). It's used by most major corporations, as well as by 90 percent of *Fortune* magazine's top-ten commercial banks, so most of us could do worse.

You can find a freeware version of the program available for virtually every computer platform, from Amiga and DOS to various flavors of Windows and the MAC OS. (A good listing of available freeware versions of PGP can be found at http://web.mit.edu/network/pgp.html).

Or if you want to spend some money and get the very newest version of the program, you can purchase it from the PGP Corporation at www.pgp.com.

The main thing to keep in mind in downloading PGP is that your source should be dependable. Otherwise, you might install a program that has been modified or to which a backdoor has been added.

Think a little before downloading security software, and you can save yourself a world of grief.

USING PGP WITH E-MAIL

Because PGP-encrypted messages consist of ASCII characters, it's possible to encrypt text, highlight and copy it, and then paste it into a text-only e-mail message. This makes it possible to encrypt e-mails even if the e-mail program you have lacks PGP capabilities.

With major e-mail programs there are plug-ins that allow you to encrypt messages without having to cut and paste text. Often all that's necessary is to select a heading on the program menu, pick the public key of the person you want to encrypt a message for, and a moment later, the coded text is ready to send, right in a new e-mail.

For those using Mozilla e-mail programs (such as Thunderbird), Enigmail is a free plug-in that permits the use of an installed version of PGP to automatically encrypt your e-mail. This program, along with the free e-mail programs that use it, is available at www.enigmail.mozdev.org.

PGP e-mail plug-ins are also available for Eudora and Outlook Express. You may have to pay for one of these (which is only fair—the PGP Corporation should make money for continued development of this software, after all). So if a little Googling doesn't locate a plugin for your email, you will either need to cut and past encryption into it or purchase a commercial version of PGP.

It should be noted that there are also programs available to employ PGP for encrypting files on a hard drive (PGPdisk) as well as to encrypt Internet phone calls (PGPfone). About the only catch with these is that encrypting or decrypting disk space on a hard drive can take time, making this useful for material you really want to protect, but not ideal for a whole hard drive that you're likely to use on a regular basis.

TIP

When generating your public and private keys with PGP, remember that the larger the key you create, the more secure the encryption will be. For example, a 40-bit key can be broken in just hours with a modern computer while a 128-bit key will take 309,485,009,821,341,068,724,781,056 times as long to break!

Steganography

Instead of attaching an encrypted e-mail to a file or encrypting files that are stored on a disk or drive, it is also possible to take encrypted messages and place them within the data of a digital photograph or picture. This technique is known as *steganography*, meaning "hidden writing" in Greek.

Currently, steganography is not practical for most people, but does lend itself to those who want to post snapshots online that can then be downloaded and a message extracted from it. Since pictures of various types are posted all over the Internet and sprinkled throughout most hard drives, messages hidden in a picture will sometimes escape undue attention (unless someone suspects that steganography might be in use, of course). Because of the possibility of discovery, it is always wise to encrypt messages hidden in pictures. While many steganography programs do encrypt data, it's better to first encrypt a message in a program like PGP and *then* hide it in a picture. That way, should the message be discovered in the picture, it still will resist being deciphered.

Among the steganography programs currently available:

- Steganography from SecureKit (www.securekit.com)
- Peter Gutmann's S-Tools (which is a little hard to find, but can generally be located with a Google search).
- 4t HIT Mail Privacy Lite (www.4t-niagara.com/hitmail.html)
- Camouflage (camouflage.unfiction.com/), which is similar in concept, hiding messages inside Word documents rather than pictures.

ISP Trail

The various techniques outlined above are ideal for protecting your computer from snoops that might enter your home and try to access files or discover detrimental things about you. But this will not necessarily stop government snoops or others with access to your ISP. In such a case, it is very possible that lists of what sites you've visited, what you've downloaded, and perhaps even e-mail you have sent and received will all be available for inspection with a court order—and perhaps even without one, should claims be made that you *might* be a terrorist, for example.

As this is written, the 1996 federal Electronic Communications Transactional Records Act is still in effect. This law requires ISPs to retain their records for ninety days if requested to do so by a federal "governmental entity." This preservation of data makes it possible for a government agency to sift it for compromising or criminal documents, or even to copy vast amounts of information that can then be stored on government computers.

There is a push to make storage of data more wide-ranging and for longer periods of time. For example, in 2006, attorney general Alberto R. Gonzales suggested that he would be engaging in some arm twisting among Internet Service Providers in order to get them to retain records for a longer—and as yet unspecified—time. This was to help in the Project Safe Childhood push to stop child pornographers, though obviously it has ramifications for all Internet users, not just those engaged in illegal activities. In an April 2006 speech, Gonzales said:[167]

> As the chief law-enforcement officer of the United States, my job is to investigate and prosecute crimes against our children. Changes in technology have made that much more difficult. And of course, privacy rights must always be accommodated and protected as we conduct our investigations. But I fear that if we do not do more—if parents, community, business, civic, industry, and political leaders do not work better together, then we will lose this fight on behalf of our children. And so today my message to the American people focuses on two categories of cases: sexual enticement of minors and child pornography. . . .
>
> As a result, I have asked the appropriate experts at the Department to examine this issue and provide me with proposed recommendations. And I will reach out personally to the

---

[167] "Prepared Remarks of Attorney General Alberto R. Gonzales at the National Center for Missing and Exploited Children," U.S. Justice Department, Alexandria, VA, April 20, 2006.

CEOs of the leading service providers, and to other industry leaders, to solicit their input and assistance. Record retention by Internet service providers consistent with the legitimate privacy rights of Americans is an issue that must be addressed.

This all sounds great. Who is going to argue that fighting child pornography is not a worthy goal?

Yet one is left with the troubling questions of whether it is really wise to let the government rather than a group protecting citizens' rights determine what is "consistent with the legitimate privacy rights of Americans," especially by a man who apparently believes that in order to deal with terrorists (and one might suspect, pedophiles), waiving a few privacy rights here and there is perfectly acceptable.

Equally vague is exactly what records will be retained and for how long. What might seem "reasonable" to those wanting to have their law-enforcement jobs made easier might be quite different from the ideals of those interested in privacy. In such a case, is it wise to let the law-enforcement community make this decision? Yet that appears to be just the course our nation is currently following.

> When you access the Internet and send unencrypted e-mail, assume that someone may be looking over your virtual shoulder.
>
> **TIP**

ANONYMOUS BROWSING

For those who want to go to the effort, it is possible to browse the Internet anonymously.

While ideally an Internet Service Provider would give you a different IP address every time you logged on, the aftermath of 9/11 —as well as the push to stop file sharing over the Internet—has led to most ISPs yielding to the pressure to assign IP addresses that remain for some time, with a specific user at a specific billing address.

This means that a variety of snoops might collect information about you and later use it against you. For example, a government agency trolling for people illegally sharing software might assemble a Web site that appears to be catering to file trading, when in fact it is a government agency running the operation, collecting the IP numbers of anyone uploading or downloading pirated software. The agency could then contact the ISP and ask to whom the IP number belongs, and then issue an arrest warrant for that person. The agency would have evidence of illegal file trading and be ready to take a culprit to court.

Much the same thing has happened with thousands of file sharers using third-party file-trading programs like BitTorrent and early versions of Napster. Record companies and movie studios went online, and then searched for the e-mail addresses or IP numbers that were exposed on these systems. The record company or movie corporation then issued some John Doe warrants in the jurisdiction where the ISP for the IP number was, and the court ordered the ISP to turn over the name and address of the file trader, who then got threatened with a lawsuit (with the options of either having to cough up a settlement of thousands of dollars or go to the expense of going to court to defend himself).

The situation is even worse in China and other repressive nations, where governments can link IP numbers to citizens visiting sites advocating more freedom or changes in government. In these nations, browsing at a verboten site can become a criminal offense that sends the user to jail.

Currently, it appears that some companies—other than ISPs—may also link IP addresses to users. There has been some speculation that some online e-mail services might link an IP to a person's name. This makes sense from the programmer's standpoint, since it would make it harder for someone to log onto an e-mail system if they weren't using the right computer—and therefore could be seen as a way to prevent hackers from gaining access to other people's accounts. But the danger here is that if a company had, say, both an e-mail service and a search engine, it might link a person's name and IP to all sorts of other information about them—from what sites they visited, to what keywords they've used in searches.

Of course, this would be a concern if you were a criminal. But criminals are not the only ones concerned with Internet privacy. In addition to dissidents, people communicating socially sensitive information in, say, a forum for rape victims, or those with serious illnesses, might prefer that the whole world didn't know their history or be able to link what they say online to a physical address.

Likewise, whistleblowers or journalists filing stories sensitive to governments would ideally not have computers shouting who and where they are. And businesses would often benefit from anonymous browsing, since it would make it harder to determine what the company might be researching or what new products it might have coming online—both of which might be betrayed by searches and visits to various sites.

It is not hard to imagine a situation where an innocent search might attract government attention. A student doing a research paper on terrorism or drug abuse might very well type in strings of words that normally would be associated with terrorists or illegal drug manufacturers. While it would be an extreme example, it isn't too far-fetched to imagine someone coming under extra scrutiny in such a case—or perhaps even waking in the dead of night to a raid by government agents.

Yes, there would be benefits in being able to hide your computer's IP address from sites you visit and searches you might conduct, even if governments around the world would prefer you weren't able to do so.

There are a few avenues that might be exploited for privacy, one being open WiFi systems that permit anyone to log onto the Internet. These are sometimes offered by coffee shops, certain areas, and entire cities. Provided a person was careful not to leave identifying tracks behind, these might permit anonymous browsing.

A second type of browsing might be done in a public library or with on-campus computers, both of which are sometimes open and can be used without a card or other ID. Some of these are "Net Nannied," however, with users prevented from accessing sites that might present legal problems to the organizations that own the computers.

The key to using such a system is to have a portable computer (one that you purchased with cash) to use with almost no user names and/or passwords that might be traced back to you, and to surf only sites that don't require passwords. Obviously this is pretty tame use of the Net, and most likely would be as easily and safely done at home.

ANONYMOUS PROXY SITES

Another way of anonymous browsing that will permit escape from some types of snooping is to connect to an anonymous proxy site (usually to be found with a Google search). These sites permit you to surf "through" them so that the only thing that is "seen" by the computer being visited is the IP number of the site hosting the proxy server. That means a government collecting IP numbers will come to a dead end, unable to go beyond that site's IP number.

One of the newer anonymous proxy systems is Tor, sponsored in part by the EFF (Electronic Frontier Foundation—arguably one of the thorns in the side of governments trying to collect data on individuals). Tor couples software on a local computer with the ability to jump from one computer to another within the Tor system. Once it makes a contact with one of the Tor systems, the data it sends is encrypted and then sent to other computers in the system. Finally, the data is decrypted and sent to the original "target" that the user aimed to contact.

This leapfrogging and encryption prevents Web sites from tracking users beyond the decryption computer, and even permits connecting to news sites, instant-messaging services, or the like in countries where these sites are normally blocked. Journalists and government agents in foreign countries also sometimes use Tor to connect to sites that are sensitive in nature. Interestingly, U.S. law-enforcement agencies also use Tor to hide their government IP addresses so they can conduct sting operations.

ANONYMOUS SURFING BROWSERS

For years there has been speculation that Microsoft software might have backdoors built into programs, or that the software was designed to hide information that could be accessed secretly by government agencies.

Whether or not this is true, Microsoft's programs often create privacy concerns, especially in the case of the Internet Explorer browser in its current and previous renditions. For this reason, those interested in security would do well to browse with a non-MS program that has tidier data storage, and is therefore easier to "clean up" after when deleting data caches, search history, what sites have been visited, etc.

By selecting a browser that is more privacy friendly, it is possible to delete files and otherwise cover your tracks on the computer you use to browse on (but not, as noted above, on the ISP side of things beyond your computer). This may be the only protection you need if you are concerned about a private detective snooping in your computer system, identity theft, or similar situations where your personal computer is likely to be the target, since the snoop won't have access to your ISPs or their records.

At this time, one good choice for increased surfing privacy is Firefox, coupled with the "Stealth" extension, a small subprogram that runs inside the browser to disable your browsing history, delete cookies when the browser is closed, delete records of downloaded files, get rid of the disk cache used by the browser, and delete information from forms filled out while online. This extension also gets rid of the "referrer" header most browsers allow, showing what site you came from when using a link to reach another site. These actions pretty much leave a clean computer, without any hints as to what sites you might have visited while you were on the Net. (However, some of this data might need to be wiped, as outlined above, in order to be completely inaccessible.)

Another option is to use the Safari browser in its "Private Browsing" mode, which does much the same thing.

ABOUT THOSE COOKIES

Most people are aware that small bits of code, called *cookies*, are often employed by Web sites to keep track of visitors. The cookie can contain a variety of information, including your name, address, passwords, and so forth, according to what forms you fill out, as well as a list of what pages you visit at a site. In theory, a cookie will only be accessed from the site that generates it, though there has always been a fear among consumers (as well as some security experts) that it might be possible for one site to access the cookies from other sites, thereby gaining information about the user.

There are advantages to using cookies, for consumers as well as Web sites and businesses. However, there is the usual downside to such loss of privacy. While it is possible to run a browser without cookies, some sites will not allow you to access them without the cookies turned on.

One useful compromise is to select the option on a browser that keeps the cookies only as long as the browser is open. (This option is available on Firefox and other browsers.) Once you're done with your session, closing the browser deletes all the cookies.

Stalkers, Here I Am

Over the last few years, the Internet has seen a variety of sites that promote the idea of being an online community. One form of this is dating sites; these promise the possibility of finding one's soul mate (or a one-night stand, depending on the site) by offering to link people not just from their own community but to other like-minded people around the world. Facebook, Xanga, Bebo, Buznet, TagWorld, MySpace, and similar sites have become popular among young people for the same reason.

Other virtual communities offer artists, nerds, or hobbyists the chance to engage in online chats with people who have similar interests, allowing them to trade ideas and pictures and otherwise carry on exchanges. They offer a sense of community, and can bring together people that are separated by continents and would never meet were it not for such online communities.

Although these sites all give the illusion that a visitor is intimate only with a few people, in truth, any pictures, home addresses, or diary-style blogs can be viewed by any visitor, including stalkers, law-enforcement personnel, or employers. Many colleges and high schools now have staff regularly trolling through student sites for possibly incriminating statements or photos.

What people, and especially teenagers, post on these sites can be nothing short of breathtaking. While most of the exchanges and postings are quite innocent, some are not. Obscene photos, suggestive messages, and compromising confessions can be found from time to time on these sites. Some high school students have even been arrested after posting photos online of crimes they've already committed, or detailed plans for upcoming crimes.[168]

Much of this material will remain online this side of forever or, even if removed from the sites, may remain in digital archives. As Professor Steve Jones, a University of Illinois-Chicago communications teacher, noted about this situation with some of these postings:[169]

> Some of these are incredibly incriminating. I wouldn't be surprised if twenty years from now, somebody who's running for an office has to answer a lot of questions as to what they had on MySpace twenty years ago. . . . In the future, if Google buys Facebook, who's to say they're not going to make all Facebook content searchable?

Actually, companies already are searching for data on employees at sites like these. In looking into this possibility, columnist Michelle Conlin discovered:[170]

> Search engines make it possible for employers to scour all manner of digital dirt to vet employees. Online profile company Ziggs.com CEO Tim DeMello fired an intern after he discovered that on the intern's Facebook profile, he divulged that while at Ziggs he would "spend most of my days screwing around on IM and talking to my friends and getting paid for it. . . ." For lawyers, Google is paradise, often delivering more damning information than the discovery process does.

Many sites encourage a feeling of safety by claiming the site is policed by people who will maintain privacy, or (as is the case with Facebook) that only people who are university students will be allowed at the site. But neither is quite the truth, since many univer-

---

[168] Jimmy Greenfield and David Haugh, "When What Happens On MySpace Doesn't Stay on MySpace," *Chicago Tribune*, April 30, 2006.

[169] *Ibid*.

[170] Michelle Conlin, "You Are What You Post," *BusinessWeek Online*, March 17, 2006.

sities permit faculty members or police departments to obtain college e-mail addresses that give them access to the system as well.[171]

Remember that any Web site allowing you to create a profile of yourself is like a public bulletin board, and one that is hanging in the seediest part of town. Anything posted at such a site may be examined by anyone, from the most innocent of individuals to stalkers or government agents. Think before posting, and never place your home address or personal details online.

It's also important to remember that a criminal can leverage even a seemingly innocent bit of information to gain an advantage over his victim. While researching this book I visited several pages designed for high school and college students (and this was *after* the big media coverage bubble of MySpace in mid-2006, when news reporters were warning that many students had entered extensive information about themselves online). Even though the sites had been cleaned of information and users warned to never post anything that was overly personal, a few dangerous tidbits were often still to be found.

For example, a high school senior (let's call her Sally Zank) posted a page listing her hometown, along with the college she was planning to attend the next fall. She gave no phone number or street address, but she did state the name of her boyfriend, Billy, who was already going to the same college.

With just these bits of information, a stalker might easily obtain her phone number, since she lives in a small town and her last name isn't common. And if it were common—say, "Smith," for example—he could simply keep calling the various Smiths in town, asking for Sally, until he gets the right house or reaches someone who knows Sally and is willing to give out her number.

Next, a stalker could use a reverse listing (available on the Internet) to get her home address by simply entering her phone number. Once he had that, he could get in his car, visit her town, and sit in front of the house and observe for a while. He could easily identify her from her picture on the Internet. He might then

---

[171] Jimmy Greenfield and David Haugh, *Ibid.*

wait until he sees her at home without her parents, and then go running to the door and hammer on it.

When she came to the door, he could say something like, "Hi. You're Sally, aren't you? I recognized you from one of the photos Billy has—I'm his friend."

At this point she may supply a name: "Harvey?"

"Yeah. Billy's been in an accident. It's pretty serious. He's asking to see you. His parents are at the hospital already—they asked me to drive over and pick you up so I can take you to see him."

At this point her defenses would be down, and he might be able to force his way into the house and rape her at knifepoint, or worse. Or, if she agreed to ride to the hospital, he might get her into the car and be halfway to his house before she's any the wiser, at which point a knife or pistol might be employed to keep her from escaping.

The act of sharing just the tiniest bit of information can place a person in danger when a criminal can exploit it toward his own ends.

BACKING OUT

If you have created an account at Facebook, MySpace, or a similar site, you should immediately remove it if possible. Barring that, go to the site and remove everything that might give information about you, including your phone number, what city you live in, where your children live, various names of family members, etc.

Have your children do the same. Even preteens can be a serious source of data leaks when they join such a site, and often they may lie about their age to do so, exposing them to possible predators.

Explain to your child why it's important not to disclose personal information, and then regularly check on children's profiles and general computer use to be sure they're not doing anything that might be dangerous.

UNLISTING YOUR PERSONAL INFORMATION

You can get your address and phone number removed from most online directories. To quickly locate any listing of information about you, go to a search engine and type in your name

SOLUTIONS

and address, or name and phone number. Then go to the pages listed. Most listings will have an "opt-out" form that you can use to remove information about yourself from their system.

Key systems that may have personal addresses and other information about you online include:

- AnyWho.com
- PhoneNumber.com
- WhitePages.com
- Switchboard.com
- YellowPages.com
- Zabasearch.com
- Various reverse phone directories
- Google's various services

A little time spent tracking down online information about you and your family members and getting the data removed will greatly increase your privacy, and might even save you a lot of time and money. In an age of stalkers and other criminal activity, it could even save your life.

CHAPTER 7 DOLLARS AND SENSE

" No American should blindly accept reduction of their liberty simply because a government official says so. The choice is a nation of laws or a nation of whims. No liberty is possible with the latter, no matter how important the cause. "

— COMMENTATOR TOM DEWEESE[172] —

There are a number of government and corporate data-collection tools that, while created for lofty purposes, can also abuse your privacy. These encompass everything from government programs to data-mining corporations, from private snoops to identity thieves.

One massive government operation for collecting information about U.S. citizens is the FinCEN (Financial Crimes Enforcement Network) within the Treasury Department, a data-collection system that was launched in 1990. The operation quickly became the world's most-effective financial investigation unit, and is credited with helping Russian president Boris Yeltsin track down stolen Communist Party funds.

FinCEN collects data from a variety of government sources, including the IRS, FBI, DEA, and the Secret Service, as well as Customs and the U.S. Postal Inspection Agency. It is believed that it also can access data held by the CIA, and possibly the NSA and

---

[172] Tom DeWeese, "Future American Lawyers Take a Stand for Freedom," americanpolicy.org/priv/main.htm, American Policy Center, April 24, 2006.

the Defense Intelligence Agency. It seems likely that it might also access data purchased from private data-mining groups.

FinCEN often snags bad guys when it compares how much they are claiming to be making legitimately to how much they are spending for land, cars, or other property. If the income and outlays don't seem to jive, then agents can dig deeper to look for possible criminal activity.

Having a system in play that can combine the various databases and private data-mining information and compile it into massive files is somewhat troubling for those concerned about a Big Brother future. Like other systems explored in this book, FinCEN can do a lot of good in bringing criminals to justice, yet also has a breathtaking potential for abuse.

Know Your Customer

In 1970 the U.S. Congress enacted the Bank Secrecy Act, which dictated that bank employees should report any transactions involving $10,000 or more in a single account during a single day, since this might occur with money laundering or when people were engaged in illegal transactions. Reports were made to the Treasury Department, which claimed that the reports, coupled with the records kept on customers by banks, would "have a high degree of usefulness in criminal, tax, and regulatory investigations and proceedings."[173]

In 1999 the state banking institutions in the Federal Reserve System launched the Know Your Customer program, which went further, including requiring banks to report anything that seemed suspicious. This measure was put into law with the USA Patriot Act in 2001, giving the U.S. Department of the Treasury the power to induce banks to collect and file data about customers for possible use by the government in criminal investigations.

The banks disliked these laws about as much as many customers did, since it transformed bank employees into virtual spies, forcing them to report even longtime customers when various criteria were met, and in the process most likely placing customers

---

[173] 112 USC Sec. 1829b and 12 USC Sec. 1951.

under varying degrees of government surveillance as if they were suspected drug dealers or money launderers.

Nor were the thresholds all that high. The Department of the Treasury requires financial institutions to report "suspicious transactions relevant to a possible violation of law or regulation."[174] According to the Treasury, reports are to be made on:[175]

- Insider abuse involving any amount
- Violations aggregating $5,000 or more where a suspect can be identified
- Violations aggregating $25,000 or more regardless of a potential suspect
- Transactions aggregating $5,000
- Amounts that involve "potential" money laundering or violations of the Bank Secrecy Act

Not surprisingly, most of those individuals reported for "suspicious activities" or who exhibit the "potential" for engaging in money laundering are just regular citizens who have come into some cash or who are getting ready to take a vacation. Consequently, there are huge backlogs of reports that have overwhelmed the system, thereby defeating its potential to actually catch criminals. Furthermore, terrorists and actual money launderers have apparently created a variety of systems, from trading gold and diamonds to nontraditional banking systems designed to circumvent the surveillance.[176]

The constitutionality of the Bank Secrecy Law was challenged in *California Bankers Assn v. Schultz, 416 US 21 (1974)*. Supreme Court Justice William O. Douglas felt the Bank Secrecy Act was unconstitutional, writing:[177]

---

[174] 31 USC Sec. 5318(g)(1).

[175] U.S. Treasury Department, http://www.treas.gov/fincen/forms.html#90.

[176] Paul Byles, "Does 'Know Your Customer' work?" Cayman Net News, www.caymannetnews.com/2005/07/886/work.shtml, July 25, 2005.

[177] Rep. Ron Paul, Joint Hearing on Bank Secrecy Act Reporting Requirements, Subcommittee on General Oversight and Investigations, Subcommittee on Financial Institutions and Consumer Credit, House Committee on Banking and Financial Services, April 20, 1999.

It is, I submit, sheer nonsense to agree with the Secretary that all bank records of every citizen "have a high degree of usefulness in criminal, tax, or regulatory investigations or proceedings." That is unadulterated nonsense unless we are to assume that every citizen is a crook, an assumption I cannot make. A mandatory recording of all telephone conversations would be better than the recording of checks under the Bank Secrecy Act, if Big Brother is to have his way.

In the same case, Supreme Court Justice Thurgood Marshall warned that such laws would cause the gradual erosion of our constitutional rights, noting,[178]

[The] crucial factor is that the Government has shown no need, compelling or otherwise, for the maintenance of such records. Surely the fact that some may use negotiable instruments for illegal purposes cannot justify the Government's running roughshod over the First Amendment rights of the hundreds of lawful yet controversial organizations like the ACLU. Congress may well have been correct in concluding that law enforcement would be facilitated by the dragnet requirements of this Act. Those who wrote our Constitution, however, recognized more important values.

During the 1999 congressional hearings into Know Your Customer regulations, Solveig Singleton, a lawyer from the Cato Institute, had these words to say (and they are every bit as relevant today as they were when he spoke them):[179]

The "Know Your Customer" proposal fosters mistrust and resentment of government. . . . People know the difference between being treated as a citizen and being treated as a suspect. Imagine the anger and fear that recent immigrants, African Americans, and Hispanics will feel, knowing their

---

[178] *Ibid.*

[179] Solveig Singleton, lawyer, testimony to U.S. House of Representatives Committee on the Judiciary, Subcommittee on Commercial and Administrative Law, Oversight Hearing, "The 'Know Your Customer' Rules: Privacy in the Hands of Federal Regulators," 1999.

banks are recording information about their jobs and patterns of withdrawals and deposits.

The proposal sidesteps the Fourth Amendment. . . . The "Know Your Customer" proposal forces banks to become agents of the police, spying and reporting on their own customers—without ever obtaining a warrant. It's an end run around our constitutional rights of privacy. Unless and until the police have probable cause to suspect someone of a crime, where he gets his money is none of the government's business. . . .

In a free society, there's no need to turn private businesses into spy agencies. . . . The "Know Your Customer" rule has no place in a free country.

Customers who are reported are never told when a form is filled out about them.[180] Furthermore, since most banks will be intent on avoiding various fines and investigations surrounding failure to report possible criminal activities, the threshold of what constitutes "unusual activities" becomes quite low. It isn't hard to imagine that the recommendation is to report anything rather than risk punishment for missing something.

Thus, there is a lot of data collected on citizens, with very little information that is useful for fighting crime. After noting that there are over 100,000 reports collected on innocent bank customers for each conviction of money laundering, Lawrence Lindsey (who became head of the George W. Bush administration's National Economic Council in 2001) wrote, "That ratio of 99,999-to-1 is something we normally would not tolerate as a reasonable balance between privacy and the collection of guilty verdicts."[181]

If it takes 100,000 searches to find a single criminal, one might argue that these searches are simply fishing expeditions, conducted

---

[180] Gregory T. Nojeim, Legislative Counsel, Testimony on Know Your Customer, Commercial and Administrative Law Subcommittee of the House of Representatives Committee on the Judiciary, March 4, 1999.

[181] Lawrence Lindsey, *The Future of Financial Privacy*, Competitive Enterprise Institute, 2000.

on a massive scale. One might also argue that Americans, by and large, must be amazingly honest given that so many who come under government scrutiny are never charged with illegal activities.

Banking and Terrorism

Most people assume that savings and checking account records are handled in-house by banking institutions. That assumption is partially true. However, a lot of data is regularly shuffled not only from branch to branch, but often across the country—or even halfway around the world—as funds and records are transferred electronically from one bank to another.

Banks work to maintain security during each step of the process in this trading of electronic data. However, like all records, banking data is regularly subjected to government scrutiny, often without any notice being given to the customer.

Some of these investigations are massive in scale. In mid-2006, it became public that following the 9/11 attacks in 2001, the Bush administration had started sifting through records handled by the Belgium-based SWIFT banking consortium (which processes millions of financial transactions daily), looking for ties between U.S. citizens and Middle Eastern terrorists.[182]

After a few brief days of coverage in the press, the story of the SWIFT monitoring was all but dropped, with the biggest uproar surrounding charges that the revelation of the operation might somehow damage government efforts to capture terrorists—despite the fact that terrorists had learned to circumvent discovery in a variety of ways, from trading drugs and diamonds to the use of informal Islamic banking systems. There was only a mild outcry because private records were being examined by government agencies with only self-imposed limitations on what might be done with the data.

Thus, it seems likely that few if any real terrorists were ever thwarted through these searches of the SWIFT data, and that by all but ignoring the revelations that such searches were being

---

[182] Paul Blustein, "Search of Banking Records Raises Privacy Concerns," *The Washington Post*, June 25, 2006.

conducted, the public once again demonstrated its willingness to trade privacy for a very modest gain in security.

USPS's Eagle's Eye

In 1997, the U.S. Postal Service adopted a system similar to Know Your Customer. The "Under the Eagle's Eye" program trains postal clerks to report unusual purchases of money orders. Here's how Representative Ron Paul described Under the Eagle's Eye:[183]

> Postal employees must report purchases of money orders of over $3,000 to federal law-enforcement officials. The program also requires postal clerks to report any "suspicious behavior" by someone purchasing a money order. . . . [T]he guidelines for reporting "suspicious behavior" are so broad that anyone whose actions appear to a postal employee to be the slightest bit out of the ordinary could become the subject of a "suspicious activity report," and a federal investigation!

> As postal officials admitted . . . the Post Office is training its employees to assume those purchasing large money orders are criminals. . . . This policy turns the presumption of innocence, which has been recognized as one of the bulwarks of liberty since medieval times, on its head. Allowing any federal employee to assume the possibility of a crime based on nothing more than a subjective judgment of "suspicious behavior" represents a serious erosion of our constitutional rights to liberty, privacy, and due process.

Information contained in the Under the Eagle's Eye training course bolster Paul's arguments:[184]

- According to the training manual, "The rule of thumb is, if it seems suspicious to you, then it is. As we said before, and will say again, it is better to report many legitimate transactions that seem suspicious than let one illegal one slip through."

- "Regina Goodclerk," an angel who appears in the training film, constantly urges an actor (who is pictured as a postal

---

[183] Ron Paul, Congressional Record, Extensions of Remarks, June 27, 2001, page E1219.

[184] John Berlau, "Postal Service Has Its Eye on You," *Insight*, July 14, 2001.

clerk) to file suspicious-activity reports on any customers who are the least bit suspicious.

- "Sam Slick," the devil, appears in the training film. He wants to give customers the benefit of the doubt by assuming they may be innocent.

- The manual instructs postal employees that anyone who refuses to produce identification and fill out a form should obviously be reported. "Whatever the reason, any customer who switches from a transaction that requires an 8105-A form to one that doesn't should earn himself or herself the honor of being described on a B form."

Exactly what happens to reports filled out by postal clerks is unclear, though it would seem likely they are forwarded to FinCEN for processing given that it is involved in sifting through and linking various government sources of information including that from the US Postal Service.

EASY DOES IT

If you're aware of the various points at which reports about cash and money order use must be reported, you can often work around them to avoid undue attention from the government. However, it is important to note that "structuring" deposits or money order purchases to avoid attracting attention is, in itself, a reason to file a report on you, and can end up attracting more attention than if you simply deposited one large amount into an account or purchased one large money order from the bank.

It also seems likely that non-banking institutions that wire money (such as Wells Fargo) work with the government and file reports, even though they are not legally required to do so, so don't be tempted to think of these as risk-free substitutes for bank or postal services.

CHAPTER 8 BIG BROTHER

" In a society perpetually altered by human innovation, we are faced with the elementary problem of keeping the law apace with technology. In particular, the explosion of video surveillance and microcamera technology has had a profound impact upon our concept of privacy. As video surveillance equipment has become smaller, more portable, more easily concealed, and more accessible to the general public, its pervasive application has contributed to today's cultural fascination with voyeurism. **"**

— LANCE E. ROTHENBERG,[185]

FORMER EDITOR OF THE *AMERICAN UNIVERSITY LAW REVIEW*

Today when a crime is committed in a public spot, day or night, chances are good that the police can obtain photos of the crime as it was committed. This is possible thanks to the huge number of cameras that now dot the urban landscape, from the inside of stores to their parking lots outside, from ATM machines that photograph not only customers but anyone within yards of the device, to individuals with cameras on their cell phones or other handheld electronic devices. In some cities, the police even have cameras mounted on street-light poles in areas with high levels of crime.

---

[185] Lance E. Rothenberg, "Re-Thinking Privacy: Peeping Toms, Video Voyeurs, and the Failure of Criminal Law to Recognize a Reasonable Expectation of Privacy in the Public Space," *American University Law Review*, June 18, 2001.

This is one of those double-edged swords that we've seen throughout this book. Although this level of surveillance is great if you wish to catch criminals, it's not so good if you wish to move about freely and privately. And the high level of surveillance would obviously be a marvelous tool for those wishing to abuse their powers at one level or another.

Nor is the trade-off as rosy as is often painted by government officials intent on putting surveillance cameras on every street corner. Over the last couple of decades, England has mounted a massive anticrime program that poured three-fourths of its crime-fighting budget, over £170 million from 1999 to 2003, into Closed-Circuit TV (CCTV) monitoring systems.[186] It was hoped that these would enable the police to stop a variety of crimes.

Despite contentions by the police that these cameras were a powerful deterrent to crime, a study conducted by the British Home Office, which evaluated twenty-two CCTV systems in both Britain and the U.S., concluded that CCTV systems prevented crime in only a very insignificant way. A second study on lighting found that improved lighting on dark streets had a much more significant deterrent effect on crime.[187]

The potential for abuse with on-the-street cameras is always a worry as well. This is not just a matter of speculation, since police officers and others charged with monitoring cameras are on occasion found to be peering into bedroom windows or otherwise spying on innocent people who have done nothing but foolishly forget about potential Peeping Toms manning police cameras. For example:

- In 2004 two CCTV operators in England were arrested for peering into a woman's flat for hours, filming her cuddling with a boyfriend, undressing, using the toilet, and having a bath.[188]

---

[186] "CCTV 'Not a Crime Deterrent'," news.bbc.co.uk/2/hi/uk_news/2192911.stm, BBC News, August 14, 2002.

[187] *Ibid.*

[188] Lester Haines, "CCTV Peeping Toms Jailed," *The Register*, January 13, 2006.

- A British film compilation called Caught in the Act was released, comprised of CCTV street videos shot by British surveillance cameras. Included were sex acts and other intimate contacts of both criminals and innocent citizens alike.[189]
- A police officer in Brooklyn, New York, complained to his superiors (with the story later getting picked up by the press) that fellow officers running surveillance cameras were regularly taking pictures of civilian women simply to collect shots of their breasts or backsides.[190]

Even if camera use weren't abused and CCTV systems acted as a deterrent to crime, one might also ask if their use was worth the cost, not only in terms of dollars but also in terms of our privacy and freedom. As journalist Jacob Sullum noted when Washington, D.C., starting placing cameras in public places,[191]

> Even in a country with a tradition of limited government, knowing that you are being watched by armed government agents tends to put a damper on things. You don't want to offend them or otherwise call attention to yourself, so you are not quite as free as you would otherwise be.
>
> When police are invisible but still watching, people conscious of the surveillance will still change their behavior to avoid being conspicuous. Meanwhile, people who don't know about the cameras or who forget about them . . . may receive uncomfortable scrutiny even though they are doing nothing illegal.

After visiting in England, journalist Jeffrey Rosen made a similar observation, noting that no matter whether the crime went up or down, more cameras were called for in public places:[192]

---

[189] Barry Steinhardt, "Law Enforcement Should Support Privacy Laws for Public Video Surveillance," Address to the International Association of Police Chiefs and the Security Industry Association, April 8, 1999.

[190] *Ibid.*

[191] Jacob Sullum, "Are You Camera-Ready?" Creators Syndicate Inc., February 15, 2002.

[192] Jeffrey Rosen, "A Cautionary Tale for a New Age of Surveillance," *The New York Times*, October 7, 2001.

Last year, Britain's violent-crime rates actually increased by 4.3 percent, even though the cameras continued to proliferate. But CCTV cameras have a mysterious knack for justifying themselves regardless of what happens to crime. When crime goes up the cameras get the credit for detecting it, and when crime goes down, they get the credit for preventing it. If the creation of a surveillance society in Britain hasn't prevented terrorist attacks, it has had subtle but far-reaching social costs. . . .

There is, in the end, a powerfully American reason to resist the establishment of a national surveillance network: The cameras are not consistent with the values of an open society. They are technologies of classification and exclusion. They are ways of putting people in their place, of deciding who gets in and who stays out, of limiting people's movement and restricting their opportunities.

Photo Radar Cameras

Of course, while the public is being sold on all the benefits of such heavy surveillance, various government agencies are careful to avoid ever mentioning the downsides to loss of privacy. For example, the National Highway Traffic Safety Administration describes the photo radar cameras increasingly being used in many urban locales:[193]

> An extension of regular radar, this technology uses photography to capture the vehicle and license plate when the violation occurs. The date, time, and speed can be superimposed onto the photograph. Some can also capture the image of the operator in the picture.

> Photo radar can be used in manned or unmanned applications. It is usually used in jurisdictions where specific legislation permits its use and where vehicles have both front and rear plates. . . . It is effective if set up properly and can also be used to photograph traffic light violators. . . .

> The potential for detection is enormous since the violators are not stopped, but a permanent record is made of each for

---

[193] *The Highway Safety Desk Book*, National Highway Traffic Safety Administration, http://www.nhtsa.dot.gov/people/injury/enforce/deskbk.html#DIPL.

processing later. Photo radar is controversial because of the photographs and privacy issues. . . .

Photo radar eliminates any arguments about the speed of the vehicle from the discussion between an officer and the violator at the scene of an arrest and moves this discussion to an administrative or court hearing. Some feel that since the photo radar does not discriminate, that this method is the most fair type of speed enforcement that exists.

Things are not quite as clear-cut as the National Highway Traffic Safety Administration might have one believe. While the system is sold as a safety device, in fact, most municipalities see it as a moneymaking device. With the ability to gain somewhere around $70 per traffic fine, some municipalities, as well as the private companies that operate the cameras, yield to the temptation to tinker with the timing of stoplights in order to enhance the numbers of drivers snared. As Congressman Dick Armey noted during hearings about this system in 2001:[194]

If you listen to local politicians, you'll hear of the significant safety benefit provided to the community [by red-light cameras], and you'll hear indignation at any suggestion that profit is their true motive.

Newly uncovered documents from red-light camera programs in California and Arizona suggest otherwise. The camera lobby has been hiding the truth about how intersections are being left deliberately mistimed—a dangerous condition—for the sake of profit. . . .

Safety was never the primary consideration. In fact, none of the devices were placed at any of San Diego's top-ten most dangerous intersections. Instead, the documents tell us how the camera operators consciously sought out mistimed intersections as locations for new red-light cameras.

Yellow signal time at intersections turns out to be directly related to "red light running." Simply put, when the yellow light is short, more people enter on red. Inadequate yellow

---

[194] Dick Armey, "The Truth About Red Light Cameras," *Freedom Works*, July 20, 2001.

time causes a condition where individuals approaching an intersection are unable either to come to a safe stop or proceed safely before the light turns red.

Though dangerous, this condition also turns out to be very profitable. Each time someone ends up in an intersection on red in San Diego, the city collects $271. And $70 of that fine is paid as bounty to the city's private contractor. Combine hefty fines with mistimed signals and you've found the formula for big money. A single camera brought the city $6.8 million in just 18 months. . . .

Red-light camera revenue dries up when the intersections are not rigged against the motorist. And when the revenue goes away, so does the true motivation for Big Brother's high-tech speed traps.

So your loss of privacy in this case isn't increased safety, or an effort to keep police officer bias from entering the picture when issuing tickets. Rather, the motive is to make lots of money through the use of poorly timed stoplights.

It is interesting to read statements from city and police spokespeople when the public is being sold on the need for red-light cameras. For example when Providence, Rhode Island, was about to install such a system, the local paper carried a statement from the mayor that every day there were "hundreds of near-accidents" at intersections, and added that the revenue brought in by fines would raise revenue without the need to raise property taxes, all the while enhancing public safety. The paper added that when the company installing the cameras saw the traffic patterns, they "were thunderstruck by the frequency of violations."[195]

There's another trade-off, since poorly timed stoplights that force drivers to run red lights are also much more dangerous than properly timed lights. This translates not only into additional tickets, but also a potentially dangerous situation.

---

[195] Gregory Smith, "Red Light Now for Real," *Providence Journal*, April 28, 2006.

There have only been a few studies to determine whether red-light cameras actually increase safety. The Federal Highway Administration claimed in its study in 2005 that broadside crashes dipped 25 percent at sites with cameras, while rear-end crashes rose 15 percent.[196] Since rear-end crashes are less damaging to both vehicles and passengers, this study argued that red-light cameras really did reduce accidents somewhat.

However, an independent group of researchers, including a traffic consultant and a former senior researcher at Northwestern University's Center for Public Safety, hired by *The Washington Post*, found that just the opposite was true. After comparing accident rates between lights without cameras and those with cameras, they found that the traffic accident rates were the same or slightly higher at intersections *with* cameras.[197]

No Small Loss

While at first it might seem that recording the license plate of a speeder is no big thing, in fact, this is not all that is recorded, and there are ramifications far beyond a traffic ticket. The cameras actually capture a wide field of visual information in addition to the license plate number, including the face of the driver, a picture of passengers in the vehicle, and perhaps even what objects might be in the vehicle. Furthermore, other drivers and pedestrians who are in the area and innocent of any crime are also caught in many of the photos.

As technology intrudes into the courtroom, there's another odd situation that has yet to be addressed. In American courts, a person charged with a crime supposedly has the right to cross-examine or question his accuser in court; yet in this case, the "accuser" is a mechanical and electrical camera system at a distant intersection.

Does this violate the constitutional rights of motorists charged with running a red light? And what are the ramifications should other crimes be electronically detected and recorded in the

---

[196] Lynn Horsley, "Caught Red-Handed?" *Kansas City Star*, April 1, 2006.

[197] Del Quentin Wilber and Derek Willis, "DC Red-Light Cameras Fail to Reduce Accidents," *Washington Post*, October 4, 2005.

future? Does this automation of the law destroy not only privacy but legal rights as well?

Suppose, for example, that a crime were committed, and the criminal had driven in a certain direction. Red-light photos might be examined, and all those captured in the shots treated as suspects, when in fact the only suspicious thing they were guilty of was driving or walking along the street. In effect, the police are encouraged to create a wide dragnet of innocents and guilty alike, rather than attempt to identify suspects by more relevant and traditional methods.

Or imagine a ticket being sent to a house where a spouse opens the mail and discovers their significant other cruising the roadway with a secret lover. While one might argue that a cheating spouse deserves to be caught, one might also ask if this is the way to go about it.

Today, there are no real checks on who can access this data; indeed, it is likely that the data is being processed by a private company which then relays it to government agencies. Nor are there legal limits on the length of time for which the pictures can be stored for later inspection.

As the ACLU noted when these cameras were first being deployed years ago:[198]

> There are two issues of fundamental fairness with the cameras that affect the right to due process under the law. First, the tickets are sent to the owner of a car, who was not necessarily the person committing the alleged violation. The burden of proof usually then falls on the owner to prove he or she was not driving at the time. This is a violation of the bedrock American principle that the accused be considered innocent until proven guilty.
>
> Second, many red-light camera systems have been installed under contracts that deliver a cut of ticket revenue to the

---

[198] Barry Steinhardt, "ACLU Urges Halt to Use of Red-Light-Cameras Until Privacy and Fairness Issues Are Addressed," Press Release, American Civil Liberties Union, August 21, 2001.

contractor. That creates an obvious incentive to contractors to "game" the system in order to increase revenue. . . .

There are also important privacy issues raised by the cameras. The ACLU is most concerned about what we call "mission creep"—that the data collected by these cameras will be used for purposes other than tracking reckless drivers. Government and private-industry surveillance techniques created for one purpose are rarely restricted to that purpose, and every expansion of a data bank and every new use for the data opens the door to more and more privacy abuses.

Similar systems have already been used to invade privacy. For example, cameras installed at the Texas-Oklahoma border have been used to capture the license plate numbers of thousands of law-abiding persons, who were subjected to inquiries about why they were crossing the border. . . .

The issue of whether or not these cameras are legal remains unanswered, though one judge has gone so far as to shut down city cameras in Minneapolis after noting that the camera ordinance was invalid. The judge felt the ordinance did not provide vehicle owners with due process rights in court since it failed to prove "beyond a reasonable doubt" who was driving the vehicle.[199]

It will be interesting to see if courts and politicians in various states address this issue of due process. But with millions of dollars being generated by the cameras, it seems likely that rights will be ignored and more cameras will continue to appear in various cities across the U.S.

TAKING THE RED OUT

Some drivers have decided to fight back. Obviously, attacking the lights themselves is not a legal tactic, though no doubt a few have been attacked over the years. Likewise, avoiding routes that take a driver through red-light intersections is not always practical, though for some drivers it might be a consideration.

[199] David Chanen, "Photo Cop Hits Red Light," *Minneapolis Star Tribune*, March 15, 2006.

A more interesting trend is that of taking countermeasures that render the pictures ineffective. Toward this end, some drivers have taken to covering tags with reflective covers or spray-painting them with a clear but reflective paint (such as "PhotoBlocker," which is currently sold online for this purpose). These measures create a bright reflection when red-light cameras flash their pictures, causing an overexposed picture that (in theory at least) obscures the tag number of the car.

Special louver covers might obscure the tag from higher angles while leaving them visible from ground level. Currently all such systems appear to be legal throughout the U.S., though one can bet if enough motorists adopt these ploys, laws will be passed to make these modifications illegal.

However, it seems that the real solution for this problem would be to remove the cameras from intersections, since the devices fail to reduce traffic accidents in any meaningful way (and perhaps even increase the number of wrecks). This is unlikely to happen anytime soon, since many towns have found the cameras very profitable, serving as another hidden tax on the populace—even if it means eroding privacy to fill bureaucratic coffers.

Little Brother Watches

Of course, the prospect of having the government, police, and/or private security cameras watching your every move is troubling. But an even greater danger to privacy is actually presented by the explosion of small, cheap cameras that are now available, and which are often attached to cell phones, MP3 players, or other electrical devices. These lend themselves to abuses of privacy.

Stories of abuse abound. Over the last ten years there has been an explosion of such stories, often luridly detailed in U.S. newspapers. Here are just a few samples:

- An ice rink worker in Rochester, New York, was arrested for photographing women hockey players in their locker-room shower.[200]

---

[200] Patrick Flanigan, "Illicit Photos Could Net Jail Time," *Rochester Democrat and Chronicle*, February 27, 2005.

- A Newark, New Jersey, kindergarten teacher was caught videotaping pupils as they undressed in a closet.[201]
- A man who tiled showers also installed a camera in the home of a friend (no doubt an ex-friend now) and secretly recorded a woman as she bathed.[202]
- Hidden cameras were found in public showers at Yosemite National Park.[203]
- Some 250 male college athletes nationwide were videotaped by hidden cameras as they undressed, used the bathroom, or showered, with the tapes being sold as gay pornography.[204]
- Fifty-eight women were videotaped while undressing in a tanning salon.[205]

Such stories inspired the U.S. Congress to pass the Video Voyeurism Prevention Act in 2004. According to this law,[206]

Whoever, in the special maritime and territorial jurisdiction of the United States, has the intent to capture an image of a private area of an individual without their consent, and knowingly does so under circumstances in which the individual has a reasonable expectation of privacy, shall be fined under this title or imprisoned not more than one year, or both. . . .

There are a couple of reasons this law has no teeth. One is that it's just one more law on top of many, since it was already illegal under state laws to take such photographs. Thus, while this might send a few more Peeping Toms to jail, it is doubtful that it will do much to put an end to such practices, especially given that the ever-greater miniaturization of cameras continues.

[201] *Ibid.*
[202] Andrea Siegel, "Secret Tape of Woman in Bathroom Recorded," *Baltimore Sun*, August 13, 1999.
[203] "Hidden Cameras in Park Showers," *LA Times*, August 6, 1999.
[204] Linda Massarella, "Nude Jocks Steamed over Raw Footage," *New York Post*, August 10, 1999.
[205] Tony Rizzo, "Taping in Secret Leads to Jail Term: Hidden Cameras at Tanning Salon Recorded Patrons," *Kansas City Star*, January 13, 1999.
[206] "Video Voyeurism Prevention Act of 2004," U.S. Federal Public Law No: 108–495.

This threat is likely to grow over the next few years as more and more cell phones become equipped with cameras, and ever more people start using a cell phone rather than a conventional landline.

The other loophole in this law is that, like most state and local laws, it leaves an "out" for government agencies engaged in the same acts. The only difference is, they are doing their work under the cloak of national security or crime prevention. Thus, within the bill is a clause that reads: "This section does not prohibit any lawful law-enforcement, correctional, or intelligence activity."[207] "*Any*" covers a lot of ground. This law may also be counterproductive in exposing any law-enforcement infractions, since rule breakers now face jail sentences for misusing surveillance cameras. Exposure would also mean no little embarrassment to police departments. While one might hope that the law would reduce the abuse of CCTV systems by law-enforcement personnel, there will also most likely be a push within the bureaucracy to either quietly reprimand those breaking the rules in-house, in order to avoid sending them to jail, and/or to classify questionable practices as legitimate and therefore above legal scrutiny under this law.

Facial-Recognition Cameras

The 9/11 acts of terrorism were soon followed by calls for the installation of facial-recognition cameras at airports and other likely terrorist targets. This technology is designed to capture a digital picture of a person's face, and then compare key areas of that face to a database of known suspects, so that the culprit can be quickly singled out. In actual practice, the technology is not perfected, with recent testing displaying an effectiveness of about 43 percent in correctly sounding the alarm when a face was in the system database.[208]

Often systems can be "confused" by a person simply donning sunglasses, putting on a hat, or growing facial hair. Thus, in the real world, the system is apt to either miss a lot of targets in the system's database, or register false positives.

---

[207] William Matthews, "Civil Liberty Warnings Raised," *Federal Computer Week*, September 21, 2001.

[208] *Ibid.*

Despite this tendency toward poor performance, Tampa, Florida, tested a system at the SuperBowl XXXV in 2001, and later covered a sixteen-square-block area of the city with thirty-six cameras, scanning faces against a database of 30,000 images of offenders, prompting House majority leader Dick Armey to ask: "Do we really want a society where one cannot walk down the street without Big Brother tracking our every move? . . . [T]here's nowhere to turn for those who value their privacy."[209]

Despite the low reliability of facial-recognition software, work continues toward developing viable systems, sometimes with results that would be amusing were the situation not so serious. For example, the facial-recognition software designed to be used with German ePassports is thrown off when a person simply smiles—prompting new guidelines that told those running the equipment to warn people they must maintain a "neutral facial expression and look straight at the camera."[210]

Despite the setbacks, governments in England, the European Union, and the U.S. are all intent on adopting facial-recognition systems. Some of the cameras you walk by in the near future may be scanning your face and attempting to determine who you are. Perhaps they'll be thwarted if you happen to be wearing sunglasses—or grinning—as you pass the lens.

OnStar Is Watching You

Over the last few years, systems such as GM's OnStar have been added to more expensive cars that track their position via satellite. These devices allow the owner of the vehicle to call in to a live operator who can then give directions, call for assistance, or handle whatever the emergency might be. The system also automatically sends a distress signal should an air bag be deployed (thereby suggesting the likelihood of an accident).

This is all well and good, and undoubtedly has helped many a motorist and perhaps even saved some lives. However, many

---

[209] *Ibid.*

[210] Robert Jaques, "Smiling Germans Ruin Biometric Passport System," VNUNet, November 10, 2005.

owners don't realize that when they sign the agreement for this service, their tracking information may be turned over to government entities.[211] This is bad news if the government is interested in keeping track of where you've been.

Many car rental companies now have this technology as well, which they may be using to collect data on users. During a court case involving Acme Rent-a-Car, it was learned that the company had not only fined a customer $450 for speeding three different times while renting a car, but it had also recorded when the car crossed from one state to another, and even permitted the company to disable the vehicle remotely.[212]

Before signing up for a system that helps you while you're motoring, it might be wise to consider just how much information you want to have collected about you every time you go out for a drive. And when you rent a car, remember that your speed and route may be monitored at all times.

Black Box Spying

As most people know, commercial aircraft operated by American companies have recording devices known as black boxes built into them. These devices continuously record the voices of the flight crew as well as various instrument readings. Should a crash occur, this data often proves invaluable for establishing what caused the accident, and may also suggest ways to make flying safer.

Recently, similar systems, known as Event Data Recorders (EDRs), have been added to some U.S. automobiles. EDRs peruse data from shortly before and during an accident, showing whether the passengers were wearing their seat belts, if the driver was exceeding the speed limit, and how soon a driver started braking before the crash.

The contention that EDRs help drivers in the same way that aircraft black boxes help pilots is often made. However, a little

---

[211] Ann March, "No Place To Hide," *Forbes*, September 22, 1997.

[212] Robert Lemos, "Rental-Car Firm Exceeding the Privacy Limit?" CNET News.com, June 20, 2001.

thought suggests that this is not likely to be the case, given that most accidents with automobiles involve human error rather than the mechanical failure or freak weather conditions that are often responsible for airplane disasters.

Thus, where a black box in an aircraft might arguably make passengers safer as unknown dangers are discovered, EDRs in automobiles aren't likely to make us safer. The only real purpose they serve is to reduce the workload for law-enforcement officers and insurance agents who settle claims. In such cases, EDRs make it easier to discover who was at fault in an accident—namely, the driver and/or the passengers. It seems likely that in many cases, the data on an EDR will be detrimental to those who own and operate the vehicle.

Sadly, the public has had little say as to whether or not EDRs are placed in the vehicles they purchase. Most buyers of new cars are unaware that the vehicle they've purchased includes a black box that is in operation whenever the car is running. Today, an estimated 40 million cars built since the mid-1990s have an EDR on board. Only a few states have laws requiring auto dealers to disclose to buyers that an EDR is present in the car being purchased.[213]

While current EDRs do not record conversations going on in a car, there's no guarantee that this feature won't be added in the future, given the added convenience this would provide to law enforcement and the insurance industry. Should this capability be added, EDRs might reveal whether the driver said anything incriminating before or after the wreck, or if they said anything incriminating before being pulled over by the police.

U.S. citizens have no advocate defending their privacy when it comes to EDRs. Insurance companies, law-enforcement personnel, and various government agencies in charge of auto safety and highway regulations are all squarely behind the idea of placing EDRs in new cars. Today, with talk about keying EDR data into Global Positioning Data satellites and adding voice-recording systems to the devices, the situation seems destined to become much worse, with little hope for safeguarding privacy.

---

[213] Rebecca Carr, "Black Boxes in Cars Raise Concerns About Privacy," *Dallas Morning News*, July 2, 2006.

Radio Frequency Identification (RFID)

Radio Frequency Identification (RFID) technology has been sold as a hi-tech replacement for the bar coding now found on most products we buy (though, in truth, it seems likely that it will be more of an addition than a replacement for some time to come). What the public isn't being told is that this technology is going to be akin to placing a bar code on the forehead of each person buying some types of RFID-marked products.

RFID technology works thanks to a transponder tag, about the size of a large postage stamp, which is placed on a product. This tag answers with a unique radio signal when interrogated by a radio transmission from a remote tracking device. This answer is a unique serial number that can then be stored in a computer, along with the place the reading was taken, the date, and the precise time of the reading.

Most RFID tags are passive—meaning that the tag has no battery and thus gets the energy for its response from the interrogation signal itself; this means the tags are cheaper to make and need no power source. As such, a passive RFID tag can lay dormant for months, years, or even decades and still be ready to respond to the proper radio transmission.

The unique serial number given with the response of an RFID tag makes it possible to identify it and link it to computer records that indicate when and where a product might have been manufactured and where it was sold, along with the time, date, and location of the actual reading. This data can then be stored on computers for a variety of purposes, from tracking inventory to identifying customers to billing products at the checkout counter.

The range at which an RFID tag can be read varies according to the amount of material between the tag and reader, whether it is a passive or an active tag (the latter having its own power supply), and whether the system uses low-frequency or longer-range, high-frequency bands. Passive tags with low-frequency systems are considered short-range, with readings taking place within just several feet or yards. However, given the right conditions and a powerful high-frequency interrogation signal, passive readings can be made as far out as 65 to 100 feet, even under current FCC power and antenna limits.[214] (And some in the industry are lobbying for a longer range in the future, so this distance may be increased at some point.)[215]

Because these readings can be taken without actually having to scan over a bar code or enter numbers manually into a computer, manufacturers have adopted RFID tagging systems for a variety of products and processes:

- Many libraries and bookstores place RFID tags in each book so they can tell whether or not it has been checked out or purchased when a patron carries it out the door.
- Cattle sometimes have RFID tags so they can be tracked.
- Shipping containers, pallets, and trailers often have RFID tags so their movements can be easily traced.
- The U.S. Department of Defense employs RFID technology to trace military supply shipments.
- Wal-Mart is requiring its top suppliers to include RFID tags in packaging.
- Around 40 percent of the cars now being manufactured in North America include RFID tags in keys to serve as ID systems to prevent starting a car without the proper key.
- ExxonMobil uses RFID in its Speedpass billing system.
- Tire manufacturers are adding RFID tags to many of their tires to facilitate easier mileage checks and easier recall of defective tires.
- Credit card companies are hoping to employ RFID tags in credit cards.
- And there have even been a few individuals who've tagged themselves with small RFID tags implanted under their skin in an attempt to discourage kidnappers.

---

[214] Mark Baard, "Is RFID Technology Easy to Foil?" *Wired News*, November 18, 2003.
[215] "Privacy Best Practices for Deployment of RFID Technology," Interim Draft, CDT Working Group on RFID, May 1, 2006.

There's also a push to tag all sensitive and legal documents, as well as passports, driver's licenses, and even money. Some of these — such as passports and driver's licenses — pose an obvious danger to privacy, as well as opening a person to a variety of scams on the part of criminals, or even terrorists. Imagine visiting overseas in a nation known for terrorism while carrying a passport that will identify you as an American when interrogated by a transponder from perhaps a hundred feet away.

In 2005, Toppan Printing developed an RFID tag that could be placed in glass sheets and glass containers, in collaboration with Nippon Sheet Glass.[216] This all but guarantees that RFID tags will appear in a variety of additional products in the near future.

The Pluses

It would be wrong to suggest that the consumer and citizen don't get some benefits from the RFID system, since it does speed products along. This makes it easy to do just-in-time deliveries that stock inventory only as it's needed, creating savings for stores, some of which will undoubtedly be passed on to the buyer through lower prices.

Since stocks in stores can be automatically filled when any given product is showing low numbers in inventory, consumers confronted by the "out of stock" notice could become a thing of the past. And a variety of savings, coupons, and other incentives may be presented to customers, based on their past shopping records and buying habits.

Government agencies such as the Federal Emergency Management Agency (FEMA) and the Pentagon can avoid many of the losses experienced in the past through waste, theft, and overstocking to avoid shortfalls during an emergency or combat. Criminals will be more easily nabbed when they try to counterfeit products, sell stolen goods, or make purchases with cash obtained at gunpoint.

The process of going through the checkout line can be streamlined with RFID technology. Ditto for returning goods for a refund,

---

[216] "Toppan Printing Develops Built-in RFID Tag for Glass Containers," Press Release, Japan Corporate News Network, March 1, 2005.

since it will be possible to quickly determine when and where something was purchased, and perhaps even who bought it if a credit card was used.

Many of the things that we waste a lot of time with, day in and day out, could be handled in the background by RFID technology.

That's the promise. But there's also a very troubling downside, and one that threatens the privacy of everyone on the business end of this technology.

Tag, You're It

With the low cost of RFID tags and the ease with which they can be read, and the introduction of cheap readers as well, it seems likely that the time when virtually every product is tagged may fast be approaching. (The low cost of equipment may also create a new route for identity theft should criminals learn how to read RFID tags on credit cards, driver's licenses, etc., and then duplicate the unique numbers on these products.)

Since many of these tags are passive and incorporated not into the packaging but rather into the product itself, these tags can be read any time a suitable interrogation signal is sent to them, whether the product is leaving the store or ten years later when the product is being driven, worn, or carried by a citizen on a busy street.

This situation in which virtually anything one might own will have a discrete serial number that can be used to identify its owner caused security expert Scott Granneman to warn:[217]

> Right now, you can buy a hammer, a pair of jeans, or a razor blade with anonymity. With RFID tags, that may be a thing of the past. . . . Once you buy your RFID-tagged jeans at The Gap with RFID-tagged money, walk out of the store wearing RFID-tagged shoes, and get into your car with its RFID-tagged tires, you could be tracked anywhere you travel. . . . Anonymity and privacy? Gone in a hailstorm of invisible communication, betrayed by your very property.

---

[217] Scott Granneman, "RFID Chips Are Here," *SecurityFocus*, June 26, 2003.

Just how intrusive this RFID invasion of one's privacy might be was noted in a technical paper from the University of Cambridge in England:[218]

> Ladies too embarrassed to reveal their dress size to their best friend will be unwittingly broadcasting that and much more, including bra cup size and whether they are wearing Bridget Jones big pants or a sexy G-string, to any stalkers within radio range. . . . Even if the game of "who's got the biggest wad of cash" is technically infeasible, what would be the obstacle to playing "who's got the Rolex" or, at less exalted levels, "who's got the trendy cell phone?"

> Since readers do not require line of sight to work, you may be silently scanned as frequently as every few minutes during the course of your normal day—and you won't know who is scanning you. Someone might aggregate these sightings to track your whereabouts, keeping a log of everywhere you have been.

> The RFID serial number of your watch or eyeglasses becomes a pseudonym that always refers to you; and location privacy researchers have proved that it is usually easy to map this back to your real-world identity. Even if there is no single object that you carry every day, you may still be tracked by the . . . "constellations" of such objects: pen, comb, wallet, clothes, etc.

Needless to say, this presents not only a huge potential loss of privacy but also a great temptation to government snoops to exploit the technology. Katherine Albrecht, director of Consumers Against Supermarket Privacy Invasion, had this to say about what might happen if people had unique RFID tags of one sort or another on their person:[219]

> Let's say you went to a gun show, or to a talk given by a Muslim cleric, or to a peace rally. At present, government agencies can't bust in and ask everyone to show their ID. But they

---

[218] Frank Stajano, "RFID Is X-Ray Vision," Technical Report No. 645, Computer Laboratory, University of Cambridge, August 2005.

[219] Kim Zetter, "Jamming Tags Block RFID Scanners," *Wired News*, March 1, 2004.

could send someone into the event with an RFID reader to identify who is there and who they are associating with.

There have been fears that criminals might employ RFID readers to select their victims by what tags respond to interrogation. This seems likely to become a real worry, given that one can already find how-to articles on the Internet that show how to program the readily available Texas Instruments S2000 Micro Reader to interrogate RFID tags.[220]

And some criminals on the street already have gadgets that enable them to clone RFID tags used as keys or identification. Others can rewrite data on RFID tags to make them respond with code that is different from their original programming, opening the possibility of cloning credit cards or identification documents with RFID tags in them.[221]

Where today you may be able to hide a wallet full of cash, a credit card, or a costly gadget in a pocket, that may no longer be the case if these items are RFID-tagged and criminals learn how to program readers to detect costly goods on potential targets.

E-Z Big Brother

While still a minority, some cars in the U.S. are already being routinely logged in at least eighteen states by RFID systems built into various bridges, roads, and tunnels requiring a toll be paid. These ETC (Electronic Toll Collection) systems include California's FasTrack system and New York State's E-ZPass, with these two systems making their way into other states as well.

Regardless of the name, the systems work in about the same way: A radio transmitter sends out a constant pulse that is answered by a transponder on the vehicle when the signal is detected. Each transponder has a signal that is unique to the vehicle it is on. The transponder is quite small, generally a small tag that affixes to the inside of the windshield. The information is encrypted and

---

[220] "Java and RFID Tags," Dr. Dobs Portal, http://www.ddj.com/dept/java/184406323, September 29, 2005.

[221] Annalee Newitz, "The RFID Hacking Underground," *Wired Magazine*, May 5, 2006.

relayed to a computer that stores the number of the vehicle's tag, the time, and location. Later this data is used to compute billing charges for the use of the toll area. This bill is then mailed out or charged against the vehicle owner's credit card.

The cautionary part of the ETC story is that when they were put into place, the public was told data collected would be kept private. But this has not proven to be the case. As crimes occurred where it was thought handy to have access to the records, data was handed over to the authorities any time they requested it, no warrant or other legal order necessary. This gave authorities not only the data collected, but also the user's address, Social Security card number, or bank account, since this information is easily gleaned from the credit card and banking accounts linked to the payment system.

As with most RFID systems, the transponder is always "on" in the ETC tag. This also makes it theoretically possible to cause it to reveal its information by simply sending the proper radio pulse that causes it to give its ID. Original ETC readers required that motorists slow somewhat in order for the data from their transponder to be read. However, newer systems have been developed that can read from a car traveling at much higher speeds, making it theoretically possible to collect data even when vehicles are speeding down a highway.

Obviously the best way to evade the privacy dangers of these systems is to avoid them altogether. If few people adopt these systems, then the police are not likely to gear up to read the few devices from the few vehicles that are tagged.

If a person must use these ETC tags, then it is also possible to purchase a carrier designed to block radio transmissions that cause the transponder to reveal its number. Placing a tag into such a bag thereby protects it. Of course, the user has to remember to retrieve it from the bag when approaching a reader; otherwise, it will fail to respond. Arguably this could be enough extra work to make simply paying the toll and forgetting the tag a viable alternative.

If the government were to require all cars to carry an ETC tag, then this could quickly become a system that would greatly degrade the privacy of all drivers. Such a proposal was made in 1997 when President Clinton suggested the U.S. interstate system should adopt an ETC system to make things "more fair" for motorists, since users would then pay an extra tax for using the roadways. Clinton's director of environmental studies at the Reason Public Policy Institute claimed, "President Clinton's proposal to allow toll collections on interstate highways could be a real boon to motorists resulting in better roads and a fairer system of funding."[222]

The measure would not have been such a boon for motorists wanting to maintain their privacy.

Mark of the Beast

Late in 2004, the U.S. Food and Drug Administration (FDA) gave its final approval to an 11-millimeter-long, glass-encased RFID tag named the VeriChip. Made by Applied Digital Solutions, the tag is implanted under the skin, thereby giving a permanent ID to that person. This tag can then be easily and quickly read by a variety of RFID devices.[223]

The tag promised an easy way to track long-term Alzheimer's patients in hospitals, as well as provide immediate positive identification of people in security positions or anywhere that a quickly verified identification might be made. Thousands of these tags are now under the skin of individuals across the U.S. There has even been talk of employing the VeriChip or similar tag as a key to open doors, as a credit system to be employed like a credit card, and as a permanent identification that would be difficult to steal (though the thought of what the owner would go through if someone decided to steal one is the stuff of nightmares).

In 2006, the CEO of Applied Digital, Scott Silverman, suggested that the VeriChip would be ideal to inject under the skin of

---

[222] "President's Toll Road Proposal is a Good Sign for Motorists," Reason Public Policy Institute, Los Angeles, CA, March 19, 1997, 15:56:57.

[223] "VeriChip RFID Tag Patient Implant Badges Now FDA Approved," Technovelgy.com, October 17, 2004.

guest workers coming into the U.S. Silverman also claimed that important U.S. congressional leaders were interested in using the chips for this purpose.[224]

Of course, immigrants coming into the U.S. were not quite so enthusiastic about the idea.

Nor were some Bible scholars and Christians. To them it sounded an awful lot like the "Mark of the Beast" described in the Book of Revelation:

> He also forced everyone, small and great, rich and poor, free and slave, to receive a mark on his right hand or on his forehead, so that no one could buy or sell unless he had the mark, which is the name of the beast or the number of his name.[225]

RFID COUNTERMEASURES

Because of the potential danger to your privacy that RFID tags present, let's consider what you can do about it. Obviously, the first thing is to resist products that have the tags built into them. This hampered with "smart" credit card systems that employ various chips including RFID tags; consumers refused to adopt these due to privacy concerns.

Industries wanting to employ RFID tags on products have been well aware of privacy concerns with the tags—and yet have done little to allay these fears. For example, in 2003, some of those making or testing RFID tags noted the privacy concerns and promised that "kill features" would be built into chips so that the tags could be deactivated once a product was sold to the consumer. At that time, it was also noted by the industry that this feature would add no cost to the tags. Thus, the MIT-affiliated standards group, the Auto-ID Center, stated that it was possible for "a kill feature to be built into every [RFID] tag. If consumers are concerned, the tags can be easily destroyed with an inexpensive reader. How this will be executed, i.e., in the home or at point of sale, is still being defined, and will be tested in the third phase of the field test."[226]

[224] James Pinkerton, "Company Says Implants Aren't Tracking Devices But Help With ID," *Houston Chronicle*, June 3, 2006.

[225] Revelation 13:16-17.

[226] Declan McCullagh, "Perspective: RFID Tags: Big Brother in Small Packages," http://news.com.com/2010-1069-980325.html, January 13, 2003.

Yet three years later, in 2006, as more and more RFID systems are actually being fielded, the "kill feature" is still missing.

This suggests that neither the government nor industrial users of RFID are apt to give more than lip service to privacy concerns with this technology. Such an assumption is pretty much supported when one reads through the various points of the Center for Democracy and Technology's statements about how privacy should be assured with RFID products. (Even the name of this group is misleading, since although it claims to be an independent think tank looking out for citizens' privacy; in fact, it works very closely with the American Library Association, aQuantive, Cisco Systems, Eli Lilly and Company, IBM, Intel, Microsoft, the National Consumers League, Procter & Gamble, VeriSign, and Visa USA.[227] Most companies on that list have a vested interest in bringing RFID online and collecting all the data possible on consumers to aid in marketing schemes.)

Thus, rather than the "kill feature" that was to be included with the RFID tagging system, the current "Best Practices,"—which are basically "best suggestions," since there are no penalties for not adopting them—is the only protection to be found. "Best Practices" are ideas that manufacturers should:[228]

- Notify buyers about whether the RFID tag can be removed or deactivated.

- "Whenever practicable" let the buyer know that an RFID tag is on a product, and that it will be used to collect information.

- Tell the consumer if the RFID information is linked to personal data— but with the companies involved "determining whether notice is necessary." (In other words, informing the consumer is optional.)

These are supposed to be the "safeguards for the consumer" as things now stand, suggesting that with protection like this, we don't need any additional dangers to our privacy.

As Jim Guest, president of Consumers Union (the publisher of *Consumer Reports*) noted about this situation:[229]

---

[227] "RFID Privacy 'Best Practices' Aim to Protect Consumers," PRNewswire, May 1, 2006.

[228] "Privacy Best Practices for Deployment of RFID Technology," Interim Draft, CDT Working Group on RFID, May 1, 2006.

[229] Andrea Rock, "The End of Privacy?" *Consumer Reports*, June 2006.

SOLUTIONS

What we need is an array of strict and enforceable state and federal laws that safeguard consumers' rights against all types of current and future gizmos. The laws should apply to any entity that collects and holds information. They should regulate, for example, the kinds of data collected, how the data can be used, consumer notification of security breaches, and consumers' ability to see and correct their information. These rights should be enforceable by federal, state, and local officials, and by consumers themselves.

Instead, consumers have received the hollow promises of the Center for Democracy and Technology's "Best Practices." Obviously those wanting to preserve at least some of their privacy will need to take additional measures.

BLOCK THAT TAG

As this is written, RSA Laboratories (174 Middlesex Turnpike, Bedford, Massachusetts 01730, 781-276-5500) has proposed a system that would use a "blocker tag," which would basically hide the privacy sections of RFID tags. These blocker tags would "answer" when an interrogation signal was presented to them. The trick here is that with current technology, only one RFID tag can be read at a time. If two "speak" at the same time, the reader can't distinguish which is which and thus can't glean information from the tags.

RSA Laboratories' blocker tag counteracts just sections of an RFID tag that might have private information, or which could be linked to private data via a computer system. At the same time, the blocker tag wouldn't cover the more general information in an RFID tag, so that some data might be gleaned from it. Thus, in theory at least, a business would have the data it needed without being able to dig into private sections of the RFID tag.

The same company has also demonstrated a "soft blocker" tag. However, this system relies on the merchant to enforce privacy policies. And it does nothing to keep other parties from interrogating an RFID tag. So this solution offers some privacy protection as long as all parties involved are trustworthy, and no untrustworthy individuals are encountered. Given the tendency of both business and governments, as well as criminals, to run roughshod over the privacy of individuals, this system seems less than ideal.

Even with a blocker tag, the "constellation" of tagged products a person carries might still give away enough data to create a unique "pattern," allowing them to be tracked.

Furthermore, sometimes the general information of a product could still compromise the privacy of the owner by announcing the waist size of her pants, or place her in danger by advertising the jewelry she's wearing.

One viable compromise to the RFID privacy problem has been proposed by IBM in the form of the "clipped tag," which is an RFID tag designed so that a portion of its antenna can be broken off. This makes it possible for a consumer to break off the antenna after purchasing something, thereby limiting the distance the tag can be read to just an inch rather than from many feet. A consumer could still return or exchange an item, since the store can still read the tag. Should the clipped tag become available commercially, it would offer a good compromise between convenience and security.

This is assuming that more powerful RFID interrogators don't become available, however. If they do, or if a criminal or terrorist were to illegally boost the power of a reader, then that one-inch reading distance might be increased to sixty-nine feet or more, giving the user the ability to sweep through crowds looking for potential targets whose various tags on driver's licenses, passports, or even sneakers may single them out for added attention.[230]

The good news is that, for the time being at least, there are a few tricks you may employ to regain some of your privacy, or to even defeat an RFID tag altogether.

PUT A SNAG IN THE TAG

Consumers can exert some influence by purchasing and using products without RFID tagging. Should there be such a backlash, manufacturers might actually get serious about addressing these concerns, rather than releasing lame "Best Practices" statements.

Rather than wait for corporations or the government to step in and protect privacy, citizens may wish to take matters into their own hands to

---

[230] Bruce Schneier, "Fatal Flaw Weakens RFID Passports," *Wired News*, November 3, 2005.

SOLUTIONS

preserve at least some semblance of privacy when it comes to RFID tags. Some of these steps may become illegal (should legislators claim it is necessary to use RFID in order to fight crimes, drug use, terrorism, piracy, or whatever the current political bogeyman might be). So these measures should be employed *only* as long as they remain legal.

Here are some steps that might be employed to protect your privacy from RFID snooping:

- When possible, purchase products that have RFID tags in packaging rather than in the product itself.

- Pay for RFID-tagged products with cash rather than a credit card or bank check, since the latter two can link data about you to the purchase.

- Avoid using discount store cards, loyalty cards, or other systems that promise in-store discounts while linking data about you to the products you are buying.

- When possible, buy or use older products that lack RFID tags. Consider shopping at garage sales to locate merchandise that has been tagged to someone else, or which lacks an RFID tag.

- Have older clothing, shoes, and other products available for your use that are RFID-free, which you can hold in reserve for use when you wish to travel or remain unidentified and untracked.

- Learn to recognize RFID tags and try to discover ways of removing them from products that can operate without them (or destroy the tag by cutting it apart with scissors if it can't be easily removed).

- If they are available, employ blocker tags to limit the information that can be gleaned from a tag. (Should these become available, they'll probably appear for sale on the Internet first.)

- Be cautious about tagging pets with a similar system, since that would basically tag anyone with the animal as well.

- Carry credit cards, passports, and other sensitive tagged documents in a shield so they can't be easily read. (These "Faraday Box" shields can be purchased or constructed, as outlined below.)

Before looking at how to purchase or make RFID shields, it should be noted that several companies have also marketed RFID jamming devices that send out signals when contacted by an interrogation radio signal. These systems work, but might easily be made illegal (in fact, it is hard to imagine that they will not be made illegal). Additionally, they might open a user to lawsuits from businesses whose readers were disrupted by the signal.

For example, a person using a jamming device enters a checkout area, possibly causing false readings to cash registers that employ RFID systems. This could jam the system and cause problems in totaling the customers' products. You can bet this would not make a merchant happy.

Shielding RFID from the interrogation beam is quite another matter, since it won't disrupt the reader or jam systems in the area. Rather, it simply cloaks a credit card or other product that has a chip so it can't be made to answer an interrogation signal. Several companies offer these devices (a quick Web search will generally uncover several). However, it is possible to improvise such a device for very little money.

While a Faraday Box won't be suitable for shielding some items, it is perfect for many others, and is capable of totally shielding an RFID tag from interrogation transmissions.

FOILING RFID TAGS

A Faraday Box (also known as the "Faraday Shield" or "Faraday Cage") is based on the research of early physicist Michael Faraday, who in the early 1800s discovered and demonstrated that an electrical charge, when it encounters a metal cage, will travel around the exterior shell without touching objects inside the shell. The electrical charge stopped by a Faraday Box can be anything from lightning to radio waves, the latter being the key to stopping an RFID signal.

Basically any electrical equipment placed inside a Faraday Box, and insulated from the metal shell of that box, will be incapable of sending or receiving a radio signal. (Which is also why Faraday Box *rooms* are created by many industrial and government departments that want to keep their computers and other equipment from being tapped or to avoid TEMPEST attacks as described in chapter 5.)

A Faraday Box is very easy to construct with metal sheeting. A variety of containers can be used as Faraday Boxes, including metal cake and candy boxes, metal filing cabinets, etc. The only two requirements are that the equipment inside the box must never touch the exterior metal shell, and that the metal shield is continuous without any gaps between pieces, or any large holes in it. The containers do not have to be airtight, but the tighter fitting the better.

The insulation between the metal exterior shell of the Faraday Box and the object inside can be a variety of materials as well, from paper or cardboard, to plastic bubble wrap, to wood or plastic structural sheets. As long as the insulator doesn't conduct electricity and is fairly durable (so it won't rip and create an electrical contact between the RFID chip and the Faraday Box exterior shell), it will work.

A quick and easy Faraday Box can be created with the Mylar plastic shipping bags many electronic components like computer cards and hard drives are sold in. These bags consist of strong polyester film with a metal layer inside the plastic. This metal film is generally thick enough to stop radio waves, making any RFID device you can fit into one of these bags safe from activation once the bag is closed. Often you can get these bags for free from a computer repair shop, or from friends who like to assemble their own computers.

A do-it-yourself Faraday Box for an RFID-equipped credit card, passport, or document can be assembled by folding a sheet of paper around the item (the paper being insulator), and then wrapping the paper with aluminum foil. Of course having to unceremoniously unwrap your credit card at the checkout counter is less than elegant. In such a case you might wish to purchase one of the small "RFID shields" offered by a number of companies, including Smart Tools (1478 Morton Ave., Los Altos, California 94024, 650-967-3875, smarttools@att.net, smarttools. home.att.net).

If you want to store RFID-equipped items in your home without fear that they might be activated, then you can create a larger Faraday Box by putting the item inside a cardboard box and then wrapping it with copper or aluminum foil. Place the foil-wrapped box inside a larger cardboard box so that the foil isn't accidentally ripped, and the equipment is ready to be stored, safe from potential detection.

THE FARADAY BOX ROOM

You likely will never need a whole storage room protected from RFID access. Yet if you should feel the need, it would be possible to create a whole storage room that would protect RFID-tagged equipment, clothing, etc., from being interrogated.

Again, the secret is the Faraday Box, this time built on a grander scale. This could be created by lining the walls of a room with copper or aluminum foil and then covering the windows, air vents, and other openings with foil or metal screen (the latter having the advantage of letting in light and permitting air flow). Be sure the screen and the foil on the doors are all connected so they form an electrical contact between the metals. The idea is to create a continuous, unbroken shell that will stop all radio waves. Remember that the floor and ceiling also need to be covered with connectors making contact between the walls. A heavy carpet should be placed over the foil on the floor to prevent tearing the foil.

A quick test of such a room can be conducted by turning on a radio inside the room or by trying to make a cell phone call. If either device is able to get an outside signal, then there are holes in the shielding that are failing to stop radio waves.

While this may be unnecessary today in terms of preventing RFID activation, such a room might be necessary for complete protection of computers or other equipment from eavesdropping. In such a case the Faraday Box room can be employed for TEMPEST protection . . . bringing us to the next danger to privacy.

While unlikely, it is not impossible that criminals might create illegally powerful RFID readers and then cruise neighborhoods looking for plasma TVs and other hi-tech items that have RFID tags. In such a case, living in a home that is not "cell phone friendly," or having a Faraday Box "treasure room" for your valuables might be a necessary measure. When house shopping, you may wish to bear in mind that earth-sheltered homes or houses with concrete walls will reduce or even stop radio waves—including those that might be produced by an illegally powerful RFID reader.

CHAPTER 9 YOUR PAPERS, PLEASE

" If Big Brother saves lives, then I'm happy to be Big Brother. "

— COMMISSIONER BURT AARONSON,

PALM BEACH COUNTY, FLORIDA[231] —

The words, "Your papers, please" have inspired fear in many a heart, whether on the streets of Nazi Germany or of a Third World dictatorship. Not without reason, since one of the tools that enables the quick assessment of a person by a government agent is a national ID card.

In the past, IDs were relatively easy to forge, giving those wanting to escape such regimes a fighting chance. That changes as hi-tech features are added to IDs, which is the route currently being adopted in various nations. These cards become progressively harder to forge, as RFID chips, holograph symbols, and biometric features are added. And, as is so often the case, such systems promise to thwart criminals and terrorists even as they create tools that might be exploited against the citizens they are designed to protect.

To date most efforts to include fingerprints or retina scans on driver's licenses and passports have failed in the U.S., in large part because too many remember the abuses of such documents in the past. Civic leader Steve Cappelli worked to prevent the

---

[231] Marc Caputo, "Conservative Pledges Clout for Traffic Cameras," *Palm Beach Post*, June 14, 2001.

inclusion of such features on Georgia's driver's licenses in the late 1990s. He noted:[232]

> [Jewish] opponents [to the proposal to include fingerprints on driver's licenses] are legitimately offended that so many would dismiss these similarities so easily. Dutch citizens were required to carry photo IDs with fingerprints at all times. In France, identification numbers on existing government records were used to round up Jews, Christians, and others on the Nazi "hit" lists. These memories have played a large role in the efforts of Western democracies to restrict the use of personal identifiers, like Social Security numbers, finger-prints, retina scans, and other biometric identifiers.

Nor are such abuses of identification cards that far removed in history. Rwandan citizens were issued national ID cards which, in 1995, proved very useful to those slaughtering men, women, and children with rapid efficiency, thanks in large part to those ID cards that tagged the bearer as Hutu or Tutsi.[233]

The push continues to create standardized cards for U.S. citizens to carry, whether for medical records, driver's licenses, or worker permits. The promise is that ID cards will fight fraud and other crimes, as well as make some tasks faster; they most likely will.

Other promises are not as likely to be kept. The contention that universal IDs (especially those based on driver's licenses, as will be covered shortly) would prevent terrorism is doubtful, given that the terrorists involved in the attacks on September 11, 2001, had valid driver's licenses. They would not have been thwarted by national ID cards. Identification papers are good for apprehending criminals or terrorists after the fact, but do little to prevent mayhem from happening.

Meanwhile, personal identification systems do aid in the collection of data about individuals, which often leads to data mining by corporations. And as noted throughout this book, such efforts can erode your privacy in subtle yet profound ways.

---

[232] Steve Cappelli, "No Fingerprints, Please!" *Fact Sheet*, Coalition to Repeal the Fingerprint Law, Atlanta, Georgia, 1998.

[233] *San Francisco Chronicle*, June 9, 1995.

Your Driver's License

Often legislation is given a name that is diametrically opposed to what the law will actually do. Nowhere was this truer than with the so-called Drivers Privacy Protection Act of 1994. This law opened the floodgates for the possibility of mining data from all the state driver's licenses issued in America.

The public got a much different spin on the legislation when it was proposed, however, with key sponsors of the Drivers Privacy Protection Act claiming the law would help prevent crimes like stalking, since it would limit who could access a state's driver's license database. The new law was meant to protect citizens from such dangers.

And some of the wording in the bill did protect, as in this section:[234]

> Sec. 2721. Prohibition on release and use of certain personal information from State motor vehicle records. Except as provided in subsection (b), a State department of motor vehicles, and any officer, employee, or contractor thereof, shall not knowingly disclose or otherwise make available to any person or entity personal information about any individual obtained by the department in connection with a motor vehicle record.

But the key word here is *except*, which, as the bill's subsections unfold, lays the groundwork for a variety of exceptions, including these:

- For use by any government agency, including any court or law-enforcement agency, in carrying out its functions, or any private person or entity acting on behalf of a federal, state, or local agency in carrying out its functions.
- For use in connection with any civil, criminal, administrative, or arbitral proceeding in any federal, state, or local court or agency, or before any self-regulatory body, including the service of process, investigation in anticipation of litigation,

---

[234] Drivers Privacy Protection Act, 18 USC § 2721 et. seq., (Public Law 103-322), 1994.

and the execution or enforcement of judgments and orders, or pursuant to an order of a federal, state, or local court.

- For use by any insurer or insurance support organization, or by a self-insured entity, or its agents, employees, or contractors, in connection with claims investigation activities, anti-fraud activities, rating, or underwriting.

- For use by any licensed private investigative agency or licensed security service for any purpose permitted under this subsection.

- For bulk distribution for surveys, marketing, or solicitations if the motor vehicle department has implemented methods and procedures to ensure that individuals are provided an opportunity, in a clear and conspicuous manner, to prohibit such uses; and the information will be used, rented, or sold solely for bulk distribution for surveys, marketing, and solicitations will not be directed at those individuals who have requested in a timely fashion that they not be directed at them.

- For use in the normal course of business by a legitimate business or its agents, employees, or contractors.

Thus, while the law did stop a variety of junk mail distributors and other groups from using driver's license records, the various exceptions—along with a clause that allows repackaging and selling data collected in one of the above exceptions—kept the door open for data miners.

One company in the forefront of this data mining was New Hampshire–based Image Data. The company was soon marketing data to private retailers who, according to the business model, could then access it from their own central database to ID customers during credit card transactions. As one might expect, there were apparently few checks on who accessed the data once it was sold to secondary companies, and little control over how the information was employed. (A troubling twist to the story is that

Image Data received nearly $1.5 million in federal funds and technical assistance from the U.S. Secret Service in 1998.[235])

A grassroots movement to prevent Image Data from harvesting the photos from driver's licenses spread through Florida, Colorado, and South Carolina. Furious citizens demanded that their states discontinue selling the information to Image Data. Image Data, in turn, announced that it was abandoning its photo database built on driver's license data (and would instead get the data from check and credit card companies).[236]

Newspapers and Private Data

Oddly enough, the Drivers Privacy Protection Act of 1994 did prevent one group from accessing data directly from driver's license records: the American press. No longer could reporters quickly find the address of someone using these state records. Instead, news organizations would be forced to buy the information from companies like Image Data.

This led to a group of newspapers asking the Fourth U.S. Circuit Court of Appeals in South Carolina to consider the constitutional legality of the new law. Their legal argument was that the Tenth Amendment's outlining of the separation of powers did not give Congress the authority to impose the restrictions of the Drivers Privacy Protection Act of 1994 on the states.

The court agreed, ruling that the information on driver's licenses, including names, addresses, telephone numbers, and even Social Security numbers, not only could not be protected, but was also far from private, and therefore not protected by the Fourteenth Amendment. Judge Karen J. Williams wrote in the decision, "We seriously doubt that an individual has a constitutional right to privacy in information routinely shared with strangers."[237] Williams's ruling stripped citizens of their most basic right to privacy.

---

[235] Robert O'Harrow Jr. and Liz Leyden, "U.S. Helped Fund License Photo Database," *The Washington Post*, February 18, 1999, page A1.

[236] Rita Ciolli, "Company Plans to Buy Drivers' ID Photos," *The Voice*, November 18, 1999.

[237] Kelvin Childs, "Drivers Privacy Protection Act Held Unconstitutional," *Editor & Publisher*, December 1998.

Not surprisingly, this case (and several similar cases) were appealed, and eventually made their way to the U.S. Supreme Court where, in January 2000, the court upheld the Drivers Privacy Protection Act of 1994, claiming that it was lawful under Congress's constitutional right to regulate interstate commerce.[238]

In the meantime, technology has permitted some groups to slowly create databases from the information on driver's licenses. This has been accomplished by marketing readers that can access the information on the magnetic strip found on the back of most driver's licenses, including height, weight, address, and other information. Clubs or other businesses may ask for driver's licenses for "age verification" before admitting people into their premises; the driver's license is then swiped through the reader, which not only checks to be sure the license is legitimate, but also collects all the information from it. This data can then be processed in a variety of ways—including selling it to data miners.

Ironically, while many states require that consent be given before adding names and addresses to marketing lists, businesses collecting data assume that if a customer doesn't ask to have their name removed from a list, they have given their consent—which is not likely to happen, given that most people aren't aware the data has been taken from their driver's license during the age-verification procedure.[239]

National ID Cards

Congress regularly trots out the idea of national identification cards as a "solution" to illegal immigrants. One such push was the Illegal Immigration Reform and Immigrant Responsibility Act of 1996, which was aimed not at creating cards for guest workers as much as making the data and layout on all state driver's licenses conform to one another (arguably an odd solution, given that most states at that time weren't knowingly issuing driver's licenses to il-

---

[238] Ray Schultz, "Supreme Court Upholds Drivers Privacy Act of 1994," Prism Business Media Inc., January 13, 2000.

[239] "Finding Pay Dirt in Scannable Driver's Licenses," *The New York Times*, March 21, 2002.

legal aliens). After many modifications, the bill finally passed, and today, the various state driver's licenses are very similar, complete with a magnetic strip containing all the data on the card. Although the card lacked some of the biometrics supporters had hoped for (including a fingerprint, voice recording, and perhaps even a retina scan), the result was nevertheless a *de facto* national ID card.[240]

In 2002, the American Association of Motor Vehicle Administrators' (AAMVA) Orwellian-sounding Special Task Force on Identification Security recommended that driver's licenses become the functional equivalent of a national ID card, recommending that Congress adopt and fund the Driver Record Information Verification System (DRIVerS).

DRIVerS basically works toward completing the standardization of one state's card to the next, to "produce a uniform, secure, and interoperable driver's license/ID card to uniquely identify an individual." It would also collect and sort data from "state agencies and federal agencies, such as the Immigration and Naturalization Service, the Social Security Administration, the Bureau of Vital Statistics, and, if necessary, the Federal Bureau of Investigation." In other words, the change would create a massive database, combining state's driver's license systems with data from a variety of federal agencies.[241]

As the Electronic Frontier Foundation has noted, such solutions to the problem of illegal immigration would bring a host of other woes with them:[242]

> A national ID card or system carries tremendous risks to civil liberties. Fundamentally, of course, an ID system aims to uniquely identify people and permits them to be tracked across their transactions and to be linked to all the informational traces thereby created. History tells us that ID systems have a strong momentum toward a checkpoint mentality.

---

[240] "Upgraded Driver's Licenses Are Urged as National IDs," *The New York Times*, January 8, 2002.

[241] "National ID Cards from DMV?" Electronic Frontier Foundation, *Action Alert*, January 16, 2002.

[242] *Ibid.*

Those who push for ID systems are well aware of this and try to start small.

During the attempt to introduce the Australia Card, one planning document stated: "It will be important to minimize any adverse public reaction to implementation of the system. One possibility would be to use a staged approach for implementation, whereby only less-sensitive data are held in the system initially, with the facility to input additional data at a later stage when public acceptance may be forthcoming more readily."

Police who are given powers to demand ID invariably have powers to detain people who do not have the card, or who cannot prove their identity. Great Britain, for instance, began issuing wartime ID cards in 1939 in order to administer rations. In 1952, the system was discontinued because police had too much discretion to stop people for ID checks.

Of course, the ends don't always need to be draconian to argue against the path being taken. Consider the last time you got your driver's license renewed and ask this question: Do we really trust the folks running the various Departments of Motor Vehicles with thwarting terrorism, fixing illegal immigration, and safeguarding our personal information?

Trusted Traveler

The legislative fallout from the September 11, 2001, terrorist attacks, as well as the public interest in illegal immigration, has brought forth another round of proposed legislation aimed at producing federal ID cards.

One organization spearheading this movement is the U.S. Department of Transportation task force, which has called for an expansion of the national transportation worker identity card, applying it to more U.S. citizens than just those working in the airline industry.

The Aviation and Transportation Security Act (passed late in 2001 following the attacks) ushered in the first leg of this expansion toward the "Trusted Traveler" card.[243]

With a goal to "establish requirements to implement trusted passenger programs and use available technologies to expedite the security screening of passengers," the Trusted Traveler cards permit passengers to bypass extensive security screening at airport checkpoints. The downside in terms of privacy is that these cards have a variety of intrusive features, including:

- Fingerprints
- An encoded biometric description of the owner
- Possibly a facial structure or irises scan
- Street address, age, and other data

Barry Steinhardt, associate director of the American Civil Liberties Union, had this to say about the Trusted Traveler card:[244]

> This is a back-door national ID. This so-called trusted-passenger card will become essentially mandatory for everyone to use not only on airlines but also buses, trains, and perhaps [when driving] over bridges and tunnels. The consequences of not having a trusted-passenger card is that you will be immediately suspect.

And Representative Bob Barr noted,[245]

> It is an unfortunate, but predictable, consequence that in the chaotic aftermath of September 11th, many in Washington are seeking to capitalize on Americans' fears by telling us a choice has to be made between security and privacy. This request is predictable because all too often in our nation's Capitol, politicians choose political expediency and rhetoric

---

[243] Tom Ramstack, "ID Card for Air Passengers," *Washington Times*, January 31, 2002.

[244] *Ibid.*

[245] Bob Barr, "September 11th Attacks Fueling Drive for National ID," http://hillsource.house.gov/barr/newsdescr.asp?N=20020118134212, January 16, 2002.

over hard work and sound policy. Instead of taking the time and thought to look at a problem and make the tough decisions needed to solve it, the typical Washington answer is to pass more and more laws, and take more and more power out of the hands of the American people. . . .

We do not need to be implementing a national monitoring system of all Americans. History is replete with dictatorial regimes that have used strict identification systems as the primary tool. With each passing day Americans' personal freedoms are eroded, the more these terrorists will have won. . . . National ID cards based on 21st-century technology, with a traceable, embedded chip, will mean the government won't even have to ask for "your papers, please"; they'll already know where you are.

Biometrics

In 2006, as politicians prepared for the next election, the new bugaboo of illegal immigration and borders that were porous to terrorists (problems that had somehow gone unnoticed in D.C. for several decades) was trotted out so legislative grandstanding could take place. Part of the "solution" offered once again was national ID cards with biometric data. Among those calling for national ID cards was New York City mayor Michael Bloomberg, who stated that DNA and fingerprint technology should be included on the cards, since "everybody's got a PC on their desk with Photoshop that can replicate anything."[246]

Which, of course, is untrue, as anyone who's used Photoshop knows. In fact, state driver's licenses are generally embossed with a holographic seal that is impossible to reproduce with the equipment and programs available to the public. Likewise, most driver's licenses have a magnetic strip that is also beyond Photoshop.

Oddly enough, what *is* easy to reproduce on Photoshop is a fingerprint, the very thing proposed by the mayor as the solution to a problem that didn't exist. (It's always hard to know whether such solutions should be chalked up to ignorance or placed in the "politician" category.)

---

[246] Sara Kugler, "NYC Mayor Advocates U.S. Worker Database," Associated Press, May 24, 2006.

It now appears that the private sector will create the biometric identification system that government officials have been longing for. Ironically, Americans may be trading their privacy without a second thought, the only payoff being the promise that they'll spend less time in the checkout line when buying groceries or other products. This event will likely have already happened as you read this paragraph, since stores are slated to be fielding these systems late in 2006. This system will actually be cardless, since it employs a customer's fingerprint to authenticate his identity and link him to a bank or credit card account.[247]

Once collected, the data linked to a customer's fingerprint can then be transferred to a variety of databases, mined, and ultimately sold to anyone from a marketing firm to a government agency. It seems likely that once this system is in place, the same ID technology might also be employed to authenticate driver's licenses or medical cards, giving industry and government snoops the biometric identification they've been pining for.

Deoxyribonucleic Acid (DNA)

Using DNA to identify individuals within a population is also not as clear-cut as many in law enforcement and politics might have you believe. Much of the genetic material within an individual's DNA is nearly identical to that of other people, and some we hold in common with other living creatures.

While current DNA samples used by law-enforcement agencies focus on only thirteen regions of genetic material, there's no guarantee the areas being examined won't be expanded, especially given that the current practice is to store whole DNA samples rather than just the markers that are now employed in crime investigations.

Should additional DNA information be sought, it becomes very specific about an individual: markers for genetic diseases, race, and perhaps even our tendencies for mental illness or to be overweight or too thin. This latter data, should it ever be computerized,

---

[247] Jonathan Curiel, "The Last Days of Privacy," *San Francisco Chronicle,* June 25, 2006.

would lend itself to anything from charging higher health insurance premiums to those with genetic markers predisposing them to disease, to quickly sorting out a racial minority from the general population.

This makes the government's collection of DNA samples into a centralized bank all the more troubling. Currently this database has over 3 million samples, with an additional 80,000 more being fed into it every month from law-enforcement offices across the nation. Most troubling is that this collection has expanded with little public debate, with many states now taking samples not only from felons, but also from juvenile offenders and those who were simply arrested and later found to be innocent.[248]

The usual justifications are heard: "If you have nothing to hide, you have nothing to fear" and "Giving up a little privacy is necessary to solve crimes." But in truth, having one's DNA in such a database transforms you from someone considered to be innocent until proven guilty into someone who is a suspect in every case in which a DNA sample has been taken, given that the existing samples are what are searched. This has led to individuals becoming suspects simply because their DNA was a close match to a criminal, especially if that criminal was related to them.[249]

Nor are DNA tests as accurate as the public is often asked to believe. Mistakes are made, sometimes on a grand scale, as in the case of the Houston DNA lab that was finally closed in 2003 after independent investigators found that out of several hundred cases, twenty-one had questionable results during DNA testing. And one individual who had been convicted of rape and sentenced to jail on the lab's DNA "evidence" was later set free.[250]

DNA testing can be useful in fighting crime. But, in the end, it seems that the promises of DNA testing as a crime-fighting tool might be overrated, and the danger to our privacy underrated. Yet

---

[248] Rick Weiss, "Vast DNA Bank Pits Policing Vs. Privacy," *Washington Post*, June 3, 2006.

[249] *Ibid.*

[250] "Grand Jury Blasts Houston Police DNA Lab," CNN.com, October 17, 2003.

sadly, politicians and law-enforcement personnel continue to sell it as the solution to many of our society's problems.

Collecting DNA from the general population—often the goal of law-enforcement agencies—has another chilling possibility, and one that recalls Nazi experiments in eugenics. That's because, while not popular, there is a school of thought which maintains that specific genes may spur violent or criminal behavior. Were this theory to gain a foothold in America, it is not hard to imagine seeing people undergo training, counseling, or perhaps even incarceration, simply because they possessed "criminal genes."

This isn't the stuff of science fiction. In 1992, the George H. W. Bush administration actually started the ball rolling with its "Violence Initiative," whose stated goal was discovering genetic predispositions toward violence and criminal behavior with an eye toward developing drugs and therapy to treat these temperaments.

A few of those championing the idea of genetic-criminal links sounded, by mischance or intent, as if they had arrived from Nazi Germany via time warp. Some speeches were laced with what could be construed as racism, with overtones of evolutionary justification. One such speaker was Dr. Frederick Goodwin, who told an audience at the National Health Advisory Council:[251]

> If you look, for example, at male monkeys, especially in the wild, roughly half of them survive to adulthood. The other half die by violence. That is the natural way of it for males, to knock each other off and, in fact, there are some interesting evolutionary implications of that, because the same hyper-aggressive monkeys who kill each other are also hypersexual, so they copulate more and therefore they reproduce more to offset the fact that half of them are dying.
>
> Now, one could say that if some of the loss of social structure in this society, and particularly within the high-impact inner city areas, has removed some of the civilizing evolutionary things that we have built up, and that maybe it isn't just the careless use of the word when people call certain areas of

---

[251] Warren Leary, "Struggle Continues Over Remarks by Mental Health Official," *The New York Times*, March 8, 1992.

certain cities jungles, then we may have gone back to what might be more natural, without all of the social controls that we have imposed upon ourselves as a civilization over thousands of years in our own evolution.

Fortunately, the cries of "racism" quickly silenced those who were intent on preventing crime by treating the innocent as would-be criminals (or monkeys, depending on how "scientific" one's view might be). That such discussions would be held, such speeches given, and such callous insensitivity expressed suggests the serpent of the eugenics movement lies just beneath the surface of our culture.

While the public candor of those involved in the Violence Initiative pretty much took it off the table for the time being, the move to create DNA data banks has been growing in the private sector. Several hospitals have started programs involving the collection of samples for medical studies.

One such group is the Children's Hospital of Philadelphia, the nation's oldest pediatric medical center. The hospital is hoping to gather 100,000 samples from children, with one of the goals being to decipher DNA encoding for genetic diseases. Meanwhile, in England, 500,000 DNA samples are to be collected for a "biobank." And the most ambitious program is California-based Kaiser Permanente, which hopes to collect 2 million samples.[252]

Given the tendency of corporations to data-mine information, one has to worry that some of this data might eventually be employed against those giving samples, or used to devise medical tests of other individuals' DNA to determine whether they were genetically predisposed to problems, thereby dictating higher medical insurance premiums, or that the candidate be rejected for a life insurance policy.

Census Data and You

The U.S. Constitution calls for a census to determine the number of voters in various districts. All that's legally asked for is a nose

---

[252] Antonio Regalado, "Plan to Build Children's DNA Database," *The Wall Street Journal*, June 7, 2006.

count. Little by little, however, census forms have gone beyond that, to a tragic point if you happened to be an American of Japanese descent during World War II. During that period, the Census Bureau was instrumental in determining where Japanese Americans were in the U.S. so they could be detained and sent to internment camps.[253][254]

Today the Census Bureau promises never to reveal your personal information. Until scholars discovered the truth, the agency also claimed it hadn't been instrumental in getting Japanese Americans detained during World War II. Not surprisingly, then, various minority groups and religious segments of the American public have been suspicious of the data the government wants to collect on them via the U.S. census.

In 2000 this distrust caused some U.S. citizens to rebel against filling out the "long form" sent to some households. This document asked a variety of intrusive questions, from the race of the family to how much income was being brought in by various members. This wasn't the first time such a form was used, but it was the first time that the Internet and talk shows were available to provide a public forum for discussion. Many questioned the wisdom of giving the government such detailed data. The result was that some refused to fill out the more detailed parts of the form, even though the government threatened to level a $100 fine against those that did not. (After weighing the hundred-dollar fine against possible required attendance in an internment camp, the decision likely seemed an easy one.)

Following this paper rebellion, the Census Bureau backed down and instituted the idea of a "perpetual census," with survey recipients selected at random every month from the agency's master address file. This "American Community Survey" is to provide "community leaders and other data users [with] timely

---

[253] Steven A. Holmes, "Scholars Study Wartime Bureau," *The New York Times,* March 17, 2000.

[254] Robyn Blumner, "U.S. Census Questions Put Your Privacy at Risk," *St. Petersburg Times,* March 26, 2000.

information for planning and evaluating public programs for everyone from newborns to the elderly."[255]

PLAYING IT SAFE

Today it may be that data given to the Census Bureau is safe. But for the cautious, it may be worth risking a small fine in order to reveal only the household head count as required by the Constitution. No more, no less.

"Private" Medical Records

Most medical records, as well as some medical insurance programs, are keyed to either your real name and/or your Social Security number. This makes linking it to information held by a variety of data banks quite simple. Should that happen, the loss of privacy could be quite profound, given the data in medical records:

- Details about sexual preferences; information about family relationships (including data on adopted children and children conceived artificially); whether a patient is infertile, has had sexually transmitted diseases, etc.

- Records of any substance abuse

- Information about emotional and mental health

- Records of family history of tendencies toward various physical or mental illnesses, from cancer to schizophrenia

- Notes by doctors, including speculations about patients which might be unfounded

Although much lip service is given to the idea that doctors will keep a patient's medical information secret, there are few actual laws to prevent the abuse of this data. In fact, insurance companies, drug companies, and other businesses have access to many records and can copy them into their own data banks, possibly

---

[255] Julie Foster, "Feds Implement Perpetual Census," WorldNetDaily.com, June 16, 2001.

sharing them with sister corporations, or even selling data on the open market.[256]

Given the intermingling of data that is ongoing in other sectors, the open question is: At what point might this data be used to your economic disadvantage?

It isn't hard to picture such a situation.

Imagine trying to obtain a loan if the bank discovered you have cancer with a survival rate of 50 percent. Or what might happen if you were trying to buy health insurance and the insurer found out that even though you're in perfect health, both your parents died at an early age from heart attacks? Such information could quickly turn you into someone without insurance or someone to whom few would want to extend credit.

There's also the small matter of human dignity. Do you want your banker to know that someone in your household buys adult diapers or Viagra? Do you want the telemarketer to be able to discuss what special needs a child taking this or that medication might have?

It appears that life insurance companies are already planning to sell such data. Recently Peter J. Albert, the corporate attorney at Progressive Casualty Insurance, stunned an interviewer when he said of his corporation's privacy policy, "The difficult part was getting our hands around our privacy practices and developing a policy that would let us do what we may want to do with information in the future."[257]

STEM THE FLOW

It may be that your medical records have already been sold. But it is wise to check with your pharmacy, medical insurer, and doctor's office to see what their policy is. Often even if information is sold, it is done with the understanding that the patient has "agreed" to this because they haven't

---

[256] Laura Beil and Charles Ornstein, "Patients' Data Not So Private," *Dallas Morning News*, September 18, 2000.

[257] *Info World*, http://www.infoworld.com/articles/hn/xml/00/10/30/001030hnprivacy.xml?1030mnlv, October 30, 2000.

specifically requested that it *not* be shared. Let them know you refuse to agree to such sharing of your private information.

You should demand that data only be shared when you request it, or when the law so requires. You may fail to prevent all leaks, but you may be able to at least stop the flood that is now ongoing with many medical institutions.

CHAPTER 10 LEAVING DODGE

❝ I know a lot of people are concerned about Big Brother, but my response to that is, if you are not doing anything wrong, why should you worry about it? ❞

— HOUSTON POLICE CHIEF HAROLD HURTT,
DEFENDING HIS CALL TO PUT SURVEILLANCE CAMERAS
IN APARTMENT COMPLEXES, ALONG DOWNTOWN STREETS,
IN SHOPPING MALLS, AND EVEN IN PRIVATE HOMES.[258] —

In the previous pages I've outlined a variety of tricks and tactics you can employ to defeat a variety of snoops, from a nosy neighbor or private investigator to an overzealous government agent. With upcoming technologies such as artificial intelligence, implanted chips on appliances (and even in people), and other dangers now on the horizon, some very profound lifestyle changes and strategies may be necessary in order to protect your privacy in the near future.

Should you come to believe that things are deteriorating to the point that you or your family may be in danger, then it may be time to simply "get out of Dodge." This is not a decision to be made lightly, and should be weighed against how overwhelming the anti-privacy measures you face may be, or how dangerous

---

[258] "Houston Police Chief Wants Cameras on Homes, Streets," Associated Press, February 15, 2006.

your government may become for a minority group you may find yourself a part of.

At that point, these may be options worth considering.

FINDING SAFE HAVEN

There are several keys to finding a safe haven from an abusive government. One is to be aware of which countries may offer you protection. This means you need to do some research with an eye toward what nations offer lower taxes (often making a government less obtrusive, as well as making your income go farther), and what extradition laws that nation has with the United States (so trumped-up charges can't be used to return you to America).

It is a lot of work finding a nation that offers more than the U.S. In fact, you probably won't find one. But you may discover one that values your privacy, and if that is your goal, then forfeiting some of the other benefits offered by living in America may be worth the sacrifice.

Living overseas may have benefits not found in the U.S. Third World nations often have very low wages, a benefit if you have a business that can draw money from customers in the U.S.

Chances are there will be a lot of fellow expats in the nation you choose if you've done your homework. Even now many movie stars, ex-politicians, retired journalists, and former ambassadors live overseas. You can join this small crowd.

When you go nation shopping, keep in mind that just as the U.S. might go downhill, so, too, might other countries. For many years Jamaica was a popular place for Americans to live; when that nation passed stringent gun-control laws, crime against white Americans skyrocketed. Suddenly many Americans were living a nightmare.

Always consider the stability of the country both politically and economically, the type of weather it has (and whether that's to your liking), and the living expenses that can be expected should you move there. If you have special energy requirements, require high-speed Internet access, or have other special business or personal needs, then these should enter into your decision as well.

THE STATE OF TAXES

In addition to greater privacy, one other key benefit to living overseas is that you can often reduce the amount of taxes you pay and do so legally. The trick is to have a business or other source of income that mostly operates outside the nation you're living in. This can allow you to avoid paying taxes in the nation you choose to live in, while paying greatly reduced taxes (or even none at all) to the U.S. government.

For example, if you were an investor who did your business via phone and Internet connections with clients based in the U.S., then you might owe no taxes at all to either the U.S. (which bases taxes on money earned within U.S. borders) or the nation in which you reside. Several nations, including Costa Rica and Ireland, currently don't tax residents' income if generated from businesses run outside their countries.

Some countries allow a business to operate as an International Business Corporation (IBC), which permits paying the United States IRS nothing. If you have a business that lends itself to this legal structure, about the only ground rules to observe are that you create your IBC in a host country that doesn't tax operations like yours, and that you never sell anything to anyone in your host nation.

Whether or not the IRS can legally tax money you're earning when working overseas is open to debate. But currently the IRS holds that the first $70,000 of income by an adult while overseas is tax-free. If you're living in a country that doesn't tax income from outside its borders, then you can make up to $70,000 without any worries.

If your spouse is working at the same job you are, then your spouse can earn an additional $70,000 of tax-free income—provided your spouse really is part of the business. Currently, in order for the IRS to consider you as living outside the U.S. (and therefore outside of its tax jurisdiction), you can own no home in the U.S., and must have a place of residence in another nation.

Additionally, you may have to pass the IRS's "physical presence test," which places you inside the U.S. for thirty days or less each year; if you're within American borders for over thirty days per year, the IRS may attempt to extract tax payments from you. And, of course, these laws and regulations can change overnight, so it is good to keep up-to-date on them.

The IRS can be taken out of the picture if you renounce your American citizenship. This is an extreme measure that may mean you "can't go home again" should things not work out as hoped for overseas. For this reason you should approach denouncing your citizenship very cautiously.

EASY AS IBC

To create an IBC, contact a corporation that handles this paperwork for businesses in the nation in which you wish to live. Obviously you should make sure the corporation is reputable, and that they are also empowered to create a bank account with a large local bank for your business. The corporation should also supply your corporate seal and other necessary devices for operating in your host country.

An added layer of protection can be enjoyed if you set up a trust to own your IBC. This makes it harder for snoops to determine who's actually running your business (and paying you a salary), and also harder for you to be sued by other parties. When you get ready to sell your business, having it owned by a trust will also simplify the transfer of ownership, whether to a buyer or to your heirs. Usually the corporation that creates your IBC can also set up a trust to own your business.

When creating a new business with funds you've saved in the U.S., document that taxes were paid on the money, keeping all IRS forms, pay stubs, and other materials so that the IRS can't challenge the money should you return to the U.S. at a later date.

As you search for nations to move to, some may seem too good to be true—because they probably are. Avoid any nations that seem to have "tax dodges" that might be illegal. You don't, for example, want to settle in a nation that's known for money laundering or otherwise protecting criminals. Such small nations are not only dangerous to live in, but they are also ripe for a U.S. invasion similar to that mounted on Grenada in 1989 to "safeguard the lives of Americans living there."

Also check into "tax-free zones," "duty-free areas," or similar arrangements within some nations that may have been created to cater to international corporations. Sometimes you can set up shop in these places, taking advantage of the tax breaks.

OVERSEAS BANKING

Banking overseas is unlike banking in the States. It can be a little risky, since many nations don't guarantee the protection of money in bank accounts. This makes a bank account more like a loan to a friend than a secure place to keep money. A good friend will pay you back, just as a trustworthy bank will.

If an overseas institution goes bankrupt, or the head of the bank runs off with all the money, bank customers are out of luck. Check the background of a bank to be sure it is aboveboard and financially sound. As with people who are trustworthy, good banks will have clients that will vouch for them. Generally, they will have been in business for some time. Do your homework, and you should be able to find a bank people trust.

Also remember that while the U.S. government tends to dismiss offshore banks as nearly illegal operations for money launderers and tax cheats, most reputable overseas banks don't have such clients. They may on occasion be tools for legal tax avoidance, but that's not the same as catering to illegal operations.

It's a good idea to avoid banks with branches either in the U.S. or in countries with close ties to the U.S., such as England, Canada, and Mexico. Swiss banks are the first choice for privacy, though Panama and Singapore have reputations that rival the Swiss and often will be easier to open accounts in.

Note that most international banks don't offer checking accounts, and generally won't accept personal checks for deposit. Be sure when setting up an account with a bank that you have a way to wire or otherwise transfer money from any U.S. accounts to your new bank overseas.

Since overseas banks aren't backed by governments, this also means they have to choose their customers carefully. Because of this, you'll generally need a personal reference from your current U.S. bank (perhaps using the form supplied by the international bank you hope to open a new account with). The trick here is that some U.S. banks may try to discourage your transferring business overseas. If so, take your money out of the bank and transfer it to a smaller, friendlier American bank that will give you a reference.

If things are really bad politically and you can no longer get an American bank to give you a reference, then you may be able to travel to Nassau or Panama City and find a business that will help you. However, you should be aware that this is the same basic route taken by money launderers and those trying to avoid taxes with the IRS, so you will likely raise some red flags in the banking industry (as well as rub shoulders with some odd characters).

Once you've secured your personal reference letter, have an IBC with the documents that show your ownership of it, and have your passport in hand, you should be ready to create an account in a bank where you're planning on living.

When you've opened your account, find out how to wire money in and out of your account, and how to write checks against money in the bank (if you aren't using an international bank). You should also be able to get a charge card issued from that bank. Ideally it will be a card that is widely accepted, Visa, American Express, and MasterCard being top contenders. The card should also function in ATMs. Since the laws regarding the loss of bank cards vary from nation to nation, know what actions should be taken if a card is lost or stolen, and how much you will be responsible for if a thief makes charges on the card.

Be aware of what delays may occur in depositing money. If you plan on doing some of your banking by phone or letter, be sure there are safeguards in place to avoid having someone impersonate you or forge your name to steal money from your account.

SAY GOOD-BYE, GRACIE

To enter most nations, you will need a valid passport. Since it may take weeks or even months to obtain a passport, it is always good to have one on hand, ready for an emergency, rather than hope to get one at the last minute. This is especially true should the political climate be deteriorating. You can find the forms needed for obtaining passports online or at your local post office.

Current law allows U.S. Customs officials to confiscate any money over $10,000. That means you'll need to make provisions for wiring most of your assets to a bank account long before you decide to leave America.

Also note that converting your wealth to gold coins, jewelry, precious metals, etc., (though often recommended by "experts") is impractical, will burden you, or will leave you with assets that are hard or impossible to exchange for cash at your destination. Unless you are unable to wire money from the U.S. to an overseas bank, don't be tempted to try such measures.

One other alternative for taking money out of the U.S. is by traveler's checks. It is best to have the checks written in the currency of the nation you're going to. If that is not practical, Swiss francs are generally accepted worldwide, with U.S. or Euro dollars being second choices.

CONCLUSION

" You already have zero privacy. Get over it. "

— SUN MICROSYSTEMS' SCOTT MCNEALY[259] —

There's always confusion in history when one observes it unfold. We may—or may not—be standing at the crossroads of history today.

Yet regardless of one's perspective on the historical landscape, it is obvious that we've sustained a great loss of privacy over the last few decades, and the threat of even more loss is imminent. This won't necessarily lead to a totalitarian society like those that have plagued mankind in the past. But the chilling possibility of Big Brother waiting in the wings, however slight, merits consideration simply because the stakes are so high.

Like all battles, the fight for privacy requires many foot soldiers, and an understanding of the price of defeat. If enough people are aware of the terrifying possibilities, more will work all the harder to avoid it.

So it is my hope that in writing this book, I may have played a small part in revealing the ongoing nightmare. I hope that enough readers will take this book to heart and make a difference—

---

[259] K. Markoff, "A Growing Compatibility Issue in the Digital Age: Computers and Their Users' Privacy," *The New York Times*, March 3, 1999.

perhaps even rewrite the ending to the morality play we have become a part of. It may very well be that this battle to regain our privacy is ours to win or lose. Perhaps enough of us will stay the course and finish the fight to make a difference, not only for ourselves, but for all of society.

Pass this book along to friends and fellow workers. The techniques outlined in these pages may help change society's direction. It may be that we can regain and preserve privacy for our children and grandchildren.

Of course, if we do nothing, we will achieve nothing.

So roll up your sleeves and get to work.

GLOSSARY

Antivirus software — A computer program designed to detect viruses and other malicious software. When running in the "background" of a computer operating system, the antivirus software may block access to infected files, clean infected files, or keep a virus from taking actions that might harm the computer or the files and programs installed on it.

Backdoor — A secret opening in security software or hardware that permits circumventing security controls, passwords, or other privacy features of the program.

BadTrans.B worm — One type of a computer virus that e-mails itself to other computers under a variety of file names. Once it installs itself on a computer, it records and logs keystrokes made on the system and may relay the data to a distant computer via an Internet connection.

Biometrics — Using physical characteristics such as fingerprints, hand geometry, eye structure, or vocal patterns to identify a person.

BIOS — An acronym for "basic input/output system." This firmware is built into most modern computers and initially links the system to peripherals like the keyboard, display screen, disk drives, and so forth.

BitTorrent — A peer-to-peer (P2P) file distribution program written by programmer Bram Cohen. The program permits trading files across the Internet. While P2P programs have legitimate uses, users sometimes illegally trade software, music, movies, or other digital files. P2P services can also become a source of viruses or other malware.

Buddy list — A collection of "handles" or screen names with contact information. Such lists are often created by programs like Instant Messenger as well as Web sites that assemble "communities" of users.

Carnivore — The codename for a program run by the FBI during the 1990s. The software was designed to check and record the e-mail address and subject headings of e-mail, and then compare these to lists of keywords that might indicate criminal activity. When suspect e-mails were located, they could then be traced to the sender and receiver by accessing account information from ISPs (Internet Service Providers).

CCTV (Closed-Circuit TV) — A video security system that continuously monitors an area, taping the view and often also being observed in real time by a security or law enforcement officer. Most cameras are designed to allow panning, zoom magnification, and low-light viewing.

CD-ROM (Compact Disc, Read-Only Memory) — A CD designed to permit information to be recorded to it for later retrieval. Once data are "burned" onto a CD-ROM, the disc cannot be erased for reuse.

Cookies — A feature of most Internet browser software that permits a visited site to place times, dates, and other information on the hard disk of the computer running the browser. These data may include a list of on-line purchases, passwords, or other validation information about a visitor. Some security experts fear such data might present privacy issues if they are accessed by other sites or if the data collected by a site should be accessed during a security breach.

Copware — Software that allows law enforcement or government agents to spy on computer users. Such programs present serious privacy issues and arguably might be misused.

Cyber Knight — An alleged code name for a program created by the FBI. It is believed that this program is an enhanced version of Carnivore (see **Carnivore**) and most likely creates its database by sorting through material from Internet sources including e-mail, chat room messages, instant messages, and possibly Internet phone calls.

Discount cards — A marketing card issued by a retail business. Customers producing the card at checkout get slight discounts on purchases; in exchange, the retailer collects data about buying habits, linking this information to a customer's name and address. These data can then be sold to information brokers, government agencies, or other businesses.

DRIVerS (Driver Record Information Verification System) — A system devised by the American Association of Motor Vehicle Administrators

(AAMVA) in 2002 to transform state driver's licenses into the functional equivalent of a national ID cards. Eventually DRIVerS may contain more than two hundred million records of American citizens and might be linked to other government databases as well.

Dynamic Host Configuration Protocol (DHCP) — A method to automatically assign an Internet Protocol (IP) address to a computer connecting to the Internet. If the IP address is not assigned randomly (and most are not), then the IP address becomes a way to identify a user by inspecting the Internet Service Provider's records.

Electronic Frontier Foundation (EFF) — Based in San Francisco, this nonprofit organization's stated purpose is to "educate the press, policymakers, and the general public about civil liberties issues related to technology; and to act as a defender of those liberties." It is supported by donations.

Electronic Toll Collection (ETC) — A system that uses an electronic tag in a vehicle to automatically debit drivers when a toll route is taken. This system allows registered cars to continue without stopping to pay cash at tollbooths.

Encryption — A procedure rendering text unintelligible to anyone not authorized to read it. Often text files are encrypted for purposes of privacy.

ePassport — A modification of conventional passports involving the addition of an electronic chip that can be read by a special reader from a distance. The chip is embedded into the cover of the passport and stores the same data that are visually displayed on the passport. The inclusion of a digital photograph may also allow biometric facial recognition technology to be used in conjunction with the passport.

Ethernet — A local-area network (LAN) protocol developed by the Xerox Corporation, DEC, and Intel in 1976. It has become the most widely implemented LAN standard for systems using cabled connections between computers.

Event Data Recorder (EDR) — A "black box" incorporated into newer automobiles. In addition to operating the airbag, the sensors in the EDR also record data on an internal recorder. These data include the car's recent speeds, engine RPMs, how far the accelerator pedal was depressed, what seat belts were in use, and when the brakes were applied. The data are continuously recorded over the same system so that only the last few minutes of driving records are collected at any given time. Such data are sometimes accessed during traffic accident investigations.

E-ZPass — One of several very similar automated toll collection systems using an electronic identification circuit mounted inside the vehicle.

Facial-recognition camera — A digital camera connected to a computer programmed to match facial images to various data banks of photos. This biometric identification is generally sold as an automated method for recognizing known terrorists or criminals.

Faraday Box — Also known as the "Faraday Cage," a metal shell designed to divert electrical waves around anything within its shell. The shield can be created from a variety of metals and from thick metal sheets to screens and thin foils.

FasTrack — One of several similar systems employing an electronic tag in a vehicle to automatically debit drivers when a toll route is taken. This system allows registered cars to continue without stopping to pay at tollbooths.

FinCEN (Financial Crimes Enforcement Network) — A division of the U.S. Treasury created in 1990. The division has created a comprehensive database of financial records of U.S. citizens with an eye toward reducing tax evasion and money laundering by terrorists and drug dealers.

Firefox — A popular browser program generally less susceptible to malicious attacks than is Microsoft's more popular Internet Explorer.

Firewall — Software or hardware that limits access to a computer or network from an outside source (generally the Internet). A firewall helps prevent malicious hackers or other individuals from gaining access to the computer it protects. Some firewalls also prevent unauthorized messages and data from leaving the network or computer, and may also block unexpected activation of software or other operations that might otherwise pose a threat to a computer or privacy.

Firmware; "flashable" firmware — Firmware is a set of instructions and data programmed directly into the semipermanent circuitry of a device's printed circuitry. This permits faster operation than when data must be retrieved from a disk drive or similar storage system. Flash-enabled or flash-upgradeable firmware can be updated with special programs designed for that purpose. Firmware is most often seen in hardware firewalls and computer BIOS systems.

Freeware — Software given away rather than sold. Though most freeware is designed by hobbyists or students wanting to attract the attention of potential employers in the software industry, occasionally malicious software may be offered as freeware to trick unsuspecting users into installing it on their computers.

Gmail — A free e-mail service operated by Google. Because the service stores a user's e-mails online and may connect personal information and keyword searches to that user, some worry that privacy may be sacrificed when using such Web-based e-mail systems.

Google (n, v); Googled — Google became the most popular search engine enabling users to find articles online easier through keyword searches. Not surprisingly the process of doing such searches soon became a generic term for conducting such searches. Thus "Googled" has become synonymous with conducting a keyword search.

Grokster — A software company that operated a peer-to-peer (P2P) file-sharing program of the same name. The software was similar to another peer-to-peer program known as Kazaa.

Hacker — A slang term for a programmer or computer user who lacks formal training and often discovers how systems work through unorthodox approaches. The term can be complimentary or derogatory, though in popular usage it generally means a malicious person illegally breaking into computer networks to steal data or damage files.

Hotspot — An area in which a wireless device can connect to the Internet or a LAN.

HTML — Hypertext Markup Language is the "language" or code for creating World Wide Web pages; this coding determines how the text, pictures, and other features will appear when the page displays on a browser.

iBill — A company that handles credit-card transactions for websites. The company made news in 2006 by inadvertently leaking the personal data of seventeen million customers.

International Business Corporation (IBC) — A legal entity for conducting business and investment activities outside the United States.

Internet Connection Sharing (ICS) — A feature in post-Windows 98 Microsoft operating systems permitting computers on a LAN to access the Internet through a single computer connected directly to the Internet. This layering provides a more secure connection for the computers operating through the single computer.

Internet Relay Chat (IRC) — A generally insecure chat service operating in real-time messaging over the Internet. Generally for online group "meetings," it also allows one-to-one communications. These latter "private messages" may be easily monitored by the company hosting the service (with the exception of "Invisible IRC" — see below).

Internet Service Provider (ISP) — A company that "delivers" an Internet connection to a user's computer thereby enabling that user to access the World Wide Web, send e-mail, and so forth.

Invisible IRC — This project (also known as "IIP") is designed to create an anonymous, real-time chat service accessed via IRC clients. Its multi-tier design conceals the IP addresses of users from other users as well as the server.

JavaScript — A scripting language originally created by Netscape and often embedded in HTML Web pages to give them greater functionality.

Key logger — Software or hardware for covertly recording key strokes on a computer. These keystrokes can later be retrieved to yield correspondence, passwords, and other sensitive information.

Keyword — The important word that relates to a specific topic. Searching for certain keywords will often yield documents closely related to those words, making keyword searches an effective way to sort vast amounts of information rapidly.

Landline — A telephone or other communications system employing cable, fiber optics, or wires to carry its signal (as opposed to over-the-air cellular, laser, or microwave systems). In theory, landlines offer a higher level of security than do over-air communications. Today many so-called landlines actually have portions of their signals sent over microwave or satellite systems if they travel any distance, making them considerably less secure than many users believe them to be.

LexisNexis — A popular data broker offering for-fee searchable archives. Content comes from a variety of sources including newspapers, magazines, and legal documents that can contain addresses, Social Security numbers, or other private information.

Linux — An open-source (and often available for free) computer operating system originally created by Linos Torvalds, who based his work on the Unix operating system. This operating system is much less frequently targeted by computer viruses than are Windows systems.

Loyalty cards — Another term for a discount card issued by a retail business. Customers producing the card at checkout get slight discounts on purchases; in exchange, the retailer collects data about buying habits, linking this information to a customer's name and address and then selling the data about the customer to information brokers, government agencies, or businesses.

Macro virus — Small subroutines written using the internal programming language of a specific application. These viruses can be designed to replicate and when in operation may do a variety of destructive actions within the capabilities of the host program. Any program with macro features is potentially susceptible to such attacks, but more commonly these viruses are targeted at Word, Excel, and PowerPoint.

Magic Lantern — Key logger software and/or hardware that the FBI is believed to use in its investigations. Once placed on a suspect's computer, each keystroke is recorded to a hidden log for later retrieval.

Malware — A computer program designed for a harmful purpose. The software can be placed on a computer clandestinely, or a user may be enticed into installing it on a computer. The software may breach privacy or damage the system.

Media fireproof box — A safe or box designed to protect computer floppies, CDs, and hard drives from the intense heat of a structural fire.

Micro-expression — An involuntary facial expression that is fleeting, lasting less than a quarter of a second. It is believed these momentary expressions reveal the subconscious feelings of people as well as emotions they may be attempting to hide.

Millivision camera — Also known as a "millivision viewer," this passive imaging device allows seeing in the millimeter wave spectrum (invisible to the naked eye). Since these waves penetrate fabric, this viewer permits seeing concealed weapons or other contraband hidden under clothing (which is made transparent by the viewer). The device can also see through wood-frame walls to determine where people and furniture may be inside a home, hotel room, or similar environments.

MySpace — An online "friends" service creating networks of people who can display photos, weblogs, user profiles, e-mail addresses, and other personal information on Web pages within the system.

Napster — The first widely used file-sharing network that permitted trading files over the Internet. While the system was useful for legally trading music or other materials, the system soon became abused by those sharing software or other materials in violation of copyright laws. Also viruses are sometimes designed to appear to be coveted files and introduced to such file-sharing operations; users may download such a file and then inadvertently install the virus on their own computers.

Net Nanny — One of several software offerings designed to "filter" what sites can be visited on the Internet. The sellers of such programs offer them as a way for parents to control what children see on the Internet. While this is a lofty goal, some have charged that such software has the potential for blocking sites due to political content, thereby becoming a form of "stealth censorship."

Networked systems — A group of computers or similar devices that can trade data over a set of cable and/or wireless connections.

Newsgroup — Also known as a "Usenet discussion group" or "user group," this is a sort of Internet-based "clubhouse" that permits members to exchange comments or files. Most newsgroups are dedicated to one topic. An individual can subscribe to different newsgroups according to his or her interests.

Next-Generation Secure Computing Base (NGSCB) — Formerly known as Palladium, this is a key component of Microsoft's proposed "Trusted

Computing" concept. Proponents claim NGSCB would increase the security and privacy of computers running the software, while critics are fearful it would result in less competition among software designers and might also present privacy issues due to built-in backdoors.

NSA — The U.S. National Security Agency captures foreign electromagnetic messages and is also charged with protecting the electronic information critical to national security. President Harry Truman secretly created the agency in the 1950s.

OnStar — A General Motors service offered with its vehicles. Global Positioning System satellite technology and a hands-free, voice-activated cellular phone link a driver to emergency services in real time. Critics fear the system might become a way to spy on or track drivers.

Pharming — The criminal process of tricking a user into visiting a counterfeit website that purports to be that of a legitimate bank or other business. Once at the site, the victim may type in passwords or other personal data that can then be exploited by a criminal to access the victim's real online account.

Phishing — The illegal process in which a scam artist, pretending to represent a legitimate business or individual, sends misleading e-mails requesting personal and financial details from unsuspecting victims.

Photo radar camera — Also known as a "red light camera," this is an automated system that takes a snapshot of cars failing to stop at a red traffic signal. The picture is then relayed to the city government, which then issues a traffic ticket for the offense and mails it to the household where the vehicle is registered.

Plug-in — Also known as an "extension," these are small bits of software operate in another program to give it added capabilities.

Pop-up — The small and generally unwanted window (generally containing advertising) that appears in a browser when a site is visited.

Pretexting — An exploit in which a criminal makes a phone call and pretends to be the representative of a company or organization in order to obtain personal information, passwords, or other sensitive data. This information can then be used for illegal activities.

Pretty Good Privacy (PGP) — Created by Philip Zimmermann, this software was designed for data encryption/decryption of messages or files. The program employs a public digital "key" along with a password-protected private key.

P2P (peer-to-peer) — An Internet-based system that permits sharing of files from one user's computer to another as if the two were on a private network. One of the first such systems was Napster.

Radio Frequency Identification (RFID) — A tagging system that couples a small computer chip with an antenna. When interrogated by a special reader, the data on the chip can be accessed from a distance of feet or even yards (via radio waves). The data from the chip can then linked to a computerized databank to determine what product has been tagged, its purchase price, or similar information.

Red-light camera program — A program that operates red-light cameras (see **Photo radar camera**).

RFID — (See **Radio Frequency Identification.**)

Rootkit — A program that installs itself at a very low level, making it hard to detect. Such programs often secure administrative-level access so they can modify a computer system, log keystrokes, or engage in other operations while remaining very hard to detect.

Roving wiretap — A special wiretap sometimes used by the U.S. Justice Department. Unlike more conventional taps that monitor only one phone, the roving wiretap gives law enforcement personnel the right to tap any phone a suspect might have access to as well as computers, faxes, or other equipment connected to such phone lines.

RPV (Remotely Piloted Vehicle) — An unmanned aircraft remotely controlled by a ground-based pilot linked to the plane via a radio. Flying RPVs are also sometimes called unmanned aerial vehicles (UAVs).

Service Set Identifier (SSID) — The unique keyword a wireless device sends to specify which Wi-Fi (wireless) network it should connect to.

Skype — Software that permits VoIP (voice over Internet protocol) phone calls between computers equipped with headsets.

Social engineering — A scam that involves posing as an authorized business employee, customer, government agent, or other person in an attempt to deceive an operator, individual, or employee into giving away passwords or other data. When this trick works, it often leads to identity theft or illicit access to computerized business systems.

Spam (n, v) — Unsolicited e-mail that is irrelevant and inappropriate and is often sent in mass quantities to thousands of e-mail addresses at once. In addition to being a nuisance, spam often presents privacy dangers when sent by scam artists.

Speedpass (ExxonMobil) — An RFID keychain device for electronic payment at Exxon and Mobil gas stations (and experimentally offered by some fast-food establishments and supermarkets).

Spyware — Software that, once installed, secretly collects information on the user and relays that data covertly, often via an Internet connection. Spyware can be installed on a computer by an intruder, but typically it is secretly bundled into other software that the user installs onto his or her computer.

Steganography — The process of using special software to hide data inside other files, typically in digital graphics, though other types of files may be employed.

TEAPOT — A program publicly mentioned only in an NSA document but believed to be software designed to covertly broadcast data from a user's computer after a program designed for this purpose has been surreptitiously installed on the target system.

TEMPEST — The code name under which the U.S. government apparently conducted research into how easily data might be retrieved from the weak radio signals computer equipment generates when in operation.

Tor — An anonymous Internet communication system employing an "outproxy" to conceal the true location and identity of a computer. Journalists as well as dissidents use Tor to avoid possible censorship, arrest, or reprisals in countries with restrictive governments.

Torrentspy — An indexing system that lists files available for downloading from various BitTorrent P2P sites.

Trojan; Trojan horse (virus) — An apparently harmless program that contains malicious code that may damage file allocation tables, format a hard disk, or do other damage. A Trojan may also distribute itself as a computer virus.

TrueType fonts — Scalable typefaces originally created for Apple systems. These fonts now are also used with other operating systems, including Windows. Because of readily available software that permits designing such fonts, a huge variety of typefaces are available, many of them available for free on the Internet. Odd TrueType fonts can lower the chances of TEMPEST-style spying on a system.

Trusted Computing Group (TCG) — An initiative championed by AMD, Hewlett-Packard, IBM, Intel, Microsoft, Sony, and Sun Microsystems as a way to assure computer users that software meets certain security standards. Critics have argued that this BIOS-based system might restrict what software a consumer could run on his or her computer, greatly limiting the choice of software and operating systems in the process.

UAV (Unpiloted Aerial Vehicle) — Also an acronym for "unmanned aerial vehicle." These small, remote-controlled planes are piloted by a ground-based operator linked to the plane via radio.

USA Patriot Act — The result of sweeping legislation aimed at fighting terrorism, this law was passed by the U.S. Congress in the wake of the 9/11 attacks in 2001. The law has since been revised by Congress. The name is actually an acronym: Uniting and Strengthening America by Providing Appropriate Tools Required to Intercept and Obstruct Terrorism.

VeriChip — An RFID identification capsule marketed by the VeriChip Corporation. This small unit is designed for implantation under the skin of a human being or animal and functions as an identification or tracking device.

Virtual Private Networking (VPN) — A network similar to a small Internet but contained with a company or other collective and used privately. The communications often travel over the Internet and therefore must be protected by protocols to keep from being compromised.

Virus — Malicious software designed to duplicate itself and then spread to other computers by copies on floppy disks or e-mail attachments.

VoIP (Voice-Over-Internet Protocol) — A system that permits making phone calls over the Internet system. These can be made via software on a computer equipped with a headset or by a phone designed to plug directly into the Internet system. For quality service, a fast Internet connection is generally required.

Webroot — A spyware removal program.

WiFi — A short-range wireless networking protocol based on the 802.11 family of standards. Signals are in the 2.4 GHz range, and data can be exchanged at broadband speeds, hardware permitting.

Wiping your hard drive — The process of recording and re-recording digital information over areas of a hard drive to make deleted files impossible to recover.

Wiretapping — The process of covertly monitoring a telephone conversation. The term originated from the original necessity of tapping off a small amount of the energy carrying a message down a telephone wire in order to listen in. Today taps can be applied without directly interfering with a signal, and cellular phones, fax messages, and other data traveling through a phone system can also be monitored.

XPdite — Software designed to remove some of the normally unused features of Windows XP to give added security to a computer.

Zfone — VoIP software that allows a user to make encrypted phone calls over the Internet. The ZRTP protocol that is the basis of the Zfone software may eventually be integrated into standalone VoIP phones.

ZIP files — Computer files compressed with the popular data compression and archival Zone Information Protocol format. A single ZIP file may contain one or more files that are compressed.

ZoneAlarm — A popular computer firewall program marketed by Zone Labs.

INDEX

ABOUT THE AUTHOR

Duncan Long is an internationally recognized technical and fiction author with over eighty books and manuals in print, along with numerous journal and magazine articles. The subjects he's written about include everything from chemical, biological, and nuclear weapons to health manuals and how-to books. Long has also authored the nine-book action/adventure Night Stalkers series (published by HarperCollins), as well as the science fiction Spider Worlds trilogy (HarperCollins) and *Anti-Grav Unlimited* (Avon Books).

Some of his manuals have been purchased for the private libraries of the United States CIA, the U.S. Marines, FEMA, and other government agencies, as well as the private library of at least one foreign embassy and the EPC (Emergency Planning, Canada). The FBI has requested that his weapons manuals be sent to their Firearms Training Unit at Quantico. Long also wrote three manuals used in International Correspondence Schools' course work.

In addition to illustrating his own technical books, Long has done a number of cover illustrations for other authors' novels, as well as CD and magazine covers. One of his illustrations was chosen for the cover of Harper Design International's *Digital Art for the 21st Century*.

Long has also been featured on radio and TV shows, and for a time hosted his own talk-radio show, named (appropriately enough) *The Duncan Long Show*.